MW00668261

**PRAISE FOR *POPCORN WITH THE POPE***

"You know *It's a Wonderful Life* and *The Wizard of Oz*, but what's *Nazarín* or *The Burmese Harp*—and why should you care? That's where this accessible, informative book comes in. Going film by film, the authors illuminate why the Vatican Film List remains an important landmark in Catholic engagement with the arts in general and cinema in particular, and how movies of all kinds reveal God speaking through beauty as well as truth and goodness."

—**Deacon Steven D. Greydanus,** creator of DecentFilms.com

"Can feature films be catechetical tools, leading viewers into a deeper appreciation of what's really important in life? *Popcorn with the Pope* suggests that the answer to that question is a resounding yes, and that the path to truth and goodness in twenty-first-century culture often begins with an experience of beauty."

—**George Weigel,** Distinguished Senior Fellow and William E. Simon Chair in Catholic Studies, Ethics and Public Policy Center

"Like the featured meal in *Babette's Feast*, this book is a sumptuous dinner for the mind and heart. Easily accessible to seasoned cinephiles and casual moviegoers alike, it is a fantastic introduction to the Vatican's Film List. Read, reflect, relish, and repeat."

—**Nick Olszyk,** film critic, *Catholic World Report*

"So many movies, so little time! How do we decide what to watch next on Netflix, Hulu, Amazon Prime, or other movie platforms? What should be on our 'must-see' list? *Popcorn with the Pope* tackles the Vatican's list of forty-five recommended titles, showing how each contributes to our understanding of religion, values, and art. All the titles on the Vatican's list date to 1995 or earlier; but movie fans can apply the same principles to find great films from the current era. So start popping the popcorn and grab a seat. The fun's about to start!"

—**Kathy Schiffer**, blogger, *National Catholic Register*

# POPCORN
## WITH THE POPE

### A GUIDE TO THE VATICAN FILM LIST

# POPCORN
## WITH THE POPE

### A GUIDE TO THE VATICAN FILM LIST

David Paul Baird

Andrew Petiprin

Michael Ward

Published by Word on Fire,
Elk Grove Village, IL 60007
© 2023 by Word on Fire Catholic Ministries
Printed in the United States of America
All rights reserved

Cover design, typesetting, and interior art direction by
Katherine Spitler and Rozann Lee

Scripture excerpts are from the New Revised Standard Version Bible: Catholic Edition (copyright © 1989, 1993), used by permission of the National Council of the Churches of Christ in the United States of America. All rights reserved worldwide.

Excerpts from the English translation of the *Catechism of the Catholic Church* for use in the United States of America Copyright © 1994, United States Catholic Conference, Inc.—Libreria Editrice Vaticana. Used by permission. English translation of the *Catechism of the Catholic Church*: Modifications from the Editio Typica copyright © 1997, United States Conference of Catholic Bishops—Libreria Editrice Vaticana.

No part of this book may be used or reproduced in any manner whatsoever without written permission, except in the case of brief quotations in critical articles or reviews. For more information, contact Word on Fire Catholic Ministries, PO Box 97330, Washington, DC 20090-7330 or email contact@wordonfire.org.

First printing, December 2023

ISBN: 978-1-68578-984-8

Library of Congress Control Number: 2022943574

# Contents

# Introduction

## THE VATICAN FILM LIST

It was not always a good thing to find yourself on a Vatican list.

From the sixteenth century onward, popes have drawn up lists of books deemed heretical or a danger to the conscience, which the faithful were forbidden to read. If a work found its way onto this *Index Librorum Prohibitorum* (Index of Prohibited Books), it was because it had been judged harmful to faith or morals.

So when the Index was dissolved in 1966, it was not because the faith had changed, or because the moral law had changed, but because the Church had resolved, largely for evangelistic reasons, to adopt a more hospitable attitude toward the wider culture. Critical evaluation remained essential, of course, and the Church remained committed to promoting a healthy culture in opposition to an insidious one, but the "finger-wagging" approach, typified in the public mind by the Index, was let go. In its place, the decision was made to spread the Good News less through frowning and forbidding and more through encouraging and celebrating, even if this meant interacting with works of culture that only partially overlapped with Christian conviction.

Eventually, this new approach led to the compilation of a list that, far from banning works, positively recommended them. This time the works in question were films, not books, and it was definitely a good thing to be put on *this* index.

This is the list to which *Popcorn with the Pope* serves as a guide.

One hundred years after the Lumière brothers held the first paid public screening of a motion picture in Paris (an occasion that is generally held to mark the birth of film as an art form), the Vatican marked the centenary of cinema by releasing a list of "some important films." In 1995, the Pontifical Council for Social Communications and the Vatican Film Library appointed a commission of a dozen international experts to compile a roll of films deemed notable in various ways and deserving of attention. The result was a list of forty-five titles organized according to three categories: religious values, human and social values, and artistic values. (In this volume, these categories are referred to as Religion, Values, and Art, and the films are ordered alphabetically within each section.)

The list was originally distributed to all the bishops' conferences in the world as part of a larger packet on discernment in film appreciation. It was not intended, as is commonly misreported, as a kind of "best-ever" register or an "Oscars of the Vatican," nor was it meant to provide an exhaustive anthology of approved works. Rather, the aim was to indicate a few examples to help educate the faithful about cinema as a kind of language and as a bearer of messages.

The entries vary widely, ranging from popular, light-hearted favorites such as *The Wizard of Oz* (1939), *Fantasia* (1940), and *It's a Wonderful Life* (1946), to rigorous documentary-like works of Italian neorealism and challenging arthouse features such as *The Seventh Seal* (1957) and *Andrei Rublev* (1966). Some films—*Nosferatu* (1922), *Stagecoach* (1939), and *2001: A Space Odyssey* (1968), for example—appear to have been chosen as milestones in the development of a given style or genre. Others, including *Rome, Open City* (1945) and *Dersu Uzala* (1975), are relatively obscure and will probably only be recognized by cinephiles and scholars.

But a good number of titles on the list are just as enjoyable as they are substantial. In the Religion category, for instance, *A Man for All Seasons* (1966), *The Mission* (1986), and *Babette's Feast* (1987) are at once pleasurable and meaningful. Likewise, under "Values" and "Art," *On the Waterfront* (1954), *The Leopard* (1963), and *Chariots of Fire* (1981) would be great places to start easing into the list, whether out of individual interest or for viewing among family and friends or in film clubs.

The list makes no claims to be universally representative. In fact, the compilers took pains to mention in a short preface that it was based on "the informed personal taste of experts, on opinion polls, and also on plain evidence," adding the important qualification that "not all that deserve mention are included."

It is worth noting, therefore, that the films chosen do reflect the sensibilities of critics of a certain frame of mind, who hail from a specific part of the world and belong to a particular generation. Many of the selections are tragic in tone—a common predilection of intellectuals. Roughly one-in-five was produced in Italy. And about one-in-six comments more or less directly upon the most catastrophic experiences of the twentieth century: the First and Second World Wars.

As a consequence, the pleasure to be had from many of these movies often comes more from reflection afterward than immediately upon first viewing. They are frequently rigorous and challenging, sometimes understated and initially underwhelming, and as a rule ask more from viewers than the average big-budget cineplex blockbuster or new release on Netflix. That said, the phenomenon of streaming means that the films on the list are now available to everyone to watch at any time (many are on YouTube), a level of accessibility that would not have been possible in the days when a large number of titles on the list were confined to arthouse theaters, film festivals, and specialty video stores.

Many of us have been brought up almost exclusively on the cinematic equivalent of junk food, but approaching every movie merely for entertainment is like treating every meal like a ballpark hotdog or every book like an airport paperback. There are, in fact, as many kinds of movies as there are types of books: superhero adventures, romance stories, and murder mysteries, to be sure, but also histories and biographies, philosophical manifestos and spiritual reflections, documentaries and gently fictionalized examinations of pressing world affairs, and so on. The Vatican Film List presents something like an exotic taster menu in the sensibilities, emotions, and beliefs of human beings from other eras and locales: some might be strange and forbidding at first, but after discovering them, sitting with them, and learning what it is they are trying to do, they become increasingly engaging, even compelling.

So, how are we supposed to know what each film is trying to do? Helping with that task is a large part of the purpose of this book. Each chapter builds a ramp for easier access to the rewards of watching a given film, illuminating what is difficult and recontextualizing what is familiar in order to make for a more comprehensible and enjoyable watching experience. Broad and suggestive in approach rather than encyclopedic or scholarly in a specialized way, *Popcorn with the Pope* offers an introductory "first pass" at these films, intended not for experts but for anyone who is interested in delving deeper into a Christian approach to movies. Each chapter offers a theologically informed reading of the film at hand, situating it in its historical context and providing questions for further reflection and discussion. Our hope is that readers will come away better equipped to appreciate the aesthetic, intellectual, and spiritual qualities in these films that the Vatican considered important enough to highlight as exemplary works from cinema's first hundred years.

But perhaps it still seems like an odd pairing, the Vatican and the movies? If so, this would be a good place to say something about the "bigger picture" of the Catholic Church's interactions with cinema, and in particular the stances taken by different popes since that first momentous Paris screening in 1895.

Admittedly, the bishops of Rome have enjoyed a rocky, back-and-forth relationship with the cinema. This is perhaps unsurprising given the immense influence for good and ill that the medium has exerted upon the tastes, opinions, and habits of people the world over. Three decades after Pope Leo XIII was filmed offering his blessing into the lens of a movie camera in 1896 (and in so doing becoming the first pontiff to appear on screen), Pope Pius XI, in his encyclical on Christian education, *Divini Illius Magistri* (1929), likened the twentieth-century appetite for cinematic diversions to "the passion for the shows of the circus which possessed even some Christians" in St. Augustine's time (a passion the saint deplored). In a follow-up encyclical specially dedicated to the motion picture, *Vigilanti Cura* (1936), Pius XI lamented the film industry's failure to police its own moral content and commended the now notorious Legion of Decency, which passed judgment on the morality of films in the United States for almost fifty years.

By the 1950s and 1960s, however, the Church's official engagement with film grew into something more complex (and arguably more important) than simply playing the part of moral referee. In a 1955 apostolic exhortation to representatives of the cinema industry and press in Italy, Pope Pius XII laid out principles for "an ideal film," which should first of all always contain "respect for man" and aim for a "loving understanding" in depicting man's condition. He also noted the longing for relief within people's souls and described film as uniquely suited to be a "respite from the pressure of real existence." Accordingly, the filmmaker, like the preacher, has a duty to offer spiritual sustenance—to point beyond this world without totally ignoring its harsh reality. The pope concluded by describing the "lofty and positive mission" of everyone who stands behind the camera: to shun easy material that appeals to base desires and "to rise to worthy ideals."

In his encyclical *Miranda Prorsus* (1957), Pius XII returned to the question of moral responsibility, focusing this time not only on filmmakers but on critics. He wrote:

> Catholic film critics can have much influence; they ought to set the moral issue of the plots in its proper light, defending those judgments which will act as a safeguard against falling into so-called "relative morality," or the overthrow of that right order in which the lesser issues yield place to the more important. . . . Quite wrong, therefore, is the action of writers in daily papers and in reviews, claiming to be Catholic, if, when dealing with shows of this kind, they do not instruct their readers concerning the moral position to be adopted.

An example of how tricky this critical evaluation can be is seen in the reception of Federico Fellini's 1963 film *8½.* One of the most famous films about filmmaking, it contains within itself the very debate about the moral and spiritual significance of cinema that Pius XI and Pius XII were wrestling with. It may not be surprising, therefore, that officials in the Church both hated and loved *8½.* More remarkable, though, is how they *first* hated it, and *then* loved it.

The Legion of Decency originally gave *8½* a C rating (condemned) and put it on the list that eventually added up to 148 films deemed unacceptable viewing for Catholics. (The condemned list, which ran from 1933 to 1980, is a hodgepodge of mediocrity, debauchery, and brilliance, ranging from gritty gangster films to two Alfred Hitchcock movies, *Psycho* and *Torn Curtain*. Sergio Leone's Spaghetti Westerns are on there, along with supernatural films like *The Exorcist* and *Rosemary's Baby*. There are also a few complete headscratchers, including the Christmas movie *Miracle on 34th Street*.) But the extraordinary thing about *8½* is that it was the one and only film on the Legion of Decency's list that would later appear on that other list—we might even say, the opposite list—which is the subject of this book.

The 1995 Vatican Film List includes *8½* under the heading "Art" rather than "Values" or "Religion," and in some ways it is readily apparent why. The film is not obscene, but it is erotic. It does not denigrate humanity or depict people unlovingly *per se*, but everyone in the picture is lost and broken. On the surface, Fellini did not follow Pius XII's advice about making an ideal film, and it was low-hanging fruit for the Legion of Decency. Yet at the same time, it is visually stunning, provokes deep contemplation about the nature of art and human existence, and contains embedded within virtually every frame the message that divine power still creates new things through broken creatures. As with Michelangelo and Mozart—imperfect men who were able to generate glimmers of perfection—so with Guido Anselmi, the fictional director in *8½*, and with Fellini himself.

The inclusion of *8½* on the Vatican Film List—as well as other titles containing potentially subversive elements—says a lot about the sophistication of the sensibility underlying its selection. Neither doctrinaire nor moralistic, this choice of films implicitly recognizes that works of art can be appreciated from various angles, and that beauty, goodness, and truth can be found among people living outside the boundaries of visible unity with the Church.

We might even identify the Vatican Film List as the opening of the gates to the kind of cultural evangelization that

Bishop Robert Barron and the Word on Fire movement carries forward today: a friendly, inquisitive, optimistic engagement with the wider culture that seeks not merely to instruct and correct but to "consolidate, complete, and raise up the truth and the goodness that God has distributed among men and nations . . . for the glory of God, the confusion of the demon, and the happiness of man."

The Vatican List was issued during the pontificate of Pope John Paul II, and four years later the poet and former theater actor released his landmark "Letter to Artists." The document does not mention cinema by name, but its general encouragement of art of all kinds might remind us of the powerful role film can play in the New Evangelization. Preoccupied less by decency and ideals than by a desire to engage and employ whatever cultural tools are available to help spread the Gospel, the Polish pope emphasizes the Church's long history as an active participant in culture. Such participation includes the biblical writings of St. Paul and St. John and the theology of St. Justin Martyr and St. Cyril of Alexandria, all of which expound eternal truth in the light of pre-Christian poetry and philosophy. It includes the medieval monks who preserved the myths of pagan peoples and the early modern Jesuit missionaries who couched the Gospel in the cultural trappings of Asia. More recently, it includes the Second Vatican Council's endorsement of a more constructive, bridge-building approach to non-Catholic traditions and cultures in order to bring the light of the Gospel to all parts of the world. In short, receiving, reflecting upon, and, where need be, reinterpreting the most beautiful products of the human imagination has long been central to the mission of Christianity.

Art needs the Church, John Paul II stresses in "Letter to Artists," but the Church also needs art. Far from being opposed to each other, the two enjoy "a relationship offered in friendship, openness, and dialogue." But how do we go about this relationship? How do we approach works of culture like the films on this list in an open, generous way, while also heeding St. Paul's exhortation, "Do not be conformed to this world, but be transformed by the renewing of your minds" (Rom. 12:2)?

One answer to this question is to take an interest in these films as studies of humanity—of those creatures whom God made and loves, indeed, loves so profoundly that he *became* human himself. However odd or unfamiliar the works of art may be—and the human lives and circumstances they represent—an honest engagement with them will grant insights into the questions and convictions that occupy the minds and hearts of our neighbors, friends, and family members.

Another answer is to engage with these films as exercises in compassion, as opportunities to expand our perspectives and stretch our sympathies in a way that prepares the natural soil of our affections for supernatural charity. With the changeless doctrines of the faith as a bedrock, we can enjoy the freedom and confidence to "go to the peripheries, not only geographically, but also the existential peripheries," as Pope Francis encourages us, sharing (and discovering as we go) the light of life even amidst "the mystery of sin, of pain, of injustice, of ignorance and indifference to religion, of intellectual currents, and of all forms of misery."

In addition to informing our minds and enlarging our hearts, there is a third reason to immerse ourselves in films like those on the Vatican List. Simply knowing about these works of culture can generate opportunities for conversation and offer points of contact and caches of shared experience that are the immemorial grounds of friendship. Of course, watching movies together with other people is also a great way to strengthen social bonds and build community.

Finally, the exercise of imagination that is required in order to enter into a fictional world, a "subcreation" as Tolkien called it, is itself a profoundly human activity and one that has an analogue in the realm of religious commitment. Willingly to "suspend disbelief"—in Coleridge's words—and freely accept the paradigm of the story being presented on screen requires a viewer to step back from his own ego and entertain another perspective. It is a kind of surrender or abdication, even a conversion—at least for the duration of the movie—to a different perspective upon reality. As John Paul II put it, "Even beyond its typically religious expressions, true art has a close affinity with the world of faith, so that, even in situations where culture and the Church are far apart, art remains a kind of bridge to religious experience."

As seen in this short survey of the Church's engagement with cinema, we have come a long way from approaching films from the vantage point of either naïve approval or blanket condemnation. Rather, as John Paul II encourages us all, the Christian filmgoer today is called "to follow the path of the fruitful dialogue between the Church and artists which has gone on unbroken through two thousand years of history, and which still, at the threshold of the Third Millennium, offers rich promise for the future." It is our hope that *Popcorn with the Pope* will aid you in this dialogue.

*Note*: To indicate who has written what, we append our initials at the foot of each piece: DPB (David Paul Baird), AP (Andrew Petiprin), MW (Michael Ward).

PART I

# Religion

# *Andrei Rublev*

## 1966

*A series of entrancing, loosely related vignettes inspired by the
life and times of the late medieval painter of icons.*

A masterpiece of spiritual filmmaking that has been
described as the *War and Peace* of Russian cinema and
the best art house film of all time, *Andrei Rublev* offers an
impressionistic reflection upon art, morality, and faith in the
context of Russia's historically Orthodox Christian past. Divided into several poetically arranged episodes, the narrative
follows the historical (albeit artistically reimagined) figure
of Rublev as he moves across a medieval landscape peopled
by fellow monks, feudal patrons, Tartar invaders, profligate
pagans, and holy fools. Across this extended, meditative film,

he walks, he ponders, he talks to a few people, and then the film ends with a visual survey of some of his most celebrated works of art. This might not sound like much of a story, and in a certain sense it isn't: the character of Rublev, who ties the project together, does not even appear in every vignette. It is nonetheless a powerfully suggestive piece of filmmaking.

It is so powerful, in fact, that it was initially banned from cinemas. As the state-sponsored production of an officially atheistic regime, *Andrei Rublev* immediately came under fire by Soviet-era Goskino censors and was proscribed after only one screening. What explains such an explosive reaction to a movie that some viewers today will likely regard as a slow-moving, relatively uneventful art piece?

The answer almost certainly has to do with the film's perceived political implications, and some of its elements do, indeed, lend themselves to such interpretation. There is a prince, for instance, who, in a fit of petty jealousy, gouges out the eyes of a group of artisans to prevent them from creating something more beautiful for their next patron. If understood as a symbol of short-sighted and worldly governing authorities in general, this could be understood as offering a comment on contemporary times. A leader of the East German Communist Party apparently understood the film along these lines, asking how a picture could be made that showed the Russian people living under such abuse and neglect. It is an ironic comment, of course, given the film's fifteenth-century (rather than twentieth-century) setting, but such extrapolation from past to present is not as far-fetched as it might seem. The film's director, Andrei Tarkovsky, spoke

> Paint, paint, paint! . . .
> It is an awful sin to deny the divine spark.
> —KIRILL

> But haven't we the same faith, the same land,
> the same blood?
> —ANDREI RUBLEV

openly about using the film's historical material as an excuse to express his own ideas and address the issues of his age, and some of its first viewers seem to have taken this as the artistic equivalent of political dissidents demonstrating in Red Square.

The real political heft of *Andrei Rublev*, though, is probably more oblique than such reactions suggest. According to intimates of Tarkovsky, the film is not fundamentally an expression of the director's political opinions (apparently, he held almost none) but his lifelong search after a true spirituality—and it was this that, in a deep way, put the director at odds with the authorities and the established materialistic ideology of the Soviet regime. Speaking about his aim in *Andrei Rublev*, Tarkovsky describes wishing to trace how the artist overcame the moral (rather than political) difficulties of his epoch. He describes Rublev's art as striving to express a "noble peace, eternity, and harmony of the soul . . . [that] made it possible for him to create masterpieces, which will always remain relevant . . . [even] at a time when the life of the people was hopeless, when they were oppressed

As late as the Second World War, many of Rublev's icons were kept locked away in the Soviet Union, inaccessible to the public, but in Tarkovsky's day they enjoyed a revival of civic interest. In 1960, a museum was opened in Moscow to celebrate the 600th anniversary of Rublev's birth, promoting him as the Russian Leonardo da Vinci.

by a foreign yoke, by injustice, poverty." Such comments apply just as readily to Tarkovsky's own work, and it is very likely this aesthetic sensibility that tripped the censors' alarm. *Andrei Rublev* is not a direct, thinly veiled critique of contemporaneous politics but a more profound, indirect, yet perhaps ultimately more

> Actor Anatoly Solonitsyn's leading role in *Andrei Rublev* was his first appearance in a feature film. He went on to play major parts in each of Tarkovsky's subsequent movies. He was also intended for the lead roles in *Nostalgia* (1983) and *The Sacrifice* (1986) but died of cancer in 1982 at age forty-seven.

powerful commentary on real beauty, which, as the radiance of goodness and truth, censures wrongdoing and falsehood wherever found.

The film's opening spectacle of a primitive hot air balloon ride *could* be understood merely as setting the tone for an imaginative foray into times past, but given Tarkovsky's metaphysical sensibility, it more plausibly suggests a launch away from strictly earthbound concerns. Such a heavenward trajectory continues across the trials of the artist-monk, then reaches a climax in a final extended meditation upon several of Rublev's actual icons, in particular his most famous, a depiction of the Trinity modeled after the Old Testament story of the three supernatural visitors to Abraham and Sarah (Gen. 18). This survey finishes, penultimately, with an icon of Jesus Christ, and then cuts, ultimately and surprisingly, to photographic footage of horses standing in the rain.

This might seem like an odd, discontinuous ending, but it takes on a rich significance when considered in a wider cultural context. Whereas most of the religious art in the Latin West since the Renaissance has been secular in character, for Orthodox Christians, icons remain sacred; that is,

> You live in fear because you know no love
> but bestial love. Carnality without soul.
> But love should be brotherly.
> —ANDREI RUBLEV

they are regarded as visual analogues to Sacred Scripture. Unlike profane images designed merely to communicate at the level of information, the icon in this tradition prompts the weightier kind of consideration appropriate to divine revelation, which invites viewers to discern traces of transcendence in and beyond physical matter. Accordingly, while this kind of art can be appreciated from a nonreligious point of view, icons are "written" (not painted) with the intention of inviting viewers into an experience of adoration. This is worship not of the image in itself, but, in accordance with the distinction set out by the Second Council of Nicaea, worship that passes from the image to its prototype—namely, the Divine persons.

By following up the iconic meditation upon the Trinity with photographic footage of four horses—animals that play an important symbolic role in the film and are arranged here in a suggestive cluster of three and one—*Andrei Rublev* seems to conclude by asking whether such a naturalistic image, too, might be regarded iconologically. Does only sacred art facilitate this kind of contemplation of the Creator? Or might the creatures before our eyes also be perceived like icons, radiating timeless beauty in and through the stuff of earth?

If *Andrei Rublev* concludes by quietly encouraging such a world-transfiguring shift in perspective, the same kind of gaze can be directed retroactively to the other images in the film. Like Rublev's iconic image of the Trinity, which adheres to the ancient custom of only depicting God the Father indirectly, so too this film's images of a man on the road to holiness might be transformed into moving-picture-meditations upon eternity in time. Viewed in this light, Andrei Rublev himself becomes the fitting subject of spiritual meditation, a sanctified life that after much strain and trial has become luminous of the divine.

A striking echo of this perspective can be discerned in the film's next-to-last sequence, which centers upon the casting of a monumental church bell. In this vignette, the stupendous physical exertions of a teenage bellmaker—digging the hole for a massive cast, erecting the primitive furnaces, smelting the enormous bell itself—become outward, concrete reflections of the spiritual tumult Rublev undergoes on the way to creating his own masterwork. They also represent the transformation of the artist himself. "In the beginning, Rublev's belief was purely intellectual. It was the ideal he had been taught in the monastery," Tarkovsky reflects. But "towards the end he believed more in the ideals of love and the brotherhood of men, only because he had been able to suffer for this ideal alongside his people. And from that moment on, which is the end of our film, this ideal becomes unshakeable for him. Nothing can tear him away from it."

In *Andrei Rublev*, the artist who faithfully perfects his art—whether bellmaker, iconmaker, or, metacritically, filmmaker—becomes in the process a more perfect work of art himself, laboring and suffering to fashion ever more luminous images of the Artist

An iconological reading of *Andrei Rublev* adds a deeper layer of meaning to its slow, sometimes almost plodding pace. Even though the "long take" was part of the general language of cinema at the time, in this film, the style takes on a profound resonance with the still, patient, focused gaze encountered in and encouraged by icons.

beyond all artists, here in the midst of his most glorious work, creation.

From a holy human life to icons and horses standing in the rain, can we discover hints of divinity in the world around us? Is God's splendor still detectable amidst our squalor and our repeated, at times programmatic, efforts to suppress and obscure it? These are some of the questions raised, quietly yet forcefully, by this film, which, as slowly as a river, carves grandeur out of the wasteland of an allegedly materialistic universe.

In an appendix to *War and Peace*, Tolstoy remarks how the sprawling shape of his novel comes directly from the decision to subordinate artistic form to the vision the book exists to communicate. Likewise, in *Andrei Rublev*, narrative becomes servant to a more urgent purpose, offering to audiences a cinematic pedagogy in a sanctified way of seeing. Such a marriage of form and function—an iconic depiction of a maker of icons—makes *Andrei Rublev* not only one of Russia's great spiritual films but, indeed, one of humanity's great works of art.

*DPB*

*(Content advisory: contains some nudity and violence)*

## DISCUSSION QUESTIONS

- Is there a work of sacred art that has provided you with a special insight into eternal things? Or has something else beautiful done so?

- Have you ever encountered a beauty that challenged your view of the world or called you to become a better human being? If so, how have you responded?

- "It is an awful sin to deny the divine spark." What special ability or desire have you been given? How have you cultivated it?

# Babette's Feast

### 1987

*In nineteenth-century Denmark, two elderly sisters welcome into their strict religious sect a refugee Parisian widow, who thanks them with a display of amazing culinary artistry.*

Of all the movies discussed in *Popcorn with the Pope*, it is *Babette's Feast* that one could most easily imagine watching while eating popcorn with the pope. Pope Francis has named it his favorite film and even referred to it in his apostolic exhortation *Amoris Laetitia* (The Joy of Love), making *Babette's Feast* probably the only film ever to be mentioned in a magisterial document.

The Supreme Pontiff is not the only religious leader who admires this movie. Rowan Williams, who as the 104th

> Through all the world there goes one long cry from the heart of the artist: give me leave to do my utmost.
> —BABETTE, QUOTING ACHILLE PAPIN

Archbishop of Canterbury was for a decade the foremost cleric in the Anglican Communion, has also cited it as his favorite film. What is it about this small-scale Danish drama, in which little appears to happen beyond the preparation and eating of a meal, that makes it so appealing to senior ecclesiastical figures?

A superficial answer to that question might be that it is simply a reimagining of the Eucharist. Just as Jesus gives himself under the appearances of bread and wine to his twelve disciples, so Babette lavishes everything she has, all her money and skill, on a dozen dinner guests. Just as the Eucharist is a communion that brings life and peace to those who partake, so Babette's meal inspires her neighbors to forgive one another and revivify their community. And just as the priest at Mass confects the sacrament while dressed in special robes, so Babette acts as a kind of celebrant, wearing a pectoral cross and a white band around her neck that resembles a clerical collar.

The first Danish movie to win the Academy Award for Best Foreign Language Film, *Babette's Feast* is based on a 1958 short story by Karen Blixen who wrote under the name Isak Dinesen and is probably best known for her memoir *Out of Africa*, which was made into a film with Robert Redford and Meryl Streep.

We might be tempted to press the Eucharistic imagery further. In Catholic theology, the Body of the Lord Jesus fulfills what had been prefigured by the manna given to the people

> Babette can cook.
>
> —ACHILLE PAPIN

of Israel after the quails visited their camp (Exod. 16:13–15), while in the movie, Babette's specialty dish is "Cailles en Sarcophage," quails entombed in pastry. The very word sarcophage (literally, "flesh-eater") brings to mind Christ's statement "Those who eat my flesh and drink my blood have eternal life" (John 6:54).

While there may be some intellectual satisfaction to be derived from drawing these Eucharistic parallels, they only take one so far, for *Babette's Feast* is much more than an allegory; and, in any case, such an approach ignores almost the entire first half of the story, where we are introduced to the main characters and their setting. It is in this larger context that the feast acquires its real significance.

The protagonists are two sisters, Martine and Filippa, so named by their father, a Protestant pastor, after the sixteenth-century Reformers Martin Luther and Philip Melanchthon, whose piety he holds in high esteem. This pastor is a "good man" who has founded a Puritan assembly in a coastal hamlet, and his daughters dutifully tread the austere path he has laid down for them. They, like him, are full of good works. They spend much of their time and almost all their little money taking food to the poor and tending the sick.

The sisters had been great beauties in their day, and each had had a suitor. Martine was wooed by a young officer, the dissolute, debt-ridden Lorens Löwenhielm. Sent by his military superiors to rehabilitate himself for three months in Jutland with his aunt (a faithful member of the pastor's flock), Löwenhielm encounters Martine and is spellbound by her loveliness. He has a vision of a future life lived alongside this gentle angel, but the pastor is opposed to any such notion, and Löwenhielm regretfully rejoins the army. He marries a lady-in-waiting to the queen and proceeds to climb the ranks.

Filippa's youthful suitor was a genial opera singer, Achille Papin, who came from Paris to perform in Stockholm and then sought solitude in Jutland to restore his energies. He hears Filippa singing like an angel in church and imagines packed concert houses applauding her as a diva. He provides music lessons in the hope of wooing her but stands no chance of gaining the permission of Filippa's father, who views earthly love as an illusion. The fact that Papin is a papist only makes it worse, and he returns home, disconsolate.

Nevertheless, Papin does not forget the peaceful refuge in Denmark. Thirty-five years later, with civil strife raging in Paris, he directs to the sisters' household a poor woman who has lost her family during the unrest and dares not stay in France. Babette Hersant was once a famous chef at the Café Anglais, but all that Papin tells the sisters—in the greatest understatement ever—is "Babette can cook." They take her in and give her a home, and she learns how to prepare their meager, unappetizing meals. Fourteen years pass.

The pastor is now long dead, and his disciples are becoming testy and querulous. Martine and Filippa are grieved by the quarrels but hope to restore unity by celebrating the centenary of their father's birth. A modest supper and a cup of coffee will suffice to mark the occasion.

Orson Welles, who made *Citizen Kane*, named Blixen his favorite contemporary writer and attempted to adapt several of her stories for the big screen.

At this point, Babette receives astonishing news from Paris: she has won the French lottery and is suddenly fantastically rich. The sisters congratulate her on her ten thousand

francs and resign themselves
to her impending departure:
"The Lord gave," says Martine,
referencing Job 1:21—"and the
Lord took away" adds Filippa.
Babette, however, volunteers
to prepare for the anniversary

> Birgitte Federspiel,
> who plays the part
> of the older Martine,
> appears in another
> title on the Vatican
> Film List, *Ordet*.

celebration "a true French meal," and they accept her offer,
little imagining what she has in mind.

When they see how extravagant the meal will be—with
turtle soup, caviar, and, worst of all, wine—they fear for their
souls. It would ruin their late father's name if they indulged
their bodily appetites. On the other hand, it would offend
their housekeeper if they declined to partake. The safest
option, they conclude, will be to eat in silence and "just as if
we never had a sense of taste."

But they have not reckoned with Babette's artistry, nor
with the insights of Lorens Löwenhielm, who is back visiting
his aged aunt and is a last-minute addition to the guest list.
As a man of means who has in the past enjoyed many a fine
meal at the Café Anglais, he alone recognizes the superb
quality of the banquet spread before them.

In another great drama set in Denmark, *Hamlet*, Shakespeare coins the phrase "caviar to the general," meaning a fine
thing unappreciated by the masses. Babette's haute cuisine
proves to be a superlative example of this—but it is also "caviar
to the General," for Löwenhielm has attained that military
rank. (Did this pun generate the whole story, one wonders?)
Gradually, the General opens the eyes of his fellow diners to
the fact that they are consuming food and wine that is almost
impossibly wonderful. Led by his enraptured example, they
learn to savor, relish, and relax. They taste and see that the
feast is good.

> Righteousness and truth have had a lover.
> —GENERAL LÖWENHIELM

In terms of the film's Eucharistic parallels, the General's role at this point provides an interesting contrast with, rather than similarity to, the Last Supper. Löwenhielm is the odd one out, a Judas figure, but Judas in reverse, a positive version of Judas, the one diner among the twelve not betraying his God-given senses.

This is not to suggest that the other eleven diners are reprobates—and indeed, it is precisely in its handling of this question that the deep gentleness of the story comes to the fore. Martine and Filippa are genuinely good people, and so are the others at table. They are God-fearing, law-abiding, humble folk, trying to follow the light that has been granted to them. Admittedly, that light is somewhat dim, a point reflected in the muted color scheme, the Vilhelm Hammershøi palette, which pervades the film's cinematography. These simple Christians know too little about the value of their God-given senses. It takes them long to learn that wine gladdens the heart (Ps. 104:15). But their limitations are depicted with quiet humor, not savage satire.

The relatively unlimited world inhabited by Löwenhielm and Papin also receives a critique. Each of these outsiders perceives the vanity of the life he has chosen and longs for the purity of heart exhibited by the golden-haired sisters. Papin, in particular, who is preoccupied with thoughts of the grave, tells Filippa (in a letter) that by renouncing worldly ambition she has chosen the better path, and that after death she will become the great artist God intended her to be, and will enchant the angels in heaven with her singing.

Babette, however, has a different view about the timeline for artistic fulfillment. She will not deny her senses or postpone her hopes: she trusts the goodness of creation, takes joy in the here and now, and transforms a mere meal into a kind of love affair. In one glorious action, she supplies both the physical and spiritual needs of those she serves, giving of her all, as in the story of the widow's mite (Mark 12:41–44).

Löwenhielm's verdict on the feast is simple: "Righteousness and truth have had a lover." He understands what has happened as an act of worship: the chef has humbly reached up toward the transcendent, forging a link between God and man. Replete with Babette's exquisite fare, the diners leave the house, hold hands, and dance around the well in the middle of the hamlet under the night sky as the stars rotate in their courses above. The circle, perfection's symbol, has become visible on earth as it is in heaven.

In the final exchange, Babette tells the sisters that the "one long cry from the heart" of every artist throughout the world is "Give me the chance to do my very best." Filippa responds through tears (echoing Papin's words), "In paradise you will be the truly great artist God meant you to be. How you will delight all the angels!" But Babette is wiser: she knows she needn't wait till then. She has already delighted the angels, both the myriads in heaven and the two angelic sisters she has come to know on earth. And of her lottery jackpot there is not one single franc left over.

*MW*

## DISCUSSION QUESTIONS

- The film shows that eating together can have a healing effect in human relationships. How realistic is this? If so, why?

- Babette treats her feast as an act both of love and of artistry. How often, if ever, have you taken a similar view of the meals you make?

- What are the chief similarities and dissimilarities between the feast portrayed in the film and the Last Supper of Jesus with his disciples?

# *Ben-Hur*

## 1959

*An epic adaptation of Lew Wallace's historical novel, set during the time of Christ, in which Prince Judah Ben-Hur is betrayed by a Roman friend and enslaved, then finds freedom and returns seeking revenge.*

*B*en-Hur was a massive gamble—and a rip-roaring success. It was a gamble because it was the most expensive movie ever made up to that point, costing over $15 million. It was a success because it won an unprecedented number of Academy Awards and became the second highest grossing movie to date after *Gone with the Wind*. It would also go on to be the only Hollywood movie included in the "Religion" category of the

Vatican Film List; its religious power, or possible lack thereof, is a question we will return to at the end of this commentary.

The commercial triumph of *Ben-Hur* was especially welcome to the production studio Metro-Goldwyn-Mayer at that point in its history. They were suffering severe financial pressure, even possible bankruptcy, because of increasing competition from television and the impact of the Hollywood Antitrust Case of 1948, which prevented studios from owning theater chains that exclusively showed their own movies. It is not going too far to say that *Ben-Hur* was a wager laid to save the studio from collapse.

MGM knew well that religious subject matter could be a profitable vein to mine. Back in 1925, they had had huge success with a silent adaptation of the best-selling American novel *Ben-Hur: A Tale of the Christ* by Lew Wallace. It now seemed due for a remake, not least because other Bible-adjacent stories such as *Quo Vadis* (1951) and *The Robe* (1953) had recently confirmed the continuing public appetite for such material. Academy Award–winner William Wyler, who had assisted with the 1925 version, was appointed director. Charlton Heston, who had recently starred as Moses in *The Ten Commandments* (1956), was cast in the lead role as Judah Ben-Hur, a prince of Judea.

In order to establish a reverential atmosphere and indicate respect for this popular "tale of the Christ," Wyler took the extraordinary step of silencing Leo, the famous lion in the company's logo. Normally, an MGM movie would be introduced by Leo's roars, but for this film a still and silent shot of the customary masthead was deemed a more appropriate way to usher in the opening peaceful scene, set in Bethlehem, where shepherds and three wise men kneel worshipfully on a star-lit night before a newborn child.

The film that thus begins with Christmas Day ends nearly four hours later with Good Friday. In the interim,

*Ben-Hur* was the first film ever to win eleven Academy Awards, a tally equalled by *Titanic* (1997) and *The Return of the King* (2003). No film has ever won more.

Jesus appears only occasionally, is shown usually from behind, and never speaks. This "tale of the Christ" is not a retelling of the Gospels but focuses instead on the fictional character of Ben-Hur and his intermittent encounters with the long-prophesied Redeemer.

The story is set mostly in Jerusalem and centers on the Judean prince's relationship with a Roman named Messala, who had been his boyhood friend but is now an officer of the occupying imperial force. Messala, anxious to make a name for himself as a commander, wants Ben-Hur to help him suppress the Judean rebels, but his former playmate refuses to be a turncoat: "I would do anything for you, Messala, except betray my own people." Enraged, Messala consigns him to slavery in the Roman navy ("By condemning without hesitation an old friend, I shall be feared"). Marched in a chain gang to the galleys and desperate with thirst, Ben-Hur is given water to drink by a mysterious stranger who emerges from a carpenter's shop in Nazareth. Meanwhile, back in Jerusalem, his mother, Miriam, and sister, Tirzah, are imprisoned, as is his household steward, whose daughter, Esther, is in love with the banished prince.

Three years elapse. In a battle with Macedonian pirates, Ben-Hur's ship is destroyed, but he escapes and saves the life of the Roman consul, Quintus Arrius, who, in gratitude, frees him from slavery and adopts him as his son.

Sextus, you ask how to fight an idea.
Well, I'll tell you how . . . with another idea!
—MESSALA

The Roman decurion's command to his men about Ben-Hur—"No water for him!"— became the on-set catchphrase whenever anyone in the cast or crew made a mistake.

Ben-Hur becomes an expert charioteer and returns to Judea where Esther tells him that his mother and sister are dead, whereas in fact (as she well knows) they have contracted leprosy. An Arab sheik, Ilderim, persuades Ben-Hur to drive his chariot in a race against Messala and thus exact his revenge: "There is no law in the arena. Many are killed." In the chariot race (one of the most thrilling live action sequences ever shot for the silver screen) Messala falls and is fatally trampled by horses. Before he dies, he informs Ben-Hur that he should look for Miriam and Tirzah in the Valley of the Lepers, "if you can recognize them."

Relieved to know that they still live but grieved to know of their condition, Ben-Hur locates his mother and sister and takes them to see a Jewish rabbi who, according to Esther, has the gifts of a healer. But this rabbi turns out to be under arrest and is shortly thereafter condemned to death by crucifixion. Carrying his cross to the place of execution, he falls in front of Ben-Hur, who suddenly recognizes the man from Nazareth who years earlier had given him water to drink. Returning that display of pity, Ben-Hur lifts a cup of water to the lips of Jesus before Roman soldiers intervene.

The climax soon follows with a thunderstorm and cloudburst as Jesus dies on the cross, the rain miraculously washing clean the leprous faces of Miriam and Tirzah. Ben-Hur embraces them and, with them, Esther, who still loves him, a love he reciprocates. The final shot of the movie, accompanied by an invisible choir singing "Hallelujah," shows three empty crosses on a distant hillside and, in the foreground, a shepherd leading a flock of sheep.

This brings us back to the question of religion. Does the final shot imply that Ben-Hur is now among the flock of those whom Christ, the Good Shepherd, has chosen? It is difficult to tell because Jesus is portrayed as such an elusive figure. His role in the story is little more than that of a roving silhouette. He is played by Claude Heater, an American opera singer, whose performance in this his only feature film went uncredited because it was a nonspeaking part.

But although Jesus never speaks, we are repeatedly told *about* things he is reported to have said. Ester informs Ben-Hur at one point: "He said, 'Blessed are the merciful for they shall obtain mercy.'" And again: "I've heard of a young rabbi who says that forgiveness is greater and love more powerful than hatred. I believe it." From an evangelistic point of view, Esther is to be lauded for her willingness to spread the word and share her faith. From an artistic point of view, however, her lines are more questionable. They are the sort of thing that a "Basil Exposition" character would say by way of providing needful background information, while not advancing the dramatic trajectory of the current scene. Esther's lines indicate the importance of being open to mercy and forgiveness, but by directly stating the issues at stake rather than suggesting them, the dialogue comes dangerously close to being didactic. And this is somewhat ironic given how indirect is the presentation of Jesus himself. The writers of the screenplay keep Jesus offstage, but then make (their distillation of) his message rather too obviously center stage. It is perhaps appropriate that the one Academy Award this

> One God, that I can understand; but one wife?
> That is not civilized.
> —SHEIK ILDERIM

> Catherine Wyler, speaking of her father, the director of *Ben-Hur*, William Wyler, said, "He wanted to make a movie that a broad audience would like, irrespective of their religious beliefs."

film was nominated for and did *not* win was Best Screenplay.

Ben-Hur finally accepts the message of forgiveness as he witnesses Christ's Crucifixion. He confesses to Esther that, "almost at the moment [Jesus] died, I heard him say, 'Father, forgive them, for they know not what they do.' . . . And I felt his voice take the sword out of my hand." The "sword" no doubt represents his hatred of Messala and his passionate desire to rid the world of Roman tyranny, by bloodshed if necessary. In the grip of that passion, Ben-Hur had earlier told Esther that it would be better if she did not love him, and she had effectively agreed: "Hatred is turning you to stone. . . . It is as though you have become Messala. I've lost you, Judah." But now, in the wake of Christ's death, she has found him again because he has found his better self. Through the shed blood of this "man who is more than a man," Ben-Hur has been cleansed from his hatred, just as his mother and sister have been cleansed from their leprosy.

His change of heart is morally admirable, but to what extent is it dramatically appreciable or, for that matter, doctrinally comprehensible? We only know that such a conversion has occurred because Ben-Hur tells Esther about it after the fact. We don't see it actually happening, at least not in any very discernible fashion. True, while witnessing the events at Calvary, Ben-Hur looks thoughtful when told that Christ's imminent death will be a "beginning," not an end, and his eyes become large and wet as he emerges out of the shadows in order to gaze upon the crucified figure more intently. These signifiers of a changing internal state may prove sufficient

> I heard him say, 'Father, forgive them, for they know not what they do.' . . . And I felt his voice take the sword out of my hand.
>
> —JUDAH BEN-HUR

for many viewers. Others may find it hard to perceive that anything psychologically significant or theologically coherent is going on. What could this predicted "beginning" mean to Ben-Hur? Has he been vouchsafed foreknowledge of the empty tomb that surprised even Christ's own disciples? The Resurrection is essential to Christian faith, but Christ is never shown rising from the dead, so it is difficult to understand the spiritual logic of the protagonist's transformation. The surging music makes it clear that something life-changing is taking place, but when one reflects upon it afterward, it feels somehow insubstantial and unsatisfactory—more *religiose* than truly religious.

*Ben-Hur* proved to be the salvation of MGM; Ben-Hur's own salvation is more debatable. It occurs in a tale of the Christ, yet Christ is hardly in the tale, and its telling does not extend to the events of Easter Day. In the end, William Wyler's Lion of Judah, like MGM's Leo, is a lion who doesn't get to roar.

*MW*

## DISCUSSION QUESTIONS

- Would *Ben-Hur* have been better, worse, or no different if the face of Jesus Christ had been shown and his voice heard?

- If you didn't know the story of Christ, how much would your enjoyment of *Ben-Hur* be affected?

- Charlton Heston, in his autobiography *In the Arena*, wrote that he would probably not have been cast as Ben-Hur in the modern age because he was not Jewish. How important is it that an actor's real-life identity reflects that of the character being portrayed?

# *The Flowers of St. Francis*

**1950**

*A series of lighthearted vignettes that focuses on the everyday experience of St. Francis of Assisi and his first followers as they live simply in community and go out to preach the Gospel in thirteenth-century Italy.*

Rare even among the famous saints, St. Francis' total love of God and neighbor has made him the subject of devotion and curiosity from his own lifetime in the Middle Ages down to the present day. Full of eccentricities but unrivaled in piety, Francis displayed a simple, active witness to the truth of the Gospel and eschewed possessions and permanence to respond in a radical way to Christ's call to discipleship and evangelization. He has long been the subject of arts high and low—from the paintings of El Greco to the ubiquitous statues of the saint in church gardens and outside private homes. Many filmmakers have focused on his life and work as well, and among them is Roberto Rossellini, whose *Flowers of St. Francis* ranks among his finest works.

Fresh off a trilogy of neorealist films about World War II, Rossellini conceived *The Flowers of St. Francis* as part of an ongoing exploration of how to live in his native Italy after the experience of Mussolini and his Fascisti, the country's alliance with Nazi Germany, and a civilizational struggle to defeat the evil that they represented. Rossellini was raised Catholic, and his childhood faith was inseparable from the institutions and values of his homeland. After the brutality of war, he believed that his people needed to rediscover the bedrock virtues of faith, hope, and charity. Moreover, after dark days, they needed to laugh and enjoy the lighter side of existence. St. Francis and his companions were just the thing for what Rossellini's daughter Isabella described as "recreating an image for Italy." Out with the political strongmen, and in with humble servant-leaders. Out with the sorrows of worldly violence, and in with the joy of the divine Gospel.

Consistent with the principles of neorealist filmmaking that Rossellini pioneered, *The Flowers of St. Francis* is radically simple and inexpensive, and the dialogue is minimal. The camerawork is neither elaborate nor intrusive, using wide and medium shots to capture people in their everyday surroundings. There are very few professional actors in the cast; in fact, St. Francis and his companions are played by actual monks who also appeared in one of Rossellini's earlier films, *Paisan*. In what is surely a rare cinematic phenomenon, most of the cast truly profess the Christianity they discuss

> Cowriter Federico Fellini described the film as "neorealism in an unlikely guise."

and enact on screen, creating a natural tenderness toward the things of faith that greatly enhances the audience's appreciation of the subject. The film is also cowritten by Federico Fellini, the director of *8½* and *La Strada*, also included on the Vatican Film List, and *The Flowers of St. Francis* maintains an intriguing dream-like quality akin to these works. Thus, between Rossellini and Fellini, there is a merger of earthiness and mysticism—a perfect combination for depicting a man and a movement that are nearly synonymous with Jesus' injunction to be in the world but not of it (see John 17:11, 16).

The nine vignettes of the movie are mostly adapted from the anonymous fourteenth-century Italian work *Little Flowers of St. Francis*. The stories are almost all lighthearted, highlighting the near reckless abandon the first Franciscans embraced in their service of Christ, and reminding today's audience of the ongoing possibility of an all-encompassing faith.

The first chapter introduces Brother Ginepro, who features just as prominently as Francis throughout the film, and whose holy foolishness is both hilarious and touching. In the fourth vignette, Ginepro attempts to help a sick, hungry brother who asks for a pig's foot. He finds a pig, cuts off its foot, and is astonished when the pig's owner expresses anger at the maiming of his animal. In the sixth story, Ginepro is left behind to cook while the other brothers preach, and he attempts to boil two-weeks-worth of vegetables so that he can join his brothers in the mission field. When Francis returns, he is at first annoyed, but is then moved with compassion, telling Ginepro that he may go out and preach, but he must begin every sermon saying, "I talk and talk, yet I

> The Italian title of the film is *Francesco, giullare di Dio*, which means "Francis, God's jester." In fact, it was Brother Ginepro (Juniper), not Francis, who was known as the jester.

> It's better to preach by example than by words.
> —ST. FRANCIS

accomplish little." In the most memorable of all the vignettes, Ginepro attempts to preach to a tribe of barbarians led by the buffoon-like tyrant Nicalaio, played by Aldo Fabrizi, one of the few major actors in the film. With physical comedy on par with Buster Keaton or the Marx Brothers, Ginepro almost gets himself executed, but ultimately disarms the warlord and turns back the marauders through a disposition of sheer humility.

The scenes that focus on St. Francis are deeply moving, and among the most striking moments is the encounter between Francis and St. Clare in the third vignette. In its depiction of the shared conversation and prayer of these two saints, the audience may better understand a partnership that would transform the Christian world. In another scene—this time without any dialogue—Francis approaches a leper, embraces him, and then collapses in tears. His heart, like the Lord's, is closest to those most in need of healing and most easily despised by the world. In the eighth vignette, Rossellini depicts one of the best-known stories of the saint: a discussion between Francis and Brother Leone on the topic of happiness. After dismissing several ideas about the true nature of happiness, Francis leads Leone to a nearby estate and knocks on the door. The proprietor throws them down a steep flight of stone steps and into the mud, whereupon Francis bursts into laughter, declaring that they have found what they were looking for.

Playfulness characterizes the life of Francis' community, as it still characterizes some of the most inspiring Christian witnesses today. When the friars get caught in the rain, for example, they choose not to curse the inconvenience, but

> O Lord, make me an instrument of your peace. Where there is hatred, let me bring love. Where there is discord, let me bring harmony. Where there is pain, let me bring joy, and where there is despair, hope. O Master, grant that I may not so much seek to be loved as to love, and may all on earth learn the secret of your peace, which is the fruit of justice and brotherly love.
> —ST. FRANCIS

rather to splash around and find joy in the experience. At the end of the film, Francis asks his followers to spin around and get dizzy in order to seek the will of the Lord. The direction they are facing when they collapse, Francis tells them, will determine where God wants them to go and proclaim the Gospel. Out of this childlike openness to the will of God, the first Franciscans show the world how fun it can be to give oneself over entirely to Christian mission. As they travel, Francis and his cohort find they always have as much as they need, and more. As Jesus says, "Strive first for the kingdom of God and his righteousness, and all these things will be given to you as well" (Matt. 6:33).

Upon seeing *The Flowers of St. Francis*, Monsignor Angelo Roncalli, the future Pope St. John XXIII, told Rossellini, "Poor man, you don't know what you've done." Perhaps Roncalli meant that no matter how high Rossellini ascended in the artistic community, he would always be considered a cheerleader for the Church after making such an overtly Christian film. But he may have meant something more, implying that through the film, Rossellini would help the world rediscover the path to holiness, in imitation of St. Francis centuries earlier. As St. Francis was tasked with rebuilding the Church in his day, an artist like Rossellini and a prelate like Roncalli were both called to the work of renewal in the violent and divisive environment of the twentieth century. As the pope

Isabella Rossellini once revealed that her father wanted to give the monks something in gratitude for their appearance in the film. Since they were bound by a vow of poverty and could not receive payment, they asked for a spectacular display of fireworks for their town, and the director agreed to arrange it.

would say in his opening address at the Second Vatican Council, the Church "extends the frontiers of Christian love, the most powerful means of eradicating the seeds of discord, the most effective means of promoting concord, peace with justice, and universal brotherhood." By bringing St. Francis into the lives of millions of ordinary people, Rossellini played his part in the same divine mission.

In *The Flowers of St. Francis*, Rossellini puts forward the best of Christianity, leaving aside abstractions, and gives the world a dose of laughter and good cheer. Amid the ups and downs of institutional Church life, the film offers refreshment for believers and nonbelievers alike, showing the love of God and neighbor in action. In the end, Rossellini's film shows that the kingdom of God is open to everyone, requiring neither money nor brainpower, but rather an open heart and an adventurous spirit.

*AP*

## DISCUSSION QUESTIONS

- Where have you witnessed radical service to God in the form of poverty, chastity, and obedience? To what degree do you embrace these virtues in your own life?

- Pope Francis' encyclical *Laudato Si* begins with these words from St. Francis: "Praise be to you, my Lord, through our Sister, Mother Earth, who sustains and governs us, and who produces various fruit with colored flowers and herbs." In what ways are we called to live in harmony not only with other human beings but with the rest of the created world?

- What is the place of laughter and humor in your spiritual life? Are you prone to take yourself too seriously or not seriously enough?

# *Francesco*

## 1989

*A jolting, discomfiting, yet illuminating foray into the life*
*of the beloved saint of Assisi.*

One of the most recent entries on the Vatican List of
notable films, *Francesco*'s original English dialogue and
cast of recognizable Anglophone actors might lead one to
expect some sort of slick Hollywood feature—which it is not.
Rather, the dialogue of this Italian production is choppy and
conspicuously overdubbed. The narrative jumps between
episodes with an almost convulsive sense of urgency. The
acting is clunky and emotionally supercharged. Yet, for all
of this, the film might also be considered a masterpiece of

spiritual filmmaking that captures the genius of St. Francis as potently and evocatively as any other work of art.

In comparing *Francesco* to the other film on the Vatican List on the same subject, *The Flowers of St. Francis* (1950), it would be understandable to mistake them for portraits of different men. Whereas the two titular figures both come across as men not of this world, each carries his otherworldliness with a distinctive kind of gait and gesture. The Francis in *Flowers* embodies this serenely, his toes scarcely seeming to touch the dust of earth. The Francis in *Francesco*, by contrast, almost seems to burst from the screen as a red-blooded son of the soil tormented by a restless, interior prodding and inescapable sense of destiny.

This interpretation of a more unruly side of the saint's personality is accentuated by the counterintuitive (yet in the end inspired) decision to cast the role of Francis with American actor and notorious bad boy Mickey Rourke. Despite the conspicuous mismatch between Rourke's public image and the preconceived idea of a saint in many of our minds, this was a bold, brilliant piece of casting because, in dramatic terms, it gives the character somewhere to go. Well-known actors all but inevitably carry some of their real-life personas into the roles they play, and if Rourke seems like a poor fit for what the saint became by the end of his life, he also supplies some startling insight into the sort of man he might well have been toward his beginnings.

> The Gospel is a strong, meek man, vigorous and tender, a man who knows how to cry and knows how to laugh, a man who can be excited or desperate, a man who faces the cross with his heart. A man like you, in other words; a man who doesn't draw back.
> —CLARE TO FRANCIS

> I thought that love had made his body identical to the Beloved's and I asked myself whether I would ever be capable of loving that much.
> —CLARE, SPEAKING OF FRANCIS' STIGMATA

Giovanni di Pietro di Bernardone (the birth name of the saint we know better by his nickname, which means "the Frenchman") was born one of several children of a prosperous cloth merchant in the late twelfth century. By all accounts, as a young man "Francesco" did not refrain from enjoying the luxuries afforded by his family's wealth, indulging in the typical diversions and expensive pleasures of the gentleman soldier and dandy. Unlike the depiction in *Flowers*, then, which introduces the man well down the rocky road to sainthood, in *Francesco* we meet him still surrounded by the silks and other exclusive comforts of high society. The offstage persona that Rourke carried with him onto the set helps root this film's portrayal firmly in this early period of Francis' life, making obvious how this one-day saint started out (like many of us) with a long way to go.

The overall impression is of a St. Francis who is ceaselessly tugged about by interior tumult and embroiled in exterior controversies he can never quite escape. If it all sounds rather tendentious and overwrought, that's because it is. But it is also certainly not boring, as depictions of the saints too often are.

The reason for this, arguably, is because too many of us approach the saints with a naïve understanding of what holiness really is. It is tempting to look back on a saint's life as a *fait accompli*, a finished triumph of static sanctity. Yet in a world where the vast majority of human beings still persistently undermine themselves

> Director Liliana Cavani made two other films about St. Francis before *Francesco*.

through complicity with sin, the kingdom of heaven suffers violence, as we read in Matthew's Gospel, "and the violent take it by force" (Matt. 11:12). Whatever our Lord meant by these perplexing words, he certainly did not mean that his followers can look forward to a life of blissfully uninterrupted walks in the park. Rather, holiness on earth is a struggle, and it is perhaps the chief accomplishment of this flawed, masterful film that it captures something of the flavor of the inescapable (but not, thank heavens, interminable) drama of sanctification.

Composer Vangelis also wrote the music for *Chariots of Fire.*

Returning to the comparison with *Flowers of St. Francis*, the saint's progress toward holiness in *Francesco* does not proceed like a kind of glassy-eyed, sad-smiled levitation over and around the troubles of this world. Rather, it conveys a sense of being dragged right through them, of getting prodded, barefoot and only half-willingly, over raw terrain. This Francis succumbs to moods, alternating between a kind of manic antsiness and a somehow even more disconcerting Olympian calm, which never attains to the transcendent composure of the earlier film. He struggles—and it is often a struggle to watch—all the way from his untidy embrace of this-worldly poverty to the epiphanic moment of the stigmata. Yet when he does get there, impressively, the miracle feels neither like an incomprehensible, alien event nor like a dismissible, mawkishly sentimental add-on, as portrayals of such moments in religious art so easily can. Instead, because this Francis attains a glory that is the fruit of an agony, the miracle feels fitting, even earned. This resurrection is inseparable from a cross, and for this reason, feels believable.

*Flowers* and *Francesco* supply us with very different portraits, yet the two individuals they give us might also be regarded as complementary angles on one mystery. Indeed,

Francesco is one of the most common male names in Italy.

some measure of outward composure and interior untidiness might well have been elements in the personality of this saint, who can sometimes seem, especially from the perspective of a purely this-worldly practicality, romantic and idealistic to a fault.

If any given artistic representation will necessarily fail to capture some dimension of so towering and complex a figure, a fruitful comparison might be made with the contrasting representations of the crucified Christ. Ancient Christians who wished to emphasize the divinity of our Lord and his triumph over death typically depicted the Cross in a style later dubbed *Christus Victor*. In this style, Christ is portrayed in total self-command, his torso and appendages arranged in clean perpendicular lines, almost seeming to levitate mid-Ascension while only momentarily pausing for this spectacle far beneath his dignity. The *Christus Patiens* of many medieval crucifixes, by contrast, emphasizes Christ's humanity and descent into our fallen human condition, his bent and bloodied body often sagging under the weight of a violent, windswept world. These diverging styles supply pictures of Jesus Christ that are almost opposites—yet both are true.

In like manner, the jagged, discomfiting portraiture of St. Francis that we discover in *Francesco* offers us an unsettling yet believable image of what human holiness might actually look like. Unofficial patron of poets, dreamers, and persons who will never quite feel at home in this world, the saint of Assisi continues to inspire but also to disrupt those of us who have grown a little too cozy in our comforts. Similarly, something about the consistently inconsistent character of this piece of spiritual filmmaking communicates at an almost visceral level the theology at its heart. Everything about *Francesco* may be just a little out of sync. Yet, rather like the extraordinary person it depicts, all of these conspicuous failures might just amount to something better than success: a seemingly impossible transformation that turns out to be just as factual as it is miraculous.

*DPB*

(*Content advisory: contains nudity*)

### DISCUSSION QUESTIONS

- Do you prefer the depiction of St. Francis in *Francesco* or *The Flowers of St. Francis*? Why?

- Is every Christian called to some kind of Francis-like poverty? How Francis-like should it be?

- If St. Francis saw how you live, would he approve?

# *The Gospel According to St. Matthew*

## **1964**

*A portrayal of the life of Jesus Christ based on texts from St. Matthew's Gospel selected by director Pier Paolo Pasolini.*

The Vatican Film List was compiled during the pontificate of John Paul II, a pope who was also a playwright and whose 1999 "Letter to Artists" indicated his interest in improving the relationship between the Church and those whose vocation is in the arts. But the Polish pope was not the first occupant of the chair of St. Peter to have such an interest. John XXIII founded the Vatican Film Library with the aim of collecting and preserving films on the life of the Church.

> To the dear, happy, familiar memory of Pope John XXIII
> —WORDS OF DEDICATION SHOWN
> AT THE START OF THE FILM

John XXIII was also indirectly responsible for inspiring *The Gospel According to St. Matthew.* In 1962, when the director Pier Paolo Pasolini attended a seminar in Assisi on the theme of "Cinema as a Spiritual Force in the Present," it turned out that the pope was visiting the town too. The crowds awaiting the papal visit clogged the streets, confining Pasolini to his room in the Franciscan monastery where he was staying. There he found a copy of the Gospels, which he read straight through like a novel, and it was this that motivated him to make his most religious film, which came out just two years later.

It is shot in black and white, with locations in southern Italy standing in for Bethlehem, Nazareth, and Jerusalem. It uses nonprofessional actors and a large cast of extras, including lots of refreshingly rambunctious children. The budget is low, with virtually no special effects: for instance, there is no star moving over Bethlehem (the arrival of the Magi occurs during the day) and the man with a withered hand is replaced by a disabled man on two sticks (presumably the unwithering of a hand would be expensive to portray). "Cast thy crutches away from thee" is the only intrusion of an obviously nonscriptural line.

The screenplay is derived (almost entirely) from the first Gospel, although Pasolini himself takes a writing credit, reflecting the fact that the texts used were selected and ordered by him. The only non-Matthaean text is a couple of verses from Isaiah, which are never quoted by the Evangelist.

These verses from Isaiah, alongside the numerous Old Testament quotations with which Matthew sprinkles his account ("a virgin shall conceive," "out of Egypt I called my son," etc.) are spoken by a narrator over the action. The most notable of these narrations comes at the Crucifixion, when the screen turns black and the voice declares, "Hearing you will hear and not understand; seeing you will see and not perceive, for the heart of this people has been hardened and with their ears they have been hard of hearing and their eyes they have closed lest at any time they see with their eyes and hear with their ears and understand with their mind." These verses (from Isa. 6) appear in the thirteenth chapter of Matthew, not in the Passion narrative of chapter 27. Their transferal to the Crucifixion scene epitomizes Pasolini's moral seriousness. Although an atheist, he was not seeking to undercut or satirize his biblical source material. By placing these words in the climactic scene, he challenges the audience to ponder their own commitment to honest, unbiased perception.

This challenging intent affects the way he shapes the entire film. From the very first scene—consisting mostly of meaningful looks exchanged between Mary and Joseph—Pasolini opts for daringly long takes. If we didn't know better, we might think at the start that this is a silent movie. But no: we are simply being required to see and perceive, and to do so at a slow, meditative pace. We will not be allowed to fall back upon a heavily articulated script that makes things clear for us, nor upon prescriptive camera angles or lighting cues; we must look carefully at the faces on screen and at their minute changes in expression, thereby involving ourselves actively in the process of interpretation.

Pasolini initially considered giving the part of Jesus to someone with a profile as a nonconformist, such as Allen Ginsberg or Jack Kerouac. In the end, he cast Enrique Irazoqui, a nineteen-year-old economics student from Spain who had never acted in a film before.

> Now all thy gates shall echo with laments, all thy cities ring with cries, and all Philistia swoon away. From the north a smoke comes ever nearer. . . . In the streets men walk girded with sackcloth. Housetop and square echo with loud crying that breaks into tears."
> —WORDS SPOKEN BY THE NARRATOR,
> TAKEN FROM ISAIAH 14:31, 15:3, WHICH ARE NOT
> QUOTED IN ST. MATTHEW'S GOSPEL

The soundtrack is another example of the way Pasolini invites the audience to participate thoughtfully in the story. Luis Bacalov's score consists of some original music but also of curated pieces drawn from a variety of traditions, including the liturgy of Yom Kippur and Bach's *Mass in B Minor*. One thought-provoking choice is the blues number "Sometimes I Feel Like a Motherless Child," sung as the wise men present their gifts to the newborn king. Who is the motherless child? Obviously not Jesus. Who then? The Magi? Mary? The viewer? Likewise, the repeated use of the Congolese "Missa Luba," accompanying both the opening credits and the Resurrection scene, emphasizes that the Christian faith is a global phenomenon, not something confined to Palestine or to white Europeans. The syncopated rhythms and the lively melodic swoops of this African piece give *Matthew* a joyous undertow that cuts refreshingly against the monochrome images of shabby townscapes, weedy lanes, and stark rooms.

The sense of a suppressed joy that might burst out at any moment is also communicated through repeated shots of children running and playing. At the triumphal entry of Jesus, a crowd of excited youngsters wave their palms, and the camera closes in on one little lad who has evidently just lost his milk teeth. His bright-eyed enthusiasm is a delight to behold, and when the shot cuts to the face of Jesus, he is for the first time shown beaming with joy; his hitherto somewhat

The film's Italian title is *Il Vangelo Secondo Matteo* (*The Gospel According to Matthew*). Pasolini was reportedly displeased when the English-language version of title was changed to include the word "Saint."

alien religious fervor gives way to straightforward human happiness. There is no doubt about what to feel or think at this moment.

It is so striking because it is a rare, perhaps unique, moment in the course of the story. Generally, the film intimates that perceiving things correctly can be difficult. "Listen, you, who have ears to hear with," Jesus declaims to a crowd, as the camera brings into shot the huge hairy ears of a donkey. At the massacre of the innocents, the director pans across the group of assembled soldiers, moving from one face to the next, but not always smoothly, sometimes actively searching for the next face to examine. Again, at the trial before the high priest, the camera is positioned within a crowd of spectators, moving back and forth along the line of heads as if to get a clearer view.

At the trial before Pilate, however, we see things through the eyes of John, drawing us closer to the heart of the drama. John, as tradition dictates, is beardless, and for once he is not alone; all the other disciples are shown beardless too, or at least none of them has a full beard. Likewise, the wise men and the scribes and Pharisees are all remarkably well shaven. Jesus is the most bearded figure, yet he is also portrayed by probably the youngest man in the cast. (Enrique Irazoqui was just nineteen when he took the role.) We *see* youth in Jesus, but we should *perceive* mature wisdom: that is surely the purpose that Pasolini has in mind here.

Irazoqui's young face and deep eyes communicate, by turns, moral innocence, spiritual ardor, righteous anger, searing accusation, and warm affection. It is an arresting visual performance. (Vocally, the role is performed by Enrico Maria Salerno.) There are scores, maybe hundreds, of other faces that also appear on screen, often in lingering close-up. And this is perhaps the secret to the oddly powerful pull of *Matthew*, for the human mind finds faces so interesting that it will see them where none exist—in cloud formations, in shadows, and on the surface of the moon (a tendency called *pareidolia*). Pasolini puts before us not the made-up countenances of the professionally beautiful, but the unadorned faces of regular people—seamed, sunburnt, fascinating, some bland, some characterful, not a few with rotting teeth. Judas has a curling lip. The rich young ruler is pale and smooth-cheeked. Salome is a fresh-faced girl. "You are all brethren alike," Jesus declares to the crowd (Matt. 23:8).

Is this focus on the crowd a giveaway? Is Pasolini more concerned with the brotherhood of man than the right worship of God? Is his Jesus more human than divine? I doubt many would think so if they did not know Pasolini to have been a Marxist in real life. True, Christ's words about the rich and his woes on the Pharisees are retained, while the Transfiguration is cut. But in a movie of this length (137 minutes), cuts were inevitable—and Jesus still walks on the water and rises from the dead! When asked why, as an unbeliever, he had made a film so sympathetic to Christianity, Pasolini said, "I may be an unbeliever, but I am an unbeliever who has a nostalgia for a belief."

> Philosophically, nothing I have ever done has been more fitted to me than *The Gospel According to Matthew* because of my tendency always to see something sacred and mythical and the epic quality of everything in even the most humdrum, simple, and banal objects and events.
>
> —PASOLINI

The director cast his own mother, Susanna Pasolini, to play the part of the older Virgin Mary.

This brings us back to John Paul II and his "Letter to Artists," where he notes that "true art has a close affinity with the world of faith, so that, even in situations where culture and the Church are far apart, art remains a kind of bridge to religious experience. . . . Art is by its nature a kind of appeal to the mystery."

That other pontiff, John XXIII, who inadvertently precipitated *Matthew*, died the year before it was released and so never got to see this stark, humane, hypnotic movie. Pasolini dedicated the film to his memory.

*MW*

## DISCUSSION QUESTIONS

- What advantages are there, if any, to telling the story of Christ from the point of view of a single Evangelist rather than synthesizing all four Gospel accounts?

- If you were making a film based on select texts from St. Matthew's Gospel, what principles would guide your selection?

- What are the benefits and drawbacks to casting non-professional actors?

# *La Vie et Passion de Notre Seigneur Jésus-Christ*

## 1903

*One of the earliest surviving cinematic representations*
*of the life of Christ.*

With this primitive silent motion picture, the oldest included on the Vatican Film List, we enter the story of cinema near the origins of the artform. Arriving on the scene less than a decade after the Lumière brothers publicly introduced the first moving photographs or "movies," *La Vie et Passion de Notre Seigneur Jésus-Christ* (The Life and Passion of Our Lord Jesus Christ) is one of the relatively few survivors from the many films made in cinema's earliest days. Arranged almost like a series of paintings in an art gallery or floats in a religious procession, the "*Pathé Passion*," as it is sometimes called (in reference to its production company), presents the major events of the Gospels in a straightforward manner that is often striking in its simplicity and at moments winsomely naïve. With compositions that often recall long-established conventions in sacred art, with clear debts to earlier representations on canvas, on stage, and in street-conducted mystery plays, they are also often spruced up by some early experiments with this uniquely modern medium.

In the opening scene of the Annunciation, for instance, a young woman with a clay vessel stands in a room (classic), only to be met by an angel who fades in holding a lily, waves his arms, and fades out again (innovation). Such "supernatural" appearance and disappearance by virtue of film that has been double exposed is a recurring favorite in the *Passion*, and even though the backdrop looks unmistakably like a stage set and there are no intertitles for dialogue, already at this early stage cinema is a vehicle for (admittedly minimal) special effects.

Other such effects include the appearance of a hand-tinted, traveling yellow star that leads the shepherds to Bethlehem; film tinted blue for nighttime as a convoy of travelers on loaded camels make their way to meet the Christ child; and chalky white liquid poured into four vessels that comes out "miraculously" dark after Jesus has prayed over it at the wedding feast. There is also a slightly more involved technique with a composite image of actual stormy surf superimposed over Christ, who thus appears to be walking on the waters.

What will immediately stand out to many viewers of *Passion*, though, are the characters' "stagey" mannerisms, which can be so-called with good reason, since they were directly inherited from the theater. Developed in a context where actors performed with large, unmistakable gestures

Ecce Homo!

—PONTIUS PILATE

to ensure their emotions could be registered as far back as the nosebleeds, these conventional gestures appear on screen as an earmark of an era when directors and performers had not yet discovered the more subtle visual language better suited to camerawork. Today, these pantomime motions teeter dangerously close to farce—for example, when *Passion*'s stage villain Judas enters clutching a bag of silver and all but twirling his mustache.

Notable, too, is the early cinematic practice of photographing characters from head to foot, at a fixed distance, and generally filling only half the frame with plenty of headroom leftover for backgrounds. In other words, they appear much as they would in the theater. In the same vein, scenes typically begin and end with the entrance and exit of the characters. Effectively, what *Passion* portrays simply *are* scenes from a play, only with a camera set up instead of an audience.

One of the few exceptions to this occurs during the trial before Pontius Pilate, which cuts abruptly to a medium shot of Christ standing in front of a sheet emblazoned with the words "Ecce Homo" (Behold, the man!). There is a similarly formatted image shortly after, where Veronica holds the cloth she has used to wipe his face during the Passion. A handful of "location shots" are also novel departures from the default setting of painted two-dimensional backdrops, as when Joseph stands outdoors, fells a tree, and then carries away the log, with a youthful Jesus struggling to heave the ax onto his narrow shoulders and follow him out.

In general, it is all quite conventional and subdued, but there is a little bit of mildly thrilling action, such as during the massacre of the innocents, when women holding infants scramble

> When the first motion pictures appeared, "the common man and his family still used kerosene lamps; none but the well-to-do had telephones; and the telegram was a form of communication seldom known in the average household except to announce serious illness or death. But this new thing—this 'living picture' affair . . . brought new thoughts to people whose imaginative world had been bounded by the village, slum, or farm." (Benjamin B. Hampton, *A History of the Movies*)

away from sword- and shield-wielding soldiers, and the latter tear the children from their arms with some surprisingly rough handling of the kiddos. In an endearing domestic scene preceding the flight into Egypt, a retinue of colorful angels plays harps and swings thuribles over the cradle of the infant Christ, fades out as Joseph arrives, and then fades back in to wake him from sleep and tell him it is time to get going. They load up onto a donkey and just make it out of sight when a platoon of soldiers arrives at their door. Then the Holy Family gets miraculously hidden from view by an angel brandishing a jagged sword, who promptly chases the soldiers away.

As its title suggests, this film concludes with scenes from the Passion, among them the Last Supper, the betrayal of our Lord at Gethsemane, and his trials before Caiaphas and Pontius Pilate. We see Jesus scourged, crowned with thorns, and spat upon, then raised up on the cross—in this case attended by cartoony lightning. Later, inside the tomb, angels lift the lid of his sarcophagus and Jesus rises out of it and continues up into the air—presumably by means of the same stage elevator that earlier hoisted him on top of the waves. Then, in departure from the written record, the sleeping soldiers guarding the tomb awake, find him levitating there, and flee in terror. The film's final tableau shows Jesus ascending via a wobbly crane platform that gradually draws him up and away from kneeling disciples toward a climactic reunion with a brightly colored heavenly company. Jesus takes a seat next to a white-bearded figure underneath a radiant painted dove—and that's the end.

On the whole, it is a forthright, relatively unembellished affair. But there will be one or two surprises for viewers, including the always fascinating appearance on screen of live animals, whose unpredictability can spice up (when they do not wholly distract from) the human performances. At the same time, *Passion* is just as notable for what it does not do when compared with other more recent cinematic representations of the Gospels. There is little sense of narrative continuity, with the action playing out like jumps between independent set pieces. For all its ties to the theater, it is not especially dramatic in the sense of a story that turns upon choices made by characters with discernible interior lives. Indeed, these actors are afforded virtually no opportunity for displays of personality; they mostly function as figures in near-static tableaux. The gesticulations are wooden and borderline ludicrous. Yet, for all this, there is also an occasional waft of air from a less world-weary age—such as the charmingly homey moment after Peter denies our Lord when a rooster gets chucked on-stage—that might be one of the principal benefits of watching.

As it is often presented today, *Passion* is a silent film in the absolute sense—lacking all dialogue, score, or sound effects. But in the early penny arcades and nickelodeons, most movies were accompanied by live music—for example, from a pianist playing sheet music or simply improvising.

Another is the chance to walk away with an impression of Jesus Christ that is significantly more

Thanks in part to its didactic quality and relatively complete story line, this film was used for years by Catholics in the mission fields.

primitive, in the best sense, than we may be accustomed to. This is how he looked to people in the past, as captured on celluloid frames like these, in the paintings and stained glass they recall, and, even further back, in the loveably comical yet somehow still dignified antics of the mystery plays. Or, most primitive of all, these moving pictures, which cram in as many people and as much action as possible, might just communicate a hint to us today of what it would have been like to be part of the jostling crowds that surrounded God when he walked the earth as a man. They saw from a distance and over the heads of others; they could not hear the words but caught oblique glimpses of wonders whose meaning they had to seek clearer explanations of elsewhere. To see as they saw, in ways both familiar and strange, highly conventional and cinematically alien, might just show us something we have never seen about the Alpha and Omega, Lord over the peoples of all times and places—and all levels of sophistication. We have come a long way since the earliest days of cinema in our tastes and expectations, but it will be useful to remember every now and again the special connection enjoyed between the highest things of heaven and the lowly things of earth, and to try to glimpse again with younger eyes, like children, the God of rustics, simpletons, and other relatively unworldly audiences still possessed of the almost miraculous ability to find fascination in the mere facts.

*DPB*

## DISCUSSION QUESTIONS

- What, if anything, strikes you in a fresh way from this depiction of Jesus Christ?

- If you are watching with children, what stands out to them as new, special, or unexpected?

- Do you have a favorite representation of Jesus Christ in film, print, or paint? Perhaps in another artform? How does it compare to the moving images presented here?

# A Man for All Seasons

## 1966

*After King Henry VIII declares himself head of the Church in England, Sir Thomas More must choose whether to support him or refuse—and risk losing his life.*

*A* Man for All Seasons tells of the clash that occurred in sixteenth-century England when coercive state power came up against a man of immovable moral conviction. The clash is symbolized by the different images with which the film opens: first, hideous stone gargoyles rearing above the roofs of a royal palace; then, inside the palace, a gold chain of office glinting on a politician's chest; finally, just coming into shot, a framed painting of Christ's Crucifixion. The dramatic conflict of the film is thus neatly summarized: on the one

> I die his Majesty's good servant, but God's first.
> —SIR THOMAS MORE

hand, monstrous political overreach; on the other hand, costly self-sacrifice; between them, the office of a statesman.

The office is that of Lord Chancellor, the king's right-hand man. In the course of the film, three very different men occupy that position. The first is the aged, bloated Wolsey, played by Orson Welles (responsible for another film on the Vatican List, *Citizen Kane*). Wolsey is seeking a dispensation from the pope to annul King Henry's marriage to Catherine of Aragon, since it has failed to produce a male heir. Wolsey sees no need to take a moral stand in defense of the marriage, even though he's a cardinal. His ugliness and unhealthiness reflect the state of corruption in the English Church. As the first line of dialogue informs us: "In this country every second bastard born is fathered by a priest."

Moreover, Wolsey is offended that his efforts to secure an annulment are not receiving support from Sir Thomas More (Paul Scofield), a member of the king's council. More points out that the marriage only happened in the first place after papal permission was obtained for the king to wed his late brother's widow, and that it is too much to ask the pope to dispense with his own dispensation. Wolsey scoffs: "If you could just see facts flat on without that horrible moral squint! With a little common sense you could have made a statesman."

But Wolsey is dying, and King Henry (Robert Shaw) thinks an annulment will be likelier if Thomas More becomes Lord Chancellor in his stead, counting on his long-time friendship with More to effect the necessary change in his opinion. As Wolsey is stripped of his chain of office, we see the words "Sic transit gloria mundi" stenciled above a doorway: "Thus

Robert Bolt, the author of the Academy Award-winning screenplay (adapted from his own stage play), later wrote the screenplay for another entry on the Vatican Film List, *The Mission*.

passes the glory of the world," a phrase spoken at the coronation of a pope to emphasize the transitoriness of all earthly honors.

Once More is elevated to the chancellorship, his loyalties to king and pope are increasingly put under a competitive stress test. The crisis comes with the "Act of Supremacy," a parliamentary maneuver that enables Henry to bypass papal authority and put himself in charge of the English Church.

If the film has a weakness, it becomes evident in this section of the story, which never clearly shows why More so ardently loves and trusts the Church—an institution that he concedes needs reform. Admittedly, we do learn that More reveres papal authority because it was conferred on St. Peter "by our Savior Christ himself." But this belief is just presented as a given, a principle to which More holds. For viewers who have no knowledge of the crucial passage of Matthew's Gospel (Matt. 16:15–19) or no sympathy for the Catholic interpretation of that passage, More's attitude will be hard to comprehend. Although we see him occasionally at prayer and making the sign of the cross, never once do we find him worshiping inside a church or receiving the Eucharist; neither are we introduced to the pope or shown images of Jesus giving Peter the keys of the kingdom. In other words, More's conviction that the king is wrong and the pope is right lacks an objective correlative: it must be taken on trust.

The film thus largely becomes a story about an individual's assertion of belief in the face of governmental pressure, and the spiritual component is downplayed. The thing that matters is not so much *what* More believes as the fact that *he* believes it. What's critical is remaining true to one's identity rather than the specifically religious nature of that identity—personal integrity, not papal authority, is what is on the line. Screenplay author Robert Bolt admitted that More is treated as "a hero of selfhood" instead of as a saint-in-the-making. For this reason, it is worth asking whether *A Man for All Seasons* would have been better categorized in the Vatican List under the heading of "Values" rather than "Religion."

But we have to take films as they come, not as they might have come, and if the protagonist of this movie is portrayed as a champion of private conscience more than as a strictly Christian martyr, he still cuts a most impressive figure whose story is intensely engaging and moving. This is the case even though his dramatic arc doesn't describe any very noticeable character development. In fact, More hardly changes at all, except insofar as he becomes increasingly resolved to stay true to himself. Under ever-mounting pressure—from the king, courtiers, churchmen, friends, and (most painfully) his own family—he repeatedly demonstrates that he prizes the value of a sincere oath above merely staying alive. He could have sworn publicly to the king's supremacy while privately making a mental reservation, but he is not the man for such self-serving dishonesty. As he tells his beloved daughter Margaret (Susannah York), "When a man takes an oath, he's holding his own self in his hands like water, and if he opens his fingers then, he needn't hope to find himself again."

More's courage here is exemplary. St. Thomas Aquinas taught that the virtue of fortitude comes in two different

> When statesmen forsake their own private conscience for the sake of their public duties, they lead their country by a short route to chaos.
> —SIR THOMAS MORE

The movie's title comes from a description of More written by Erasmus in 1521: "It would be hard to find anyone who was more truly a man for all seasons and all men." The allusion is to St. Paul's words in his First Letter to the Corinthians: "I have become all things to all people, that I might by all means save some" (1 Cor. 9:22).

modes—attack and endurance—and argued that endurance is the morally higher form. By this ranking he did not mean to suggest that in every case it is braver to endure than to attack, but that fortitude in its purest form consists in the willingness to suffer when it remains the only possible way of resisting evil. And it is the courage of endurance that Thomas More displays. He knows that it is "our natural business" to escape martyrdom if possible, and he would have gladly sworn the oath if he could; indeed, he minutely scrutinizes the wording to see precisely what it would have committed him to, in the hope that he could have found some honest way of taking it. But he concludes that should God bring him to the point where there is no escape, he must let go of his grip on life before he lets go of his true self.

As it happens, it is not precisely More's refusal to swear the oath that results in the sentence of death, but rather the perjury of another man, Sir Richard Rich (John Hurt), a spineless careerist. At More's trial, Rich betrays him with a patent lie that sends him to the executioner's block. Asked by the judge three times whether he wishes to amend his testimony, Rich replies, "No, my lord," echoing St. Peter's threefold denial of Christ. But unlike Peter, the first pope, who wept bitterly at his actions and was restored by thrice confirming his love for the Lord (John 21:15–19), Rich shows no remorse at all. Rather, he goes on to scale the heights of worldly honor. In the film's closing voiceover, we learn that "Richard Rich became Chancellor of England and died in his bed"—the words spoken with biting scorn. Rich has become rich, but More had more.

The shot used for the title of the movie depicts reeds swaying in the sunlit river Thames. Robert Bolt said that the metaphorical figure he used for the story's "superhuman context"—the transcendent realm, the divine dimension— was water (rivers, tides, currents, etc.), while human society was figured as dry land. Tellingly, a lot of activity occurs on the Thames (boats shuttle back and forth on it, ducks swim and quack on it), but only reeds grow in it. Thomas More is one such reed. He is a man rooted in water—that is to say, at home in the spiritual world, gaining nourishment from its depths, not just skimming its surface. There is surely an allusion here to Christ's words about John the Baptist: "What did you go out into the wilderness to look at? A reed shaken by the wind?" (Matt. 11:7). John the Baptist, like More, suffered death by beheading—a terrible tragedy from one point of view, but also a holy sacrifice that would inspire others.

"We've been cutting reeds. We use them for fuel!" explains Margaret in one scene, as she and her new husband,

> In 1935, four hundred years after his death, More was canonized as a martyr by Pope Pius XI. In 2000, Pope John Paul II declared him the patron saint of statesmen. In 2010, Pope Benedict XVI gave a speech in Westminster Hall, the very location of More's trial, saying, "I recall the figure of St. Thomas More . . . who is admired by believers and nonbelievers alike for the integrity with which he followed his conscience, even at the cost of displeasing the sovereign whose 'good servant' he was, because he chose to serve God first."

> Your taste in music is excellent.
> It exactly coincides with my own.
> —KING HENRY VIII TO SIR THOMAS

carrying sickles, run laughing and panting into the house. (In the original play script, they cut *bracken*; Bolt evidently elected to make reeds significant only when writing the screenplay.) In other words, symbolically speaking, moral exemplars like Sir Thomas are "fuel" for others to live by. More himself told his daughter that the stance he was taking was finally "a matter of love." His love of truth, outweighing his love of life, gave her heart to hold on to the old faith even after his brutal execution; it stoked her devotion. With the subtly poignant reed imagery, Bolt reworks Tertullian's immortal statement: "The blood of the martyrs is the seed of the Church."

*MW*

### DISCUSSION QUESTIONS

- After he was condemned to death, More finally spoke his mind about the king's claim to supremacy over the Church. Was he wise to keep silent until that point?

- Is More presented primarily as a Christian martyr or a hero of individual conscience? What is the difference, if any, between these two kinds of person?

- Robert Bolt described himself as "not a Catholic nor even in the meaningful sense of the word a Christian." Would it have helped or hindered Bolt if he had shared the beliefs of Sir Thomas More?

# *The Mission*

## 1986

*Jesuit missionaries to South America in the eighteenth century struggle to preserve a religious outpost against the political hostility of Portugal and Spain and the prudential interests of the wider Catholic Church.*

The legendary film composer Ennio Morricone remarked that he only ever wept in public twice: once when he met Pope Francis, and once, years earlier, when he first saw *The Mission*, for which he wrote the acclaimed soundtrack. Tears and *The Mission* go well together, as we shall see.

The opening words of Robert Bolt's screenplay are: "Your Holiness." They are spoken by Cardinal Altamirano (his name means "high aim") as he dictates a letter to the

> The Mission screenwriter, Robert Bolt, also wrote the screenplay for another title on the Vatican Film List, A Man for All Seasons.

pope about the Jesuit mission to South America in the 1750s. Altamirano (Ray McAnally) has to decide whether the Jesuit mission established above the Iguazú Falls among the Guarani Indians on Spanish territory should continue once the land is transferred to the Portuguese under the terms of the Treaty of Madrid.

If the mission continues, it will offend the Portuguese, because it is a flourishing enterprise that competes with their own colonial efforts, and also because they would like to enslave the Guarani people, given the chance. The Spanish colonists, though officially opposed to slavery, connive at and profit from the Portuguese slave trade and therefore have no interest in supporting the mission either. Cardinal Altamirano fears that if the pope continues to support this unpopular outpost of the Church, it could result in the Jesuits being driven out of Portugal, then Spain, and then any number of other European countries. Which side will he come down on?

That the story is oriented toward Rome might make it seem an obvious choice for inclusion on the Vatican List. However, there is nothing self-satisfied about the perspective it adopts vis-à-vis the Church. The picture painted is "warts and all." The movie lets none of the clergy off unquestioningly, not even the most heroic of them, Father Gabriel (Jeremy Irons). His is the way of forgiveness and nonviolence. It was he who sent to the Guarani people Father Julian, the priest we see bound to a cross in the opening sequence, who was martyred by being dispatched over the Iguazú Falls. However, the death of Father Julian has not caused Gabriel to give up on the Guarani, nor has it engendered in him a vengeful spirit.

On the contrary, it fills him with a new missionary purpose, and he bravely risks his own life in order to bring them the Gospel. That he shares his name with the angel who brought glad tidings to Mary is highly appropriate. In an early scene, after his beautiful oboe playing has won him a hearing from the musically gifted Guarani, we see the tribes-folk admiring pictures of the Virgin and Child. The joyful mysteries of the faith are taking root in them freely and without coercion.

It is because Father Gabriel has such evident moral stature that he is called upon to minister to Rodrigo Mendoza (Robert DeNiro), a mercenary and slave trader. Mendoza is crushed by the guilt of having killed his own brother in a duel and wants to die. Gabriel challenges him not to take the cowardly way out, but rather to be brave enough to be penitent. Mendoza, supposing no penance could be sufficiently harsh for the sins he has committed, decides to follow Gabriel up to the mission above the falls, dragging behind him a massive weight of armor and weapons from his days as a mercenary. The burden repeatedly causes him to fall or get stuck, but he will not let it go. When another priest, Father Fielding (Liam Neeson), cuts him free of the load, Mendoza refuses to be let off so easily and reattaches the rope. "How long must he carry that stupid thing?" Fielding asks. "God knows," replies Gabriel.

Eventually, Mendoza climbs high enough to encounter the Guarani people, whom once he would have captured and enslaved. One of the Indians comes at him with a knife. Instead of attacking him, however, the man hacks at the rope and rolls the huge burden into the river. On this occasion,

MENDOZA: For me, there is no redemption.
FATHER GABRIEL: God gave us the burden of freedom. You chose your crime. Do you have the courage to choose your penance?

because the relief is offered by a representative of those he has hurt, not imposed by a neutral third party, Mendoza accepts his deliverance and begins weeping with sorrow and joy. But one small Indian boy looks on with puzzlement. This boy becomes a permanent companion to him.

Having portrayed Jesuit priests in *The Mission*, Jeremy Irons and Liam Neeson both went on to do so again in, respectively, *The Man in the Iron Mask* (1998) and *Silence* (2016).

Mendoza enters the Jesuit Order and is ordained a priest. He turns away from violence so completely that he will not even participate in the killing of a wild boar. He reads aloud St. Paul's hymn to love (1 Cor. 13), but as he finishes that great celebration of charity with the words "the greatest of these is love," we see his familiar Indian boy spearing a fish, a sign of the ambivalence that remains in Mendoza's heart.

His ambivalence is mirrored by that of Altamirano, who prays for hours but cannot come to a decision about the future of the mission. Gabriel invites him up to see the place for himself, believing that, in situ, the cardinal will receive the "strength and the grace" to do what is good, whatever it costs. After seeing the wholesome character of the mission and the genuine piety of the Indians, Altamirano nonetheless decides it must close. He prioritizes the safety of the Jesuit Order in Europe above the life of this godly community of converts.

Gabriel cannot accept Altamirano's verdict and decides to resist the Portuguese authorities—peacefully—when they come to close things down. Mendoza refuses to follow Gabriel's lead and resolves instead to oppose the incoming Portuguese by force. His faithful Indian boy retrieves the sunken sword from the penance burden and cleans it up for him to use in the looming confrontation.

> If might is right, love has no place in the world.
> —FATHER GABRIEL

Gabriel tells him to help the Guarani "as a priest" and not to die with blood on his hands. Mendoza has promised to serve God—"and God is love," Gabriel insists: "If might is right, love has no place in the world." Yet, even as he says this, he mutters under his breath, "It may be so, it may be so," indicating that for him, too, there is an interior struggle.

In the climactic scene, Father Gabriel, surrounded by the noncombatant members of the mission, walks forth holding aloft the Blessed Sacrament in a huge monstrance. Meanwhile, as the battle unfolds, Mendoza kills a number of Portuguese soldiers and is eventually shot as he saves one of the Indian boys. He lives long enough to see Gabriel mown down by the barrage and collapsing on top of the monstrance. However, he dies before he can witness other people take over for the fallen priest and continue the Eucharistic procession, even as the mission burns to the ground around them. Later, on hearing of this bloody and destructive outcome, Altamirano laments, "Thus have we made the world. Thus have I made it."

In the closing scene, the only survivors appear to be a small group of young children. We see a naked girl walking out of the ruined village in a shot deliberately reminiscent of the famous photograph from the Vietnam War of the "Napalm girl" (the nine-year-old Phan Thị Kim Phúc). She salvages a broken violin from the water and climbs into a boat, which a naked boy then punts down the river. Has the innocence of Eden returned, or is the cycle of endless conflict in human affairs simply starting again? As they fade into the distance, the screen freezes over a biblical caption: "The light shines in the darkness and the darkness has not overcome it" (John 1:5). After the credits, the very final shot of the film is of a silent Altamirano staring directly into the camera with an ambiguous expression. Is he remorseful, guilty, calloused, or all three at once?

The complexity of his gaze is reflected in the complexity of the music over the closing credits: a mix of Gabriel's oboe theme and tribal chants from the Guarani, punctuated by deep plosive sounds suggestive of cannon fire. The soundtrack is one of the movie's major strengths; indeed, it has been described as one of the greatest pieces of film music ever written. As noted above, composer Ennio Morricone found that *The Mission* moved him to tears, and many other viewers have found the same, not least because of his score. Tears are a natural response to *The Mission*—not only on witnessing the joyful deliverance of Mendoza from his burden but also because of the tragedy of the overall story line and the beauty of the Iguazú Falls, which provides its stunning backdrop. These falls might even be seen as an objective correlative of what Altamirano calls "the everlasting mercy of God," always flowing above and despite human folly, a torrent of inexhaustibly bountiful divine love. Wisely, though—like Gabriel's oboe playing, which allures and does not compel— the director Roland Joffé resists drawing attention to such symbolic values and leaves it to viewers to perceive them or not as they choose.

The film's symbolic subtleties and complexities are reflected in its title. Which "mission" is *The Mission* really about? There are three possibilities. The first is the framing device, the mission that Altamirano is on as a papal legate. The second is the Jesuit mission itself, the community that is built and destroyed. But the third mission is that of the

> *The Mission* won the 1986 Cannes Film Festival Palme d'Or and the Academy Award for Best Cinematography.

> Thus have we made the world. Thus have I made it.
> —ALTAMIRANO

Church, more broadly construed as the carrying forward of the Incarnation through space and time. Christ's life, death, and Resurrection—the divine mission of self-sacrificial love—is the central, overarching, and undergirding mission. And this mission, so the film suggests, is indefectible. One way or another, the Good News of Jesus Christ, centered in the Blessed Sacrament, will advance, even amid death and destruction—indeed, precisely as the antidote to death and destruction—and the darkness will not overcome it.

*MW*

*(Content advisory: contains nudity and violence)*

### DISCUSSION QUESTIONS

- With which character do you sympathize most? Gabriel, Mendoza, Cardinal Altamirano—or a different character? Why?

- The final shot of the movie, after the closing credits, is of a silent Altamirano staring directly into the camera with an ambiguous look in his eyes. How do you read his expression?

- Is disaster inevitable when members of the Church get involved in secular politics? Could the destruction of the mission have been avoided?

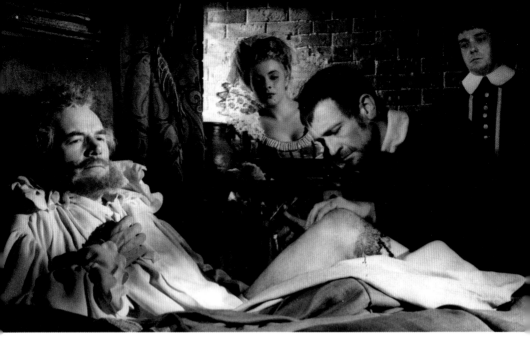

# *Monsieur Vincent*

### 1947

*A challenging portrait of the life and work of the canonized
seventeenth-century priest Vincent de Paul.*

"Be perfect, therefore, as your heavenly father is perfect."
With these words recorded in Matthew's Gospel (Matt.
5:48), our Lord brings to its climax a discourse on godly love,
or what the Latin-influenced tradition often calls *charity*.
Something more profound than simply handing over loose
change to someone on the street or donating pantry items to
a soup kitchen—although it might include these—charity in
the theological sense is the underlying substance, historically
speaking, to charity in the social sense. As commanded in the
Gospels, this love lends expecting nothing in return and is the

86

same semi-miraculous power by which Christians love their enemies (see Luke 6:27–29). Both presuppose a generosity whose origin and justice, so to speak, are found beyond the horizon of history. Such transcendent standards might seem at first blush as intimidating and out of reach as they are difficult to imagine, but the latter difficulty, at least, might be helped by a film like *Monsieur Vincent.*

Best known to many people today for the food banks and thrift stores established in his name, St. Vincent de Paul's legacy remains tied up with his many practical works of mercy and the numerous foundations he established to improve the material well-being of the poor. At our stage in history, many such efforts—soup kitchens, hospices, orphanages, care homes for the elderly, etc.—have been secularized, commercialized, or taken over by the civil government. But this film underscores how most of these institutions began—namely, as conscious and often personally costly labors of Christian charity. As one character in the film asks, "What will people say in the future when they learn that a single man had the desire to create what seems so normal and so just today?"

The real heft of the film, though, comes from the unflinching and unromanticized way it depicts such ministry. For instance, after Vincent renounces his worldly goods to live in greater solidarity with the wretched of this world, he rents a ramshackle room and finds he can hardly sleep at night because of his neighbors' crying baby, domestic disputes, and a woman who laughs maniacally every quarter hour. When Vincent allows a homeless

*Monsieur Vincent* won an honorary Oscar for Best Foreign Language Film in 1949. It was honorary because, at the time, non-English-language films were not a regular part of the Academy Awards but handed out on an *ad hoc* basis.

man to share his quarters, the latter comments on the cacophony, "The poor don't sleep at night. They work. They
insult each other. They fight. They cough. They make more
poor people. You can't let that get to you. You have to do like
everyone else and not care." This counsel of despair redoubles
Vincent's resolve to do something helpful, and he begins on
his knees, begging forgiveness for living so long in complete
ignorance of such misery.

He starts small, but his influence spreads, and when
volunteers trickle in to aid his efforts, another kind of squalor
surfaces. When two men fight tooth and nail for the chance
to die in a bed in an overcrowded hospice, a volunteer nurse
at wits' end cries out to Vincent, "They demand things, they
insult us, they spit on us! How could I possibly love them?"
"They can be tough and unfair, but we have to serve them
and love them like we would our masters," he returns. "The
uglier and dirtier they are, the more unfair and vulgar they
are, the more love you'll have to give."

Here the future saint calls attention to one of the more
arduous and less publicized characteristics of truly Christ-like
charity: as a Christian's love of neighbor participates more
purely and completely in the Creator's love for his creatures,
the more one-sided and unreciprocal it becomes. In other
words, the poorer a person is in exterior tangible things (and
even more so in interior intangible ones), the less resources (or
even gratitude) he or she will have to offer anyone in return.

However, since natural love spontaneously expects *some*
sort of reciprocity, to love such persons with the tender and
persistent solicitude God extends toward each of us, the giver

> You are not as poor as they are, so you owe
> them everything.
> —ST. VINCENT DE PAUL

of charity must necessarily tap into something deeper than mere emotion—deeper, even, than anything merely natural. Indeed, it is arguably *impossible* to love the poorest in this world simply on our own strength as creatures; to love as God loves, we must cooperate with God's own love. "Apart from me you can do nothing" (John 15:5), and nowhere is this more painfully and urgently obvious than in the attempt to love those we instinctively find unlovely.

If there is a shortcoming in this film, it is on this point: for all its emphasis upon corporal works of mercy, its overall depiction of the saint makes scarcely more than passing reference to the spiritual and sacramental dimension that without doubt animated his lifelong charitable activity. Although Vincent alludes to saying Mass, for example, he never does so on screen, nor does he do much by way of prayer, formal preaching, or administration of the sacraments. The only time he enters the vicinity of a confessional is to pull out its sitting priest and summon him to more practical duties. He also washes linens by hand, insisting that hiring a maid would cost money that could buy physical bread. But why, in

Although set several hundred years in the past, some elements in *Monsieur Vincent*—for instance, the maimed ex-soldier with whom Vincent de Paul shares his first presbytery and other images of wartime violence— would have resonated in a special way with post-WWII audiences. The film's themes also readily converge with Italian neorealism's unromanticized lingering over the squalor of many lives in late-1940s European society. Such convergences illustrate the ongoing appeal of a saint like Vincent de Paul, whose perennially valuable example is lent fresh significance by changing historical circumstances.

light of Jesus' teaching in John 6, is he never shown, even once, providing spiritual bread to the poor he serves with such all-consuming passion?

No one artistic representation can be expected to capture the entirety of the Christian life, of course. But by failing to prioritize—frankly, failing even to recognize—the interior supernatural communion that is the source of all outward acts of Christian charity, the film seems to promote a kind of living sacrifice that is subtly secular, forbiddingly rigoristic, and ultimately foreign to Christianity. The kind of service this film shows us may be extraordinarily human, but it is less than fully divine.

So when Vincent tells a struggling fellow worker that "it is not enough to do a little good," and that "you have to take on a little more every day," we might agree. But the characterization goes too far when, as an old man, he laments how little he has accomplished and insists it amounts to nothing. He makes this complaint in a private audience with the Queen of France, where she quite naturally compares his achievements to her own: "You've given your whole life, you've given up happiness and power forever, you've built more than useless palaces, more than vain glory. Do you also feel, now that death is near, that you're leaving nothing but an empty hole behind?"

"Yes, Madame," he responds. "I haven't accomplished anything." Agitated, she asks, "What is one supposed to do in life, then, to accomplish anything?" His answer is as simple as it is devastating: "More."

"You will soon realize," he later tells one of his helpers, "charity is a heavy load to carry." But is it? What about the

> Believe me, you need your poor.
> At least as much as he needs you.
> —ST. VINCENT DE PAUL

> What will people say in the future when they learn that a single man had the desire to create what seems so normal and so just today?
> —CARDINAL GRAZIANI

yoke our Lord describes as easy and the burden he promises is light (Matt. 11:30)?

In response to this question, something might be said on both sides. On the one hand, there is Mother Teresa of Kolkata, the most celebrated missionary of charity in modern times, whose private journals disclose few if any feelings of natural consolation across most of her adult life. As her experience suggests, one of God's most severe mercies is to entrust some of us with a share in his own interior poverty expressed at the cry of dereliction from the cross. On the other hand, in the wake of the Resurrection, no cross need be carried alone. However toilsome and demanding my particular call to charity may be, I can depend upon some sense of Christ's companionship to lighten the load.

So what do we make of this film's insightful, imperfect picture of saintly service? Even if it does fall short of presenting a full-bodied—better yet, full-Spirited—portrait of Christian charity, *Monsieur Vincent* portrays at least one thing perhaps better than any other film: what might be called an *unsentimental* love of the poor. Charity, it shows quite clearly, can never be just a feeling. At the same time, it can never be a merely human effort. If God himself as a man had "no beauty or majesty to attract us to him, nothing in his appearance that we should desire him" (Isa. 53:2 NIV), how much more will we need to deepen, strengthen, and transfigure our finite affections and natural attractions when attending to the needs of "the least of these" (Matt. 25:40)?

The Society of St. Vincent de Paul, which operates in many dioceses around the world today and for whom "no work of charity is foreign," was founded by a group of lay students in Paris in 1833. It forms part of the "Vincentian Family" alongside the two congregations founded by St. Vincent de Paul: the Congregation of the Mission and the Daughters of Charity.

We have already spoken of the supernaturally empowered love that gives alms and prays for its persecutors, but the Gospels also describe charity in even more mysterious terms. It is so far removed from relying upon human reactions like appreciation or even acknowledgement, we read, that it can be compared to the rain that nourishes everyone on earth, righteous and unrighteous alike (Matt. 5:45). Showing such perfect mercy is a high calling and, if it were intended as a strictly natural self-sacrifice, would seem impossible. But what makes it possible, and what *Monsieur Vincent* helps us begin to imagine, is how everything God demands of us he firstly gives. The work of charity may be a heavy load to carry, but it is a load shared by God himself. Even more fundamentally, it is an invitation into an ever-dependent, divinely emboldened participation in God's own love, which the servant of true charity will find to be as unostentatious, abundant, and ultimately—miraculously—indifferent to creaturely thanks as the weather.

*DPB*

## DISCUSSION QUESTIONS

- How do you react to the unglamorous and often un-thanked service of the poor by St. Vincent de Paul and his companions? Do you find it inspiring or discouraging? How would you respond (or hope to respond) in comparable circumstances?

- Does this film present a well-rounded view of Christian charity? What, if anything, is missing?

- Which is worse in your view: material or spiritual poverty? What is the best way to help with each?

# *Nazarín*

## 1959

*An idealistic priest faces numerous hardships while ministering to the poor in Mexican villages in the early twentieth century.*

Luis Buñuel was a celebrated and controversial twentieth-century filmmaker. Born and raised in Aragon and educated by Jesuits, he was quintessentially Spanish and Catholic. But as a young man, Buñuel ended his formal relationship with the Church as he moved to Madrid and then to Paris, before retreating to the United States and Mexico as the Spanish Civil War and World War II raged in Europe. He was close friends with the Spanish playwright Federico García Lorca and the painter Salvador Dalí, and he dabbled in surrealism, communism, and atheism. Despite Buñuel's adult critiques of

Catholicism, the faith of his youth did not entirely leave him. Buñuel once summarized his spiritual ambivalence saying, "I'm an atheist, thank God."

In his 1959 film *Nazarín,* Buñuel depicts an honorable and charitable priest who is determined to proclaim the Gospel despite many obstacles. Father Nazario, played by Francisco Rabal, is a Spaniard who, like Buñuel, finds a new home in Mexico. Nazario chooses to live in a poor community, styling himself in name and attitude after the image of the itinerant son of a Galilean carpenter, possessing nothing and living off the generosity of neighbors and parishioners. His door is literally always open, and at the beginning of the film various visitors come in and out to make demands of him. Government officials mill about the village, popping in to tell Nazario of the eventual plans to modernize and improve conditions. But Buñuel's depiction of life on the ground in rural Mexico is so difficult that one cannot imagine anything short of a miracle could turn things around. In this almost hopeless context, Nazario labors on faithfully, but he is soon implicated in harboring a fugitive prostitute named Andara, who in one scene hallucinates that an image of Christ is laughing at her. When the authorities come to get her, she enlists the mentally unstable Beatriz, and the two women burn down the priest's lodgings, destroying the evidence of Andara's presence. For his part in the scandal, Nazario is stripped of his license to minister, and he is sent to the open road in civilian clothes, penniless.

*Nazarín* was one of the ten favorite films of Andrei Tarkovsky, a director of two films on the Vatican Film List: *Andrei Rublev* and *The Sacrifice.*

Nazario is a thoroughly guileless man, and he reframes his misfortune as an opportunity to live a more detached existence in even deeper imitation of his Lord. But immediately, his ideals clash with harsh reality. The

> Night carries yesterday's sorrow and the hope and
> joy of a new day. That's what death is like.
> Joyous and sorrowful.
> —FATHER NAZARIO

last thing Mexico seems to need is another beggar or another idealist. When Nazario asks for food in exchange for manual labor, the other workers revolt against their foreman, and as the priest wanders off the job site dejected, we hear a barrage of gunfire, presumably causing deaths. When Nazario goes to a plague-stricken town to help tend to the sick and bury the dead, a dying woman tells him she does not care about heaven but only wants her husband Juan, who suddenly returns, kicking Nazario out of the house. As the story unfolds, bad things keep happening wherever he goes, to almost comedic effect.

Beatriz and Andara accompany the priest on the road, becoming his eager disciples but also contributing to unwarranted suspicion that Nazario is behaving unchastely or otherwise manipulating people. In one scene, a woman begs him to cure her sick daughter, and he reluctantly prays over her. When the girl recovers, Beatriz and Andara believe Nazario to be a miracle worker, but he strongly protests, disabusing the women of what he believes to be superstitious piety. He intends his ministry to focus on this-worldly accompaniment, not supernatural intervention; however, the healing is the only thing that ever seems to go right for Nazario. It is as if the people around him are wondering: What other use could there be for a holy man? In a later scene, an angry colonel pulls a gun on him for defending a rude peasant, but another nearby priest tells the officer to leave Nazario alone. He is "a heretic, an errant preacher," the priest says. Like Jesus among the Pharisees and Sadducees, Nazario is not what anyone wants or expects him to be.

> Asked about the main character, Father Nazario, Buñuel once said, "I really like that guy."

Eventually, the authorities catch up with Nazario, Beatriz, and Andara, and the priest is thrown in prison, where he is badly beaten by a cruel, blasphemous man who mocks Nazario's principled outlook on life. Buñuel does not glamorize his protagonist as a martyr; instead, he depicts how the abuse he receives creates a crisis within him. The priest shouts at his attacker, "For the first time in my life, I find it hard to forgive. . . . I scorn you! And I feel guilty, not knowing how to separate scorn from forgiveness." Offering up our own suffering for sanctification is not easy. Another cellmate comes to Nazario's defense, but in this action, Buñuel defies the expectation of the viewer, who might want a bit of dialogue akin to that of the thief on the cross who defends Jesus against the mocker on the other side and who is assured of his place in paradise. Instead, Nazario asks the man if he would like to be "good" and to change his life. The inmate replies cynically, "All I do is bad deeds. And what good is your life? You on the good side, and me on the bad side. Neither of us are much good at all."

The final scene of *Nazarín* may be difficult to interpret definitively, but it clearly offers room for hope, in contrast with the fatalism that pervades much of the rest of the film. Being led down a dirt road by a policeman, Nazario stops at a produce cart, where a woman offers him the gift of a pineapple—a strange choice among the other things more easily consumed by a hungry man in transit. Uncharacteristically, Nazario refuses her charity, marching on with an anguished look on his face that the audience has never seen up to this point. He then turns around, changes his mind, and accepts the fruit, telling her with a kindly countenance, "May God repay you, ma'am."

Although never fully explaining the ending, Buñuel remarked in an interview that it encapsulates the struggle between faith and doubt, saying, "It's like someone falling asleep in bed. You fall asleep in bed with a cigarette. It might go out, or it might burn the house down. Doubt is like that cigarette. It could be nothing, or it could destroy everything." After so many failures, Father Nazario's refusal of the woman's impractical gift may represent a momentary temptation to despair. He briefly lets down his guard to doubt, perhaps believing the chatter he has long heard about his ministry (what's the point?) and about Christ himself (what good is he for my everyday life?). But then the priest recommits himself to his vocation. The doubt is extinguished, and his house of faith remains standing, even as he faces more difficulty. Maybe Nazario needs to try receiving for a while instead of giving.

*Nazarín* is a great realist work that evokes aspects of the novels *The Power and the Glory* by Graham Greene and *The Diary of a Country Priest* by Georges Bernanos. In all three works, there is a palpable sense of the weight on the shoulders of men called to the priesthood; but there is also a challenge to ordinary Christians not to sentimentalize religion. In some ways, life is short, and therefore faith should come easily, since it will decide eternity. But in other ways, life can feel long and arduous, and keeping the faith over years and decades can seem impossible. Moreover, in *Nazarín*, people live in harsh circumstances that continue to characterize the existence of untold millions in the world today, where the promises of civil authorities too often fail

The film was adapted for the screen by Buñuel and Julio Alejandro from the novel by Benito Pérez Galdós, a nineteenth-century realist regarded by many as second in importance among Spanish writers only to Miguel de Cervantes.

and brutal opportunists prey on the most vulnerable. Where is God then? Today, as in Buñuel's time, the Church carries on its work, often under duress and with scant evidence of any success, sometimes even making existing problems worse. But despite all hardship, Christians keep moving on the pilgrim path and receiving grace, both in the guaranteed means of the sacraments and in truly inexplicable ways, like receiving a pineapple from a stranger on the road.

Finally, in *Nazarín,* the Catholic piety of Buñuel's childhood and the surrealist aesthetic of his young adulthood converge: What if a joyous, life-giving faith feels more real when presented as a largely painful if not pointless quest—the way of the cross instead of a happy, user-friendly enterprise? In fact, Jesus seems to endorse this upside-down strategy, telling the disciples, "If the world hates you, be aware that it hated me before it hated you" (John 15:18). Accordingly, Jesus describes worldly failure as heavenly success: "Blessed are you when people revile you and persecute you and utter all kinds of evil against you falsely on my account" (Matt. 5:11).

*Nazarín* is a gritty story of faith and doubt, a spiritual classic told by a true intellectual with a heart for humanity. It remains today among the best films addressing the extreme difficulties of this life in the sometimes dim but never-failing light of the Gospel.

*AP*

## DISCUSSION QUESTIONS

- Have you ever tried to live out difficult ideals only to find that everything goes wrong? What do you count as a success or failure when it comes to your call to serve God?

- What are some different Christian responses to helping the poor? If you are or have been poor, what role has the Church played in alleviating your suffering?

- Have you had moments when you doubt your faith or doubt the importance of what you believe God has called you to do? If so, how did you get through?

# *Ordet*

## 1955

*Against a backdrop of household strife and community discord, members of a rural Danish family explore the nature of Christian faith and the possibility of miracles.*

Carl Theodor Dreyer's *Ordet* (The Word) is a masterful work of Christian thought that demands careful attention and evokes deep contemplation. Based on the 1932 play by Kaj Munk, a Lutheran pastor, it is the story of the Borgen family, whose patriarch, a hard-headed widower named Morten, has three sons: Mikkel, a hard-working skeptic with a delightful, prayerful wife named Inger; Johannes, a mystic whose study of theology has left him believing he is Jesus

Christ; and Anders, a fretful romantic who struggles both to please the father he adores and to pursue his own happiness.

The strange dynamics of the Borgen family become immediately apparent. Anders, who wakes up to find Johannes missing and probably wandering alone among the nearby dunes, rouses the other men of the house, and they bundle up and head out to retrieve him. With wild eyes and an unnaturally high voice, Johannes finally appears, preaching to the wind his own version of Jesus' "Woe unto you" speech from Matthew 23. When the four men return home, Johannes continues speaking as if he were Jesus, and Morten comments that he had once hoped to see his son's interest in theology blossom into a true prophetic ministry, "the spark that could fire Christendom from this farm." The old man tells Mikkel, "What we need is someone who can shake people up." Later, Morten tells the town's new pastor that the writings of Søren Kierkegaard are to blame for Johannes' delusions, which the family can no longer bear. Contrasting with the intellectual rigor of the Borgen men is the heartfelt, radiant faith of Inger, a mother of two children, pregnant with a third.

Morten, a relatively prosperous farmer with a healthy brood, embraces a philosophy of joyous, this-worldly Christianity, and behind his dining table hangs a portrait of the liberal Lutheran philosopher N.F.S. Grundtvig. Morten reminds his family with pride that he has prevailed in a parochial struggle with a dissenting group of believers, led by Peter Petersen, a modest tailor with one grown child, Anne. Peter presides over an Inner Mission group, a conservative movement

Birgitte Federspiel, who plays Inger, was actually pregnant during filming, and she allowed Dreyer to make audio recordings of her labor sounds, which were later used in the soundtrack for the labor scene in the film.

> I believe a lot of little miracles happen secretly.
> —INGER BORGEN

within Danish Lutheranism that sought to evangelize existing Christians, particularly poor, uneducated people. In the relationship between the two families, we may find a microcosm of contemporary religious controversies. In modern times, Christians are divided for myriad reasons, with individual religious identities and fierce allegiances to theories, as in Morten's case, and to sects, as in Peter's case. Dreyer depicts the struggle among Protestants, but it applies to inter-Catholic strife and ecumenical relations as well.

In a version of the ages-old forbidden love story among rival families, Anders Borgen seeks to marry Anne Petersen, and after strategic coaxing by Inger, Morten agrees to the match. Peter, however, refuses unless the Borgen farm becomes a beacon of a more Puritanical version of Christianity. Deeply angry, Morten barges into an Inner Mission meeting, declaring, "I can't stand your undertaker faces." Morten and Peter briefly start shoving each other before a disturbing phone call comes through. Inger's baby is coming, but there are complications: both woman and child are fighting for their lives.

*Ordet*'s reputation as one of the most compelling and nuanced Christian films becomes readily apparent in the tense scenes in which Inger's life hangs in the balance. As Morten and Anders return to the farmhouse, they find Inger and Mikkel in agony—she in physical pain, he in spiritual turmoil. As the doctor treats Inger, Morten tries to pray, and Johannes wanders around the house muttering apocalyptic sentences. Inger's baby dies, but it appears Inger will live, and the doctor, the pastor, and Morten celebrate with coffee, cigars, and theological discourse. The doctor expresses skepticism of miracles, asking whether it was his treatment

There are only three close-up shots in the entire film, a complete contrast with Dreyer's 1928 film *The Passion of Joan of Arc*, also on the Vatican Film List, which consists almost entirely of close-ups.

or Morten's prayers that saved Inger. The pastor maintains that miracles are possible but unlikely, opting instead to emphasize *ora et labora*—that is, Christians pray and work, never sure precisely how good things come about. Despite the death of the child—a sad but common occurrence in earlier times—all three men laugh over their academic differences, happy that Inger is on the mend. But then, Johannes' strange voice reemerges. As the doctor and pastor leave together, their car lights shine into the room with an eerie glow. Johannes prophesies Inger's death just as she suddenly passes away, and he slips out the window.

The last few scenes of *Ordet* put every character's theoretical notion of God's love, will, and power to the test. The whole town gathers in the Borgen's farmhouse, as Inger lies dead in a stark, white room with light pouring in through the windows on either side of her coffin. Peter Petersen enters, begging Morten's forgiveness, and offers Anne to Anders so that "Inger's place shall not stand empty." It is nothing short of a miracle of reconciliation. And then, Johannes returns, speaking in a more normal voice and bearing a more serene countenance. "Your eyes are as they were before," Morten exclaims. It's another miracle. The pastor and the doctor both sit by as Mikkel weeps at Inger's side, and Johannes slowly approaches, telling him tenderly to trust in God. Johannes holds the hand of his niece, who expects yet another miracle—a full-fledged New Testament raising of the dead. Johannes prays, "Jesus Christ, give me the Word," and what follows is one of the most astonishing moments ever put on screen. As Mikkel continues to weep, Johannes commands

Inger to rise, and the child smiles. Inger's hands move, her eyes open, and she sits up. Mikkel tells her that their baby is alive with God, and they embrace in a renewed bond of faith. Even on repeated viewings, the audience may watch in rapt attention, amazed at something too good to believe, but presented too powerfully to dismiss.

In an interview near the end of his life, Dreyer described *Ordet* as a movie of "radical simplification," which is apparent in the scenery as much as in the relations between the characters. In the Borgens' kitchen, for example, Dreyer asked the prop mistress to fill up the set with every possible thing she thought a good country kitchen required. Then, before filming began, Dreyer and his cameraman methodically took away items one by one until they achieved an aesthetically minimalist look, preparing the audience to focus on the "one thing" that Jesus describes to Martha at Bethany in Luke 10:42. The film simplifies as it intensifies, with the characters growing toward spiritual unity, as two families become one, grounded in a shared supernatural experience. Mikkel expresses a newfound solidarity with his reanimated wife, telling her, "I have found *your* faith," while Morten and Peter agree that the God of old has manifested himself among them, "eternal and the same." Individual opinions, petty grievances, mental anguish, and even well-formed ideals seem insignificant or incomplete compared to an encounter with the living Christ, the Word.

*Ordet* was filmed in part in Vedersø, the village in western Denmark where the original playwright, Kaj Munk, served as a pastor. Munk preached against Danish collaboration with the Nazis, and he was arrested and murdered by the Gestapo in 1944, making

None of the actors or crew are credited, with the only credit given to Kaj Munk, the author of the play on which *Ordet* is based.

*Ordet* the work of a martyr-like man, reminding future generations that the faith represented in this tale is always worth dying for. Moreover, Munk, a Protestant, died for the same devotion to Christ in the same era as Catholics like St. Maximilian Kolbe and Blessed Franz Jägerstätter, reminding all Christians that, in the face of the direst challenges in the world today, reunion of disparate believers is not only desirable but possible, as seen in the rapprochement of Morten and Peter in the film. As Pope St. John Paul II wrote in his 1995 encyclical on ecumenism, *Ut Unum Sint*, "Every factor of division can be transcended and overcome in the total gift of self for the sake of the Gospel."

*Ordet*'s cinematography has influenced the work of many filmmakers, including Ingmar Bergman, Andrei Tarkovsky, Lars von Trier, and Terrence Malick, and its long scenes—some lasting up to seven minutes—may take some adjustment for modern audiences used to quick cuts and fast action. Just as Christianity is accessible to all while always rewarding deeper exploration, *Ordet* may not come across as a crowd-pleaser, but patient audiences will likely savor its themes of faith, family, and community and find more to appreciate on repeated viewings. Its images are unforgettable.

Quite simply, *Ordet* is among the best religious films ever made, and it richly rewards the effort required to watch it.

*AP*

## DISCUSSION QUESTIONS

- The family has been the basic unit of order in most societies throughout history. What do the similarities and differences in the three Borgen brothers say about modern life? Does *Ordet* spur contemplation about your own family dynamics?

- How do you relate to people who have strongly opposing religious views to yours yet claim to be of the same Christian faith?

- What do you think about miracles? Did they happen more in earlier times than now? Have you ever witnessed or experienced an astonishing event that seems to defy ordinary explanation?

# *The Passion of Joan of Arc*

## 1928

*In fifteenth-century France, Joan of Arc is put on trial for heresy by cruel accusers but remains committed to the mission the Lord has given her and dies a martyr.*

A teenage heroine of the Hundred Years' War between England and France and a mystic guided by heavenly visions, Joan of Arc is a woman whose story continues to inspire and perplex the world. Surprisingly, for all that Joan has meant to French people and to Catholics, one of the greatest works of art about her martyrdom was made by a Danish Protestant, Carl Theodor Dreyer, whose 1928 film *The Passion of Joan of Arc* is a riveting depiction of the saint's courageous witness. Starring Maria Falconetti in a

> To save France . . . that's why I was born.
> —JOAN OF ARC

one-of-a-kind performance, Dreyer's film is a jewel in the crown of silent cinema. It intersperses title cards containing the actual text from Joan's trial with intense close-ups on the faces of Falconetti and the actors playing her ecclesiastical accusers. Falconetti manages to express an extraordinary range of human feeling, with Dreyer saying about her, "There was a soul behind that façade."

The first major theme of the film, as indicated by the title, is passion. On the one hand, Dreyer affirms that Joan was indeed a martyr and that her story of suffering and death follows the example of the Passion of the Lord Jesus. Her death is noble and holy, and she has received her heavenly reward for it. But Dreyer also depicts a young woman *with* passion, an intense patriot and a zealous mystic whose decision to leave her village, don a soldier's clothes, and speak to the king himself are not meant simply to make a political statement or express her unique identity but to obey divine promptings and serve at any cost. In this way, Joan calls to mind biblical figures like the prophet Samuel, King David, the Blessed Virgin, and even Jesus himself when he wanders away from Mary and Joseph in Jerusalem, later asking them, "Did you not know that I must be in my Father's house?" (Luke 2:49).

A second theme of the film is honesty, which is established at the beginning when Joan swears to tell "rien que la vérité" (nothing but the truth) before a collection of men whose severe faces filmed from unusual angles call into question any possibility of fairmindedness. Joan's interrogators attempt to entrap their young prisoner with her own words by highlighting the stark difference between safe, simple knowledge and dangerous, complex feelings. But the plan fails out of the gate, as the simple questions posed to Joan require nuanced, even speculative answers. One of the priests asks, "How old are you?" to which she replies, "Nineteen, I think," eliciting uncomfortable laughter from the buffoon-like men. Even her name is not a settled matter: "In France, they call me Jeanne. In my hometown they call me Jeannette." Joan then affirms that she has been catechized, but she defiantly refuses the bishop's request to recite the Lord's Prayer on command, prompting another interrogator to ask derisively, "Do you presume God sent you?" This time, Joan nods her head affirmatively, eyes blazing, and fires back with absolute assurance, "Oui." Then, in a beautiful shot, Joan gazes upward, tears streaming down her face, and elaborates, "To save France . . . that's why I was born." In the questions that follow, Joan's accusers become more agitated, and in a roomful of cynical old men supposedly doing the work of the Church, it is the perceived weakness of Joan's age, sex, earnestness, and outsider status that shine the light of Christ on their sin.

Two more related themes in the film are deception and coercion, tactics to which the ecclesiastical authorities resort upon Joan's rhetorical victory in the straightforward interrogation. "We must use wiles," one of the men says. Although there are a couple of men sympathetic to Joan, there is broad agreement that she must be stopped. Joan is presented with a false letter from King Charles VII before being taken to a cell where, in a disturbing scene, torturers mock her, putting a straw

> The original version of the film was heavily edited by French censors. In 1981, a print of Dreyer's intended cut was discovered in a mental institution near Oslo, Norway, then restored and rereleased as the definitive version of the movie.

crown on her head and an arrow in her hand. When she faints, they bleed her before sending for the Sacrament, which is then cruelly denied her when she revives. The bishop tries to appeal to Joan's piety, inviting her back to the mercy of the

The film was originally accompanied by live music in the movie theater, but there is no definitive musical score for the film. Over the decades dozens of new soundtracks have been compiled or composed for it, including Richard Einhorn's *Voices of Light*.

Church to avoid being burned and, much more crucially, eternally damned. Joan looks at a maggot-infested skull and, contemplating her mortality, temporarily relents, signing a false document before being taken away to have her head shaved—an emotionally gripping scene that concludes with Joan's return to her original resolve. She makes her confession, receives the Viaticum, and heads to the stake. Again, following in the footsteps of Jesus and all the holy martyrs, it is the condemned one whose righteousness convicts her accusers, as the Church's leaders are deceived, failing to see the power of God at work in his chosen vessel. The bishops, priests, lawyers, soldiers, and politicians are the ones who have been coerced by worldly forces promising safety and prosperity, if only the outlying voices of dissent can be silenced.

A final theme of the film, encapsulated in the horrifying scene of Joan's execution, is the nature and evaluation of history. In many respects, *The Passion of Joan of Arc* is a timely movie, reflecting post–World War I tension that may not be immediately noticeable a century later. In 1928, for example, the anachronism of the soldiers in the film wearing World War I–era British Army helmets would have been spotted right away. More importantly, the film was released just eight years after Pope Benedict XV canonized Joan, and just six years

> You have burned a saint!
> —UNNAMED BYSTANDER

after Pope Pius XI had declared her a patron saint of France. When Dreyer made his movie, Joan had recently become a focal point of national unity for the French and an inspiration for Catholics, but more broadly, she stood as a symbol of hope for a world that seemed determined to keep making the same gruesome mistakes. "You have burned a saint!" a man cries out as Joan dies.

Today's viewer knows that it was only in the decades *after* Dreyer's film had come out that the most violent period in human history, the most prolific era of Christian martyrdom, and arguably the most scandalous behavior ever committed by churchmen would take place. When the soldiers turn their spears, maces, and cannons on the crowd mourning Joan's demise, it is an eerie reminder of the high cost of recognizing and publicizing truth in every age. However, the final title card reads, "The protective flames surrounded Joan's soul as she rose to heaven," offering the consolation of an eternal solution to the intractable problems of worldly injustice.

Dreyer shot the film almost entirely in closeups and medium shots—there is no establishing shot, for instance, of the town or the castle where the interrogation of Joan takes place—which helps create a sense of relentless intensity between Joan and her interrogators.

But Dreyer's tale of St. Joan of Arc is finally an invitation to put the ideals of faith into action in the present—both to reject the notion of a purely private religion and to be open to the possibility of God's call to extraordinary public service. This courtroom drama vividly depicts the active, holy life that inspires the masses but may confound great thinkers. "Joan of Arc," G.K. Chesterton noted around the same time as Dreyer's film, "was not stuck at the cross-roads, either by rejecting all the paths like Tolstoy, or by accepting them all like Nietzsche. She chose a path, and went down it like a thunderbolt."

*The Passion of Joan of Arc* would prove to be Dreyer's last silent film and a swan song for the early film era, as the industry would soon embrace talking pictures. Even after many subsequent films about Joan, Dreyer's achievement remains arguably the very best, and it is rightly included in discussions of the most mesmerizing pieces of contemporary art from any medium. Although the film offers a very different experience than modern moviegoing, it will still be appreciated a hundred years from now, and the example and prayers of the Maid of Orléans will continue to bless the world amid its ongoing crises.

*AP*

## DISCUSSION QUESTIONS

- Watching Joan's passion, you may well be inspired to ask searching self-critical questions: For what purpose were you born? For what would you give your life?

- How is watching a silent film different than watching a talking picture? Do you appreciate the images more? Is there a place for new silent films in today's cinematic landscape?

- Dreyer's depiction of Joan's story certainly highlights her sanctity, but it also features unjust, even wicked churchmen. How does the holiness of the saints both uphold and challenge the status quo in the Church?

# The Sacrifice

## 1986

*A dramatically minimalist, symbolically abstract meditation on humanity's natural fear of death, hope for salvation, and world-altering power of total self-gift.*

"External chains of events, intrigues and causalities have come to mean less and less with every film I make." These words from director Andrei Tarkovsky fittingly describe the aesthetic of this, his final film. It is perhaps the most formally demanding work on the Vatican Film List, and during significant stretches the visible elements on screen seem to give way almost entirely to arcane, subjective significances. Nonetheless, for a patient, sensitive, and sympathetic viewer, *The Sacrifice* may well deliver a profound portrayal—albeit

Raised Russian Orthodox, Tarkovsky expressed to several friends an interest in becoming Catholic. At one time or another, he was also interested in Islam, yoga, transcendental meditation, and parapsychology, and, near the end of his life, he continued to treat very seriously a séance that predicted (accurately, as it turns out) that he would make a total of seven films.

oblique, stripped bare, and highly metaphorical—of that all-consuming self-gift that our Lord describes in superlative terms: "No one has greater love than this, to lay down one's life for one's friends" (John 15:13).

Also appearing under the heading "Religion" on the Vatican List alongside Tarkovsky's other, better-known film, *Andrei Rublev*, *The Sacrifice* utilizes the medium of cinema as a vehicle not so much for drama or documentary realism as abstract symbolism and searching philosophical dialogue. It opens with a selection from Bach's *St. Matthew Passion*, whose aria "Erbarme dich" (Have Mercy on Me) establishes a tone of direct, supplicatory appeal to God. The accompanying visual of a slow, meditative survey of Leonardo da Vinci's painting *Adoration of the Magi* adds a theme of double sacrifice. Man offers his this-worldly gifts to God in the treasures these kings offer to the Christ child; and God offers an other-worldly, mysterious gift to man in the impending sacrifice of this child grown into a man.

A slow camera tilt up the trunk of a tree in this painting cuts to footage of a tree—really just a leafless stalk—in the real world, which is being planted amidst a desolate landscape by the film's central character, Alexander. A once-famous actor turned theater critic and university lecturer in aesthetics—as well as a practical atheist (he does not formally disavow belief in God but mentions he does not pray)—Alexander reveals his searching spiritual sensibility and penchant for preaching as he recounts a parable to his mute son, Little Man. There once was an old Orthodox monk, he narrates, who planted a barren tree on a mountainside and then asked a younger monk to water it every day until it came to life. Each day for three years the younger monk did so, until one day he climbed the mountain and found the tree was in full bloom. A little later in *Sacrifice*, Alexander orates again while sitting under another tree with Little Man on his lap. He launches into a lengthy harangue about the maladies of their civilization: how it only contributes violence to the world, had been built around unnecessary things, and lost sight of spiritual goods in its obsession with material progress. The film captures each of these speeches in a single long take, cementing the impression that in this film, as one critic comments, Tarkovsky's already slow cinema grinds almost to a complete halt.

In between Alexander's monologues, we are introduced to the members of his household—his wife and daughter, a pair of maids, the mailman, and a doctor (apparently his wife's lover)—as well as to the claustrophobic atmosphere that has been described as the real protagonist of the film. When fighter jets race over the house and a flickering television announces an imminent nuclear missile strike, the characters each respond to this descending mood of existential dread. Alexander, for example, quietly reflects that his whole life has been waiting for this moment, whereas his wife dissolves into hysterics that are only quieted, in a troubling scene, by a tranquilizer injected against her will. The rest of the party languishes in a taut, nauseous atmosphere as if in fear

> Every gift involves sacrifice.
> If not, what kind of gift would it be?
> —OTTO

of the impending Final Judgment—or perhaps its secular analogue, death perceived as an absolute end. (The film's Cold War context is notable here, as many persons at that time lived in fear of "the ultimate war," as Alexander later describes it, in which "there will be no victors and no vanquished.") For these characters, an almost palpable sense that the end could come at any moment builds toward a half-suppressed kind of frenzy and a crisis of urgent, decisive choice.

Shot in Sweden, *The Sacrifice* employed many of the same crew members as Ingmar Bergman's films; even Bergman's son Daniel assisted on location. Tarkovsky referred to them as "Bergman's mafia."

Alexander's crisis comes when he retires from the rest of the group and, alone in a sparsely furnished room, sinks to his knees and prays the Lord's Prayer. This practical atheist then begs God to restore things as they were before, offering in return everything he has: "I'll destroy my home. . . . I'll be mute, and never speak another word to anyone. . . . Just let me be rid of this deadly, sickening, animal fear!" Then he crawls onto a couch and sleeps.

At this point things get bizarre. Possibly in a dream (critics debate which parts of what follows, if any, take place outside the confines of Alexander's mind), Otto the mailman advises Alexander that he should sleep with the maid, Maria, as a way to resolve all their problems. Alexander sneaks away to do just this and tenders his request for physical intimacy while holding a gun to his head. She complies, and jets again fly overhead, which are then followed by several abstract images, including the lovers tangling on a levitating bed and a crowd running chaotically through trash-strewn streets. Alexander wakes up on the couch where he had fallen asleep, proposes

> I'll be mute, and never speak another word to anyone. . . . Just let me be rid of this deadly, sickening, animal fear!
> —ALEXANDER

that everyone else in the family leave for a walk, and, while they are away, burns their house to the ground.

It is an extraordinary climactic sequence. Filmed in the days before computer-generated imagery, a single protracted shot of over six minutes literally burns down the set. In fact, Tarkovsky and his crew burned down two sets, since the camera jammed the first time around and rendered the footage unusable. Some ruthless negotiating with the producers enabled Tarkovsky to build a second house (which his crew did in only two weeks), then they completely reshot the scene (significantly running over the film's original two-million-dollar budget).

The family returns to the site of the conflagration and scrambles around in anguish. Alexander gets transported away in an ambulance (for some reason already on site). The film then concludes with Little Man, who carries pails of water to the withered tree planted in the opening scene. Lying down with his head at its base, Alexander's son speaks for the first time and quotes the opening lines of John's Gospel: "In the beginning was the Word," followed by a lingering question: "Why is that, Papa?" The final shot of the film mirrors the first: a slow tilt of the camera climbs the trunk of the tree, and over the final frame a superimposed dedication appears: "to my son Andriosha with hope and confidence."

As these concluding words suggest, much could be made of the way the incidents and imagery in *The Sacrifice* reflect the intimate circumstances of Tarkovsky's own life. Each of the characters in Alexander's life is allegedly based upon a person in Tarkovsky's. For example, at the time of shooting, Tarkovsky's own son was forcibly prevented from joining him abroad by Soviet officials in retaliation for the director's refusal to return to Russia—not unlike the way Little Man remains almost entirely off screen yet constitutes a kind of silent center of the whole film. Also, like Alexander's tryst with the maid Maria, Tarkovsky was actively involved in an affair while working on *The Sacrifice* with a Swedish woman who later bore him a child.

It is as if, through the medium of this film, Tarkovsky renders his most intimate, otherwise intangible interiority in concrete, publicly accessible terms. He shows us a desolate landscape weighted by the fear of a looming death; an almost madly hopeful anticipation of restorative love, at once physical and otherworldly; a man's overriding desire to summarize the significance of his existence through a single, consummate gift of self. These concerns are intensely personal, and the result is a strange and in many ways forbidding film. But it is *so* deeply personal that it also edges upon the universally human, to the extent that it touches upon impulses fundamental to our nature as persons. Made in the image of a God who, in loving his creatures, holds back nothing but gives himself without reserve, so we, too, Christian tradition tells us, beneath all our short-sighted desires and calculated reservations, want more than anything to give all that we are.

Tarkovsky used to say that art is a prayer, an

> The various references throughout the film to Japanese culture—the withered tree compared to *ikebana*, Alexander's musical recording, and the kimono he wears during the conflagration scene—are deliberate gestures of respect for another director on the Vatican Film List, beloved by Tarkovsky, Akira Kurosawa.

expression of human hope, and anything else is not art. In this particular work of art, Alexander (in the fictional world), and through him Tarkovsky (in the actual world), burns a microcosm of the whole world, in the ultimate hope of somehow, unforeseeably, receiving back in the same measure. Both men give up everything, in a gift that amounts to a grand, some might say quixotic, gesture. But love not infrequently masquerades as folly. Indeed, if there is one certain sentiment expressed in *The Sacrifice*, it is this: that everything amounts to nothing compared to the chance, however fleeting, to give one's entire life to and for the ones we love.

*DPB*

## DISCUSSION QUESTIONS

- Have you ever been in a situation that demanded everything from you? How did you respond? How did it turn out?

- How do you think about potentially world-ending catastrophes, like nuclear war, meteor strikes, or an uncontrollable pandemic? Are these real possibilities? How should we prepare (physically, spiritually, etc.)?

- Is giving up a thing the same as giving it as a gift? Are there circumstances where one is more powerful than the other?

# *Thérèse*

## 1986

*An impressionistic, aesthetically unconventional representation
of one of the most popular saints of modern times:
the "Little Flower" of Lisieux.*

As a rule, mysticism is difficult to photograph, but this film makes a good show of it with some striking artistic choices. Entirely shot on what appears to be a single, sparsely adorned sound stage, *Thérèse* powerfully communicates a sense of the renunciation involved in the spirituality it depicts. But the "no" to the world at the center of this film perhaps grants too little insight into the great "yes" at the heart of this saint—that is, the positive choice of that pearl of great price: true charity, communion with God, call it what

> To evangelize the evangelists—that's the chief object of all the prayers we offer and all the sacrifices we make. We've got to pray for them while they're busy bringing souls to Christ by their preaching, and still more by their example.
> —ST. THÉRÈSE OF LISIEUX

you will, which makes all earthly gain count as loss. *Thérèse* is a mystical film—achingly, almost devastatingly beautiful and suffused with a sensation of being lifted to dizzying, almost asphyxiating spiritual heights—even if on the surface it is all very simple and down to earth.

Eschewing a naturalistic (let alone lavish) visual style, *Thérèse*'s minimalistic sets follow one after another like a succession of still-life paintings. A father uses an old-fashioned bedwarmer to cozy up the covers for his two young girls and kisses them good night: "Nice and warm," he says, with good-natured simplicity. A gilded clock ticks under a glass dome. The sisters sit at a table and play a game of checkers with a vase of flowers and bowl of fruit between them. One of these girls is, of course, Thérèse (played by Catherine Mouchet), who reveals her youthful evangelistic zeal by asking for a Mass to be said for an unrepentant murderer sentenced to die. After his execution, she reads in the paper that just before dying he kissed the crucifix. "He's saved! I saved him! I won!" she celebrates.

Shortly thereafter, Thérèse and her sister Céline (played by Aurore Prieto) visit the Carmelite monastery where their two older sisters are already cloistered. They indicate a desire to join too—Thérèse, in particular, speaks of her vocation like an engagement, expressing a wish to know Christ as her husband and to be his alone—but everyone thinks she is too young to enter. Her sisters tell her not to worry: "You'll never meet the boy who could satisfy you. He doesn't exist. . . . Eat sweets, enjoy yourself. . . . Have fun. Go to Paris with Dad." The priest responsible for the convent tells her no, as does the bishop, so she appeals directly to the pope. She gains an audience and, when the time comes, blurts out her request and clings to his robes, enthusiastically disregarding official protocol. Returning home, she learns that the choice has been entrusted to Mother Superior at the convent, who eventually relents.

When the day comes, Thérèse approaches the altar dressed in a white dress and veil. The priest asks what she desires. "His mercy. The poverty of the Order and company of the sisters," she replies. Then, through happy tears, she kisses her natural family goodbye and is greeted with welcoming kisses by her new supernatural family. They sheer her hair, dress her in black and white, and garland her with a crown of white roses. That night a sister reads from the Song of Songs: "My beloved speaks. He says, 'Come, my beloved, come.' Winter is over. The rain has stopped." "How I've longed for this day," Thérèse prays. "I'll give my life for you. I'll be yours forever. I am not perfect. . . . Help me to do good, to help others . . . to please you. I wish I were already up there to see you."

She joins the sisters' silent regimen of Scripture reading and sharing simple meals. She assists the older, physically less capable sisters, walking with them and giving them sponge baths. She does laundry and stitchwork during the community's social hour. In between these examples of "the little way"— doing small things with great

Thérèse was canonized in 1925, only twenty-eight years after her death. To mark the occasion, Pope Pius XI revived an old custom of filling St. Peter's Basilica with lamps, torches, and candelabras—a labor that took three hundred men over two weeks.

love—the film interposes additional recitations from the Song of Songs, and the rhythmic back and forth conveys a sense of ordinary, daily tasks steeped in a whispered spiritual romance. "I sleep, but not my heart. I hear my beloved

For her leading role in this film, Catherine Mouchet won the 1987 César Award for Most Promising Actress and went on to act in over fifty-four films, most of them French language.

knock. Open, my sister, my friend, my dove, my perfection. For my head is covered with dew, my curls glisten from the night." "My beloved, come into your garden. Take the fruit of your trees." "My beloved instructs my soul, speaking to it in silence and in darkness."

Even a convent is not free from troubles, though, and when Thérèse's father suffers a debilitating malady, Céline whispers through the grill at the convent: "Everyone thinks it's your fault. . . . Especially you, Thérèse. That you killed him." Then she adds a censure still leveled against those who take religious vows today: "That you're selfish, useless, and crazy." Not much later Thérèse also gets sick and collapses while, in a bit of girlish fun, she gets her photograph taken dressed up as St. Joan of Arc in armor made of foil. She is confined to the infirmary, bleeding from her mouth. A doctor inspects her and gives his diagnosis: tuberculosis. He prescribes fever cups and morphine shots for the pain, but the convent's superior adopts a different perspective on a disease that at the time was regarded as incurable. Her exchanges with the doctor are terse and telling:

> Superior: "There's no need."
> Physician: "There is."
> Superior: "She'll refuse them."
> Physician: "I'll ask her."

Superior: "We're on earth to suffer as our husband did."
Physician: "He suffered only a day."
Superior: "He's in agony till the world ends. For you, for me, for all our crimes."
Physician: "Suffering is hideous."
Superior: "Not here."
Physician: "They ought to burn this place down."
Superior: "They probably will."
Physician: "You're dangerous."
Superior: "No, the salt of the earth."

The biblical recitations resume, this time interspersed with images of the hardships involved in the sisters' austere manner of life. "He brought me to his wine cellar. He poured his friendship in me. Sustain me with flowers, strengthen me with fruit. I pine away for love." Some of the sisters fasten themselves with rough burlap bands and crosses with punishing metal spikes. "His left hand touches my head, the other embraces me. Downpour cannot extinguish love, nor floods submerge it." The water in a wash basin is completely frozen, and Thérèse has her fingers wrapped against chilblains. "I opened the door to my beloved. I turned around and he had vanished. What despair! I fainted. I looked but couldn't find him. I called, he didn't answer. I ran into the night watchman. They beat me, they wounded me." Thérèse's illness gets worse. "Please, if you meet my beloved, tell him I'm ill with love." A sister attends to her but says, "I can't pray for you. We all agree, you deflect the prayers onto others. You pass on all your gifts." Thérèse becomes too sick to receive Communion and coughs up the

> Please, if you meet my beloved
> tell him I'm ill with love.
> —ST. THÉRÈSE OF LISIEUX

Thérèse's parents, Zélie and Louis Martin, were the parents of five nuns and were beatified in Lisieux during the year of their 150th wedding anniversary. Seven years later, on October 18, 2015, they became the first spouses to be canonized together.

consecrated Host. "I'd cross mountains and plains in search of my love. I'd go see the shoots in the valleys, the budding vine, the blooming pomegranate trees."

Before her untimely end, Mother Superior hands Thérèse an empty booklet and asks her to write her feelings and memories. This is a nod to the origin of Thérèse's autobiography, *Story of a Soul*, the spiritual classic upon which the film is based. After she finishes writing, puts away her notepad, and slides closed her pencil box, text on the screen informs us, "After her death, Thérèse's notebook was published and translated in several languages. Her tomb is often visited. In 1925, she was declared a saint and canonized." And that's where the film ends.

It is a beguiling, even entrancing portrait of the person Pope Pius X called the greatest saint of modern times. But how well does it capture the spirit of the young woman who lived only twenty-four years yet, within decades of her death, was declared co-patron of world missions with St. Francis Xavier, co-patron of France with St. Joan of Arc, and the thirty-third Doctor of the Church?

For all it does well, one thing *Thérèse* almost certainly underplays is all that is *gained* in consecrated life. "I felt charity enter into my soul," Thérèse writes in *Story of a Soul*, "and the need to forget myself and to please others; since then I've been happy! . . . He desires only our happiness." She later adds, "Often during my Communions, I repeated these words of the *Imitation*: 'O Jesus, unspeakable sweetness, change all the consolations of this earth into bitterness for me.'" To focus solely on the last part of the final quote and forget all that was said before—about charity and happiness, Communion and sweetness—is to miss the most important point of a life dedicated to God.

Carmelites in particular model their spirituality upon the Old Testament prophet Elijah and his intimate encounter with God recorded in 1 Kings: he withdraws from society; endures tempest, earthquake, and fire; and finally, amidst "a sound of sheer silence" (1 Kings 19:12), hears the still small voice that created the heavens and earth. This is the treasure Thérèse forsook all passing earthly pleasures to cherish, a joy as subtle and elusive as it is superlatively real. Film, as a visual medium, necessarily deals in the outside appearances of things, but to go deeper into the real meaning of the hidden life of a saint like Thérèse, it becomes necessary to discover what no eye as yet can see—that Great Fact that another Carmelite beloved of Thérèse, St. John of the Cross, describes as a flame only "seen" with the heart, which "lit and led me through / More certain than the light of noonday clear."

*DPB*

## DISCUSSION QUESTIONS

- Cardinal Francis Bourne once said, "I love St. Thérèse of Lisieux very much because she has simplified things: in our relationship with God she has done away with the mathematics." Could your relationship with God benefit from a simplification? In what areas is your life (or religious life) overcomplicated?

- Mother Teresa of Kolkata chose *la petite Thérèse* as her namesake because she did ordinary things with extraordinary love. Where are you called to practice fidelity over small things?

- On the occasion of proclaiming her a Doctor of the Church, Pope John Paul II described Thérèse as a model of missionary commitment even though she never left the cloister at Lisieux. How might you help advance the Church's missionary endeavors, even without leaving home?

# PART II

# Values

# *Au Revoir les Enfants*

## 1987

*A beautiful coming-of-age story, where upper-class boys adapt to the everyday realities of life in a Catholic boarding school in Nazi-occupied France.*

Near the end of his career, director Louis Malle returned to his native France to tell a story that had been on his mind and in his heart for decades. After early success as part of the French New Wave movement, Malle made several films of varying quality and success in Hollywood before finally undertaking his masterpiece, *Au Revoir Les Enfants*, a largely autobiographical tale of his own experience in a Catholic boarding school outside Paris during the Nazi occupation in the Second World War. Set in the winter of early 1944, just months before the liberation of France, the film depicts ordinary juvenile rivalries and hijinks as well as the heroic virtue of a priest, Father Jean (Philippe Morier-Genoud), who hides Jewish boys from the Gestapo among the ranks of France's elite sons.

Father Jean's heroics are mostly in the background, as the film focuses primarily on Julien Quentin (Gaspard Manesse), a sensitive boy from a wealthy family, who is modeled after the young Malle. At the beginning of the movie, Julien is upset at his fur-clad mother and absentee industrialist father for sending him back from Christmas break to a new semester in the spartan dormitories of a Carmelite school during difficult wartime conditions. But once returned, he settles into a normal routine with his classmates, and they all marvel at the arrival of a new boy, Jean Bonnet (Raphael Fejtö), who does not know Catholic prayers and shares only the vaguest details about his past. Jean is an excellent student, displacing Julien at the top of the class and outdoing him at the piano, inspiring both fascination and envy. Although Julien is mature for his age, he occasionally wets the bed—a reminder that everyone must go through the inanities and ignominies of childhood, not avoid them. Even amid monumental world events, kids are kids.

Father Jean perceives Julien's potential for compassionate leadership, and he encourages him to look out for Jean Bonnet, saying, "The others look up to you. I'm counting on you." Julien subsequently discovers his classmate engaging in an unfamiliar prayer routine, and he later snoops in Jean Bonnet's locker to confirm his Jewish identity and learn his real surname, Kippelstein. Father Jean's challenge to Julien is put

> I don't mean to shock you but only remind you that charity is a Christian's first duty.
> —FATHER JEAN

The piano teacher, Mademoiselle Davenne, is played by Irène Jacob in her feature film debut. In one scene, she accompanies the silent picture *The Immigrant*, written and directed by Charlie Chaplin, whose work inspired Jacob to begin acting.

to the test when the boys get lost in the frigid woods after dark. No sooner does Jean Bonnet ask, "Are there wolves in these woods?" than German soldiers approach in a jeep. One of the soldiers congratulates himself for showing kindness to the boys by returning them to the school and tells the priest that he is a Catholic from Bavaria. One doubts, however, whether the soldier's faith would have informed his decision to help the boys if he had known that one of them was Jewish.

The film also tackles the controversial issue of French collaboration with the Nazis. At the parents' weekend, Father Jean poses a challenge to the boys' wealthy families, many of whom profit in various ways from the war. In his homily at Mass he says, "Those who should guide us betray us instead." One man stands up and walks out of the church in protest, but Father Jean is unmoved, confident in his convictions.

And then there is the pitiful character of Joseph, a young disabled man who trades black-market merchandise with the schoolboys. Although Joseph is shown great charity by the priests who employ him at the school, he is often ridiculed by the students, and he is keen to position himself above anyone he considers to be lowlier than he is. He makes fun of the cook, for example, who seems to have a drinking problem, and he expresses disdain for the young Frenchmen pressed into service as manual laborers in Germany. He reserves his most vicious rhetoric, however, for Jews. When Joseph's black-market business is discovered and he is fired, he informs on Father Jean to the Gestapo, reappearing at the school in a

suit and overcoat and handing out the cigarettes that are the spoils of his treachery.

In contrast to Joseph, Julien's mother represents a high-minded attitude about the German occupation, quietly hoping it will end soon, trying not to rock the boat. And although she finds anti-Semitism distasteful, she still does condemn one Jewish person: the former socialist French Prime Minister Léon Blum. When she treats Julien and Jean Bonnet to a fancy lunch, she does not hide her disapproval of collaborators, but she chastises her other son, François, for antagonizing French militia men as they attempt to remove a Jewish patron from the restaurant. François represents a young layman's version of Father Jean's principled resistance to evil: he discusses Thomas Aquinas, gives Nazis bad directions to where they are trying to go, and tells his mother he plans to join the Resistance. One can imagine a privileged idealist like him making a difference in the world as an educator or a statesman after the war.

The friendship between Julien and Jean solidifies as the film nears its end, as, for instance, they both delight in watching Charlie Chaplin's silent classic *The Immigrant*, complete with live piano and violin accompaniment. Julien's experience of comradery through cinema is perhaps a nod to Malle's own early inspiration to pursue filmmaking. Later, when Julien is being punished for his involvement in Joseph's black-market scheme, he and Jean hide out in the music room, playing jazz together on the piano. The boys also bond with each night after lights out, reading aloud

> In the film, the boarding school is run by Carmelite priests who are "discalced"–that is, they do not wear shoes. A close examination of even snowy outdoor scenes will show the priests wearing simple, open-toed sandals.

> I'm the only one in this school that thinks about death.
> It's incredible!
> —JULIEN QUENTIN

from the Muslim classic *One Thousand and One Nights* and swapping grins at provocative passages. In these simple scenes of camaraderie, Malle shows us how art has the power to transcend differences and unite people in brotherly love.

As a result of Joseph's betrayal, the Nazis finally raid the school and bring the story to its tragic but not entirely unpropitious ending. The head Gestapo agent, Dr. Müller, barges into the school and angrily removes the pins representing Allied victories from the classroom map. He then takes Jean out of class and locates the other two Jewish boys hiding on the premises before closing the school and sending all the students back home. As Jean packs his belongings, he tells Julien in resignation, "They would have gotten me no matter what." He then gives him his personal books, which he sadly but correctly suspects he will never need again. One panicked teacher attempts to escape to the roof of the building, telling Julien "Adieu," indicating a final farewell. In contrast, as the Nazis take away a serene Father Jean, the boys call out to their beloved headmaster with the much more hopeful valediction "Au revoir"—"Until we see each other again." He responds in kind: "Au revoir, les enfants," adding, "A bientôt"—"See you soon"—a further emphasis on the expectation of reunion, whether in this life or in the next.

The film's concluding voiceover states that Jean and the other two Jewish boys died at Auschwitz and that Father Jean died in another camp, Mauthausen (as did Malle's real-life headmaster, the similarly named Father Jacques). In Yad Vashem, Israel's official memorial to the victims of the Holocaust, Father Jacques de Jésus, OCD (the Order of

Discalced Carmelites), is counted among the "Righteous Among the Nations," a list of non-Jews that took heroic risks to save Jews from the Nazi atrocities. Also included on the list is Oskar Schindler, the famous subject of *Schindler's List*, which is also on the Vatican List. More than twenty years before the landmark Catholic document

> The film was nominated for Best Foreign Language Film at the 60th Annual Academy Awards but lost to *Babette's Feast*, another film on the Vatican List.

*Nostra Aetate*, the Declaration on the Relation of the Church to Non-Christian Religions, Father Jacques demonstrated one of its most important teachings: "In her rejection of every persecution against any man, the Church, mindful of the patrimony she shares with the Jews and moved not by political reasons but by the Gospel's spiritual love, decries hatred, persecutions, displays of anti-Semitism, directed against Jews at any time and by anyone."

Like the work of some of Malle's French filmmaking peers, especially Robert Bresson and Éric Rohmer, *Au Revoir les Enfants* presents the Church in a positive light. And while Malle's personal piety in his adult years is uncertain, his boyhood encounter with a saintly priest clearly stuck with him throughout his life. When he died in 1995, his funeral Mass was held in the Church of Saint-Sulpice in the Latin Quarter of Paris.

Amid Malle's many cinematic accomplishments, few would deny that *Au Revoir les Enfants* is his greatest work. A religious film of the highest quality, it continues to have the power to touch the heart and inspire Christ-like charity.

*AP*

## DISCUSSION QUESTIONS

- Have you ever jeopardized your own safety for the sake of someone else?

- As a child, did you know anyone of a different religion or ethnic background? In your experience, does the encounter with someone of another faith strengthen, weaken, or make no difference to your own?

- In the film, Joseph chooses to hurt others in response to his own deep hurt. How might he have reacted differently? How would you have reacted?

# Bicycle Thieves

## 1949

*A paradigmatic example of Italian neorealism in which a man and his son traverse an impoverished, war-stricken Rome in pursuit of a stolen bicycle.*

"No doubt one's first and most superficial reaction to everyday reality is that it is tedious," writes *Bicycle Thieves* screenwriter, Cesare Zavattini, and at first glance the film he has written would seem to confirm this impression. For viewers unaccustomed to Italian neorealism's understated style, a first viewing will almost certainly be an underwhelming cinematic experience. How is it that this film, whose action is pretty nearly exhausted by its one sentence summary, has been called the film that granted legitimacy to Italian cinema and is consistently held up next to *Citizen Kane* as one of the twentieth century's two most important films? The answer almost certainly has to do with its revolutionary departure from the kind of movies that came before it, as well as, perhaps, the aesthetic intention behind its superficially lackluster presentation, which, in the words of director Vittorio De Sica, was to "reintroduce the dramatic into quotidian situations, the marvelous in a little news item . . . considered by most people throwaway material."

This is the most classic example of Italian neorealism on the Vatican List—a socially minded story about desperate lower-class characters shot on location with nonprofessional actors and available light. *Bicycle Thieves*' preoccupation with the everyday, even mundane lives of relatively unremarkable poor folk is established straight away: a busload of men crowd the steps of an unemployment office, and one lucky chap, Antonio Ricci, lands a job—on the condition that he owns a bicycle. After retrieving his bike from a jampacked pawnshop (at the cost of trading in his bedsheets), Antonio returns home to celebrate the windfall: his son Bruno cleans the bike, Maria prepares egg sandwiches for his lunch, and the next day the family is all smiles as he pedals away into a brighter future. Antonio drops Bruno at the gas station where the boy works as a (startlingly underaged) pump attendant, but he only has the chance to ply his new trade pasting up American movie posters for about five minutes before a thief makes off with the

According to actor Enzo Staiola (who plays Bruno in film), the crowd of persons in the church scene were really homeless people, not extras dressed for a part. "They'd get angry because we kept redoing scenes," he recalls, remembering their shouts: "I want a shave. I want to eat. Who cares about some film?"

> I have to find that bike.
> —ANTONIO RICCI

linchpin of his employment. Antonio chases after it (to no avail), files a complaint with the police (also useless), and then spends the rest of the film hunting it all over Rome.

From the bustling marketplace in the Piazza Vittorio, through the halls of a homeless shelter and the chambers of an alleged clairvoyant, to a final confrontation with the thief in the middle of a crowd of his outraged neighbors, Antonio exhausts himself to retrieve the bicycle before, finally, he fails. In the film's final moments, desperate and apparently left with no other recourse, Antonio steals someone else's bicycle. Bruno watches in horror as an angry mob chases his dad and only elects not to drag him off to jail when the offended owner spies Bruno's tears and opts not to press charges. The film then ends with a final glance at the shame-stricken father and son as they disappear, hand in hand, back into a crowd.

Dramatically it is just about as spare as a film can be; even co-screenwriter Suso Cecchi d'Amico has admitted that *Bicycle Thieves* did not really have a story line. Yet as French critic and neorealist champion André Bazin observes, "The thesis implied is wondrously, outrageously simple: in the world where this workman lives, the poor must steal from each other in order to survive." Going on to describe it as the only valid communist film of the past decade, Bazin argues that the primary aim of *Bicycle Thieves* is not to tell the story of a man who loses his bike, but to transform a world in which losing a bike condemns a man to poverty. In other words, like the social novels of Dickens and Steinbeck, it is a film meant not to entertain (at least principally) but to agitate its audiences in the service of political reform—and given the historical moment in which the film was produced, it can be

admitted that hope for some such sort of reform certainly seemed warranted.

When neorealist films started appearing on the cinematic scene in the late forties and early fifties, Italians had already endured twenty years of fascism, occupation by the Nazis, and a pulverizing war that left their homeland in ruins and hundreds of thousands dead. People everywhere were looking to make a fresh start, including a subset of Italy's *avant-garde* filmmakers who were profoundly optimistic about the potential to effect social change through cinema. And the revolutionary way they hoped to do this? Simply by filming, in Zavattini's favorite expression, "life as it is."

Documenting the real character of the world without sentimentality, as if the camera had just happened to be present at a nonfictional event, the intent behind neorealism is reactionary on two fronts. On the one hand, it was meant as a counterpoint to the ideological super-spectacles of the Mussolini-era 1930s, deliberately rejecting, for instance, the grandiosity of ancient Rome in favor of contemporary stories showing day-to-day life. On the other hand, neorealists also desired to challenge what they perceived as the cinema of complicity and vain distraction coming out of Hollywood, whose imports occupied up to three-quarters of the

> Before the annual award for foreign language films came into existence in 1956, *Bicycle Thieves* was granted one of eight Honorary Academy Awards. The first of these was bestowed upon the Italian neorealist *Shoeshine* (1946), whose accompanying citation applies just as readily to *Bicycle Thieves*: "The high quality of this motion picture, brought to eloquent life in a country scarred by war, is proof to the world that the creative spirit can triumph over adversity."

Italian box office at the time. The chastened documentary style advanced by the neorealists, then, was an idealistically charged indictment of both European fascism and American fantasy. It deliberately departed from the cultural legacy that had produced the war and its atrocities, but it also attempted to circumvent commercial cinema's escapist stereotypes and engage more directly with reality.

So the classical Italian neorealist style was largely a product of ideals, but it was also, at least initially, a matter of sheer necessity. With the post-war economy in ruins and up to 7 percent of the population still living homeless, there was very little movie-making equipment, funding, or even film stock available to filmmakers. "There wasn't even a trace of an organized movie industry," De Sica writes, and as a result, "the problem of costs was without a doubt the determining factor that encouraged . . . these attempts to make movies no longer inspired by fiction but by real life." Many of the stylistic hallmarks of Italian neorealist cinema were thus simply the result of situational imperatives; it was only later that they became elements of a conscious aesthetic.

Many Italian critics, filmmakers, and scholars refer to the neorealist period as simply "The Golden Age." Its influence is notable upon other Vatican List films, including *The Flowers of St. Francis* (1950), *On the Waterfront* (1954), *Ordet* (1955), *The Tree of Wooden Clogs* (1978), and *Dekalog* (1988).

This might raise the question: If the roughhewn minimalism of these films was mostly a matter of making do, does this cinema retain any relevance once the constraints of its particular time and place are lifted? Does a film like *Bicycle Thieves* have anything more to say than providing a kind of artistic witness to hardships long past?

Quite possibly. The movement has been called a deeply ethical initiative, saying, for instance, that people were important in the wake of a war that made many of them voiceless, faceless, and nameless victims. Relatedly, such films might continue to startle audiences today with their radical commitment to a belief in the dignity, even sacredness, of everyday life.

Perhaps not especially obvious on a first viewing, this aspect of *Bicycle Thieves* finds energetic articulation in Zavattini's theoretical writings, which describe how he sets out in his screenplays, in a way comparable to other modern storytellers like Joyce, Proust, Kafka, Mann, etc., to transform our perceptions of everyday life into epic. In the influential essay "Some Ideas on the Cinema," Zavattini writes that the most pressing moral and artistic demand of his day resided in the ability to observe reality, not to extract fictions from it. "I am bored to death with heroes more or less imaginary," he complains. "The time has come to tell the audience that they are the true protagonists of life." The secret, he continues, is learning to notice that certain flashes of daily life are charged with a powerful poetry of their own. When viewed from the vantage of its true historical importance, every human life at each minute will become spectacular "not through its exceptional but through its normal quality; it will astonish us by showing us so many things that happen every day under our eyes, things we have never noticed before."

This is a beautiful idea. At the same time, there may be a flipside to such optimism about the endless fascination of the everyday lives of ordinary people: Bazin drolly remarks, for instance, that Zavattini's greatest dream is to make a ninety-minute film about a man to whom nothing ever happens. Such a film will presumably never actually be made—it is difficult to imagine what that would even look like—nonetheless, it is tempting to suggest that *Bicycle Thieves* comes pretty close. Strictly speaking, of course, it is untrue to say that *nothing* happens; *things* happen, some of them of world-altering significance for the hapless protagonist. Only they number among the sort of things that many viewers today (just as much, I suspect, as in Zavattini's day) are un-accustomed to regarding as cinematically interesting. But is this a deficit in the spectacle or in us, the spectators? This, in the end, may be the most interesting thing about *Bicycle Thieves*: precisely the way it questions its viewers' indifference and challenges us, ultimately, to care as much as God does for every sparrow that falls from the sky—or even some obscure Italian fallen on tough times.

*DPB*

## DISCUSSION QUESTIONS

- Do you find this film fascinating, boring, or both? Why?

- Have you ever found yourself in such desperate circum-stances that you compromised your ideals? How do you think back on that decision today?

- Does the drama in this film prompt any new thoughts about the plight of the poor? Is there something you might do to help a struggling individual or to improve a problematic situation?

# *The Burmese Harp*

## 1956

*A moving historical drama in which a unit of defeated Japanese soldiers leaves Burma at the end of the Second World War while one of their number stays behind to bury dead comrades.*

The opening titles of *The Burmese Harp* appear over a fixed shot of a dusty, empty landscape that stretches far away to a flat horizon beneath a blank sky. Not a soul is to be seen. The earth is pitted and heaped in mounds. Dotted here and there a few small scrubby bushes poke out; otherwise, everything is lifeless. Smoke drifts from something burning off-screen. The only thing to be heard is plangent strings and deep rolling drums on the soundtrack.

Music—stirring, mournful music—continues to make its presence felt once the action gets under way. The scene is Burma during the dying days of World War II. A company of Japanese troops, there to fight the British, sings songs to the accompaniment of a harp, played by a young soldier named Mizushima. The men have been trained to sing well by their leader, Captain Inouye (played by Rentarō Mikuni), who was a musician before the war began. But their songs are not hearty, tub-thumping morale-boosters. The lyrics are full of sorrow and longing:

> A night in late autumn:
> the solitary traveler
> looks up at the sky
> with a desolate heart—
> his beloved hometown,
> his parents dear.
> The path of his dreams
> is one that leads back home.

But back to which home? Japan? The song is so impassioned, so indelibly sad, that mere patriotism seems inadequate to account for it. The emotion speaks of something else, a deeper yearning. When the soldiers stop off in a village one night, a local graybeard declares that "the Himalayas are the home of the soul" but are too far away to be seen: "We long to see them, even if just once."

That same night, Captain Inouye and his

The screenplay was written by Natto Wada, a graduate in English Literature from Tokyo Woman's Christian University, who married director Kon Ichikawa in 1948. They collaborated on numerous film projects from 1949 until she retired from writing screenplays in 1965.

> It's no use fighting our fate. Far better to accept
> it like men. . . . If we die here in Burma, we'll die
> together. But if by chance we're able to return home,
> we'll do so together, leaving no man behind.
> —CAPTAIN INOUYE

unit realize they've been surrounded by advancing British
forces in the jungle. To pretend they haven't detected the
stake-out, the men give a heartfelt rendition of "There's No
Place Like Home"—a song evidently known in the East as in
the West—hoping thereby to forestall an attack while they
retrieve their ammunition. Surprisingly, the Brits echo it back
to them, in English. (Both armies, by the way, make the song
sound genuinely meaningful, not the trite jingle it usually
resembles.) Mizushima on his harp joins in to signal friendship and the two armies find themselves singing together.
Why such nonbelligerence? Imperial Japan surrendered to the
Allies three days ago. The homeland of Inouye and his men
is in ruins, and they are no longer combatants but prisoners
of war.

However, not all Japanese forces in Burma are willing to
give up the fight; a detachment in the mountains is holding
out. Mizushima, the peacemaker, offers to go up and persuade
them to surrender, knowing that he has only half an hour
before the British will obliterate this nest of snipers. His
mediation meets with resistance, and, within minutes, the
entire band of die-hards is destroyed; Mizushima alone
survives. As the camera pans over the corpses, we hear the
Passion Chorale from Bach's *St. Matthew Passion*: "O sacred
head, sore wounded."

This musical invocation of the suffering of Christ is
an intriguing development for a story with a Buddhist and
Burmese context, for, as we are told, "Burma is the Buddha's

At the 1956 International Venice Film Festival (the world's oldest film festival), *The Burmese Harp* was awarded the San Giorgio Prize. Ichikawa remarked, "I heard that San Giorgio [St. George] was the name of an Italian man who dedicated his life to peace. Since *The Burmese Harp* is about a soldier whose actions speak for peace, I think they saw a connection."

country." A little later, Mizushima overhears the singing of a funeral hymn by British hospital workers in a neatly tended cemetery with crosses at the head of every grave. The reverence shown by these Westerners for their dead does not provoke his conversion to Christianity; on the contrary, Mizushima soon starts to dress like a Buddhist monk and takes refuge inside a huge statue of a recumbent Buddha. But evidently the Christian funerary rites that he witnesses spur on his own attempts to honor the Japanese dead with appropriate burial and prayer.

He finds corpses everywhere: on the mountains, in the jungle, by the coast. These bodies—forgotten, rotting, carrion for birds—he begins to bury or burn. He realizes that his newfound vocation, to honor his deceased compatriots, is more important than rejoining his living comrades. When, by chance, he meets them on a bridge outside their prisoner-of-war camp, he avoids their eyes and pretends to be someone else; with his freshly shaven head, his monk's habit, and a parrot on his shoulder, he could pass for a stranger. His former friends look at him, puzzled by this familiar but unresponsive figure, and go on their way.

Captain Inouye struggles to concede that Mizushima could still be alive, for that would mean he was now a deserter. No, he must have died nobly in the mountains. But then he hears a few notes floating on the breeze from this mysterious monk strumming his harp and recognizes the musical skill of his former fellow soldier. He trains a parrot to say, "Let's return to Japan together!" and arranges for this "brother of the monk's bird" to be sent to the distant, solitary figure.

Through barbed wire, the prisoners catch sight of Mizushima with a parrot on each shoulder. They sing loudly to him, "There's no place like home," but he has a vacant look and doesn't approach. Rather, he sends to them his own bird, which he has taught to say, "No, I can't go back!" He also sends a letter, knowing that their repatriation order has come through and soon they will be heading home. The old lady who serves as letter-carrier for Mizushima says to the prisoners, "Since it's the last thing I can do for you, I brought it." The "last thing" she can do for them—are they then dying too? Captain Inouye saves the letter to read aloud on the ship back to Japan.

The climactic scene occurs on board deck as Inouye asks his men, "Is everyone here?" With the sea glinting in the sunshine over his shoulder, he reads what Mizushima has written: "The captain's words that we should all return and work together to rebuild our country are still fresh in my memory. But when I saw how many dead were left behind, I could no longer feel the same way. I will stay behind to create a place where those thousands of young souls can find repose. . . . There is no end to words of farewell."

Mizushima is effectively saying farewell to the dead and to the living at the same time. He is facing both ways at once, torn in two directions: dead to the living and living among the dead. The film's final image revisits the stony landscape with which it opened, again with the poignant soundtrack

> No, I can't go back.
> —MIZUSHIMA'S PARROT

*The Burmese Harp* was originally to be shot in color, but that plan was abandoned for practical and technical reasons: color cameras were too big to carry to remote locations and would have been almost impossible to repair if they broke down. In 1985, Ichikawa remade the film, this time in color. It was the number one box office hit in Japan that year.

by Akira Ifukube, but this time a caring human figure walks between the mounds of earth.

When director Kon Ichikawa read the source novel upon which *The Burmese Harp* is based, he was inspired: "I just felt I had to make it into a film. I felt this strong sense of mission, a call from the heavens." He did not specify the religion that these "heavens" and this "mission" pertained to. As noted, the story has a Buddhist context, but the issue at its heart is a matter of concern to all people, whether they be religious or not—namely, burial of kindred and respect for their memory. How we deal with bodily remains is a perennial, universal human problem. Hence, this film appears in the "Values" section, not the "Religion" section, of the Vatican List.

Nonetheless, there is a lot of religion in this movie, both explicit and implicit. Explicitly, it deals with what Christians view as one of the corporal works of mercy. From Abraham to Jesus, proper burial is understood to be a godly undertaking (Gen. 23; Luke 23:53), whereas leaving the dead untended is a sign of being accursed (Deut. 28:26; Ps. 79:3). Implicitly, the fact that Mizushima occupies a liminal space between the realms of the living and the dead suggests something of a purgatorial subtext. This is a film for watching on "a night in late autumn," during November, the month of the Holy Souls, when the Church calendar directs our minds especially to remembrance of those who have gone before us.

> There is no end to words of farewell.
> —FROM MIZUSHIMA'S LETTER

*The Burmese Harp* closes the same way it opens: with a caption that reads, "The soil of Burma is red and so are its rocks." This line is hard to understand. The geological meaning is plain, but what is its symbolic meaning? Symbolically, the soil is red because it has been stained with blood, yes—but why should the *rocks* be red too? What does that mean? That the film never provides a clear or easy answer reflects its many intriguing qualities. Profundities and ambiguities are being explored, and whatever resolutions are offered at the end—insofar as they amount to resolutions—remain subtle, communicated through emotion and image, not expressed through reason and articulation. This is a deep, gentle, poetic piece of cinema, with an intensely moving climactic scene: at once an elegy for the dead and a eulogy to inarticulate love.

*MW*

### DISCUSSION QUESTIONS

- How do you interpret the opening and closing caption, "The soil of Burma is red and so are its rocks"?

- Would you feel differently about the film if it had been shot in color?

- "There's No Place Like Home" features in both *The Burmese Harp* and another film on the Vatican List, *The Wizard of Oz*. Compare and contrast the different purposes it serves in each film.

# *Chariots of Fire*

## 1981

*Based on real-life events at the 1924 Olympics, a pair of British athletes contend with social pressures as they prepare to run for king and country.*

The first words of the screenplay for *Chariots of Fire* are taken from the Old Testament Scriptures: "Let us praise famous men and our fathers that begat us" (Sir. 44:1). This biblical opening not only strikes a religious note that will continue throughout the movie but also establishes its celebratory and commemorative, even somewhat nostalgic, tone. This is a story about heroic figures from the past and the different ways in which they showed their greatness.

> I believe God made me for a purpose . . . but he also made me fast. And when I run, I feel his pleasure.
> —ERIC LIDDELL

The story, which is loosely based on historical fact, opens in London at a 1978 memorial service for the recently deceased Harold Abrahams (played by Ben Cross), who had been part of the British athletics team at the Paris Olympics in 1924, the year in which most of the film occurs, through a prolonged flashback.

Abrahams, a Jewish student at Cambridge, finds himself the target of much casual anti-Semitism. He acknowledges that athletic success will be a way for him to defeat prejudice and demonstrate his loyalty to England. In order to gain victory, he is prepared even to transgress the gentleman-amateur ethos of his day and hire the services of a professional trainer, Sam Mussabini.

The other leading British athlete of the time, Eric Liddell, is a Scotsman and the son of Christian missionaries to China. A man of devout faith, he feels God's pleasure when he runs and intends to use the fame attendant on his sporting prowess as a means of spreading the Gospel, despite the fears of his sister, Jennie, that he is too interested in worldly success.

At the Olympics, Abrahams wins the hundred meters final, proving his point. Liddell withdraws from the sprint competition, having discovered that the heats are to take place on a Sunday, which he sees as a breach of Sabbath law. Instead, he races in the four hundred meters, a place having been generously made available to him by the aristocrat sportsman Lord Andrew Lindsay who has already won silver in the hurdles. Despite not having trained for the longer distance, Liddell wins the gold medal. Meanwhile, another teammate named Aubrey Montague comes sixth in the steeplechase. Montague, a seemingly minor character, serves to bring out one of the principal themes of the movie, as we shall explore further in a moment.

Abrahams and Liddell, the Jew and the Christian, are strongly contrasted. Abrahams is stylish, urbane, attractive, and successful as a suitor, dating a famous actress, but also driven, hurting as a result of anti-Semitic prejudice, and willing to adopt professional means in order to achieve the success he seeks, even if that might seem undignified to those of a more leisured mindset. Liddell, on the other hand, is tweedy, traditional, moral to the point of scrupulosity, keen to preach the Word of God (in the rain if need be), careful to respect the concerns of his conscientious sister, and attended by no love interest, save for some star-struck school girls.

The differences between Abrahams and Liddell emerge chiefly in their approach to running. Abrahams runs on his nerves—compulsively, discontentedly. He is determined to justify his existence through excellence. Having attained his end, he duly becomes "the toast of England" and marries his girlfriend. Liddell runs on his guts—passionately, even worshipfully. He sees sport as a way of honoring God but also as something that he will readily lay down when the time comes to return to the mission field.

The two men are faced with diametrically opposite moral challenges. Whereas Abrahams fights against the prejudice and snobbery of university dons in order to *achieve* his aims, Liddell fights against the nationalistic and morally compromising British Olympic committee in order to *destroy* his own hopes: "I told myself, if I win, I win for God . . . and now I find myself sitting here destroying it all, but I have to. To

> The title of the film derives from the account of the prophet Elijah's ascension into heaven (2 Kings 2:11).

run would be against God's law." Abrahams' success comes about through strength, through the intelligent deployment of expertise and technology. Liddell's success comes about through apparent weakness and as a result of the unforeseen generosity of Lord Lindsay.

The interesting thing about the contrast between the two men is that it is not presented as an "either/or." Although Liddell comes across as a more rounded and less conflicted person than Abrahams, Abrahams' approach is shown to be warranted, explicable, and successful. The message seems to be "both/and," celebrating not only the input of needful human effort but also the intervention of unaccountable, unexpected providence.

As the film returns to the present day and the framing device of the London memorial service, we see two choirboys standing next to each other; they are evidently real-life twins. This is a little nod to how we should read *Chariots of Fire*. Its two lead characters are neither antagonists nor buddies but, as it were, brothers. Their dramatic trajectories are peculiar, yes, but also intimately related. Abrahams and Liddell appear together in very few scenes, yet the implicit tension between them is what gives life to the symmetries of the screenplay.

These choirboys, like the entire congregation, are singing the patriotic hymn "Jerusalem" (by the poet William Blake) about Christ's legendary visit to Britain. Jesus may not really have "walk[ed] upon England's mountains green," but the hymn imagines a new Jerusalem being built there by one who carries a "bow of burning gold" and who steers a "chariot of fire," the latter term derived from the account of the prophet Elijah's ascension into heaven (2 Kings 2:11). Although, religiously

> ABRAHAMS: If I can't win, I won't run.
> SYBIL: If you don't run, you can't win.

*Chariots'* iconic beach scene became so famous after the movie's success at the 1982 Academy Awards that plaques were installed on both the beach where it was shot (St. Andrews, on the east coast of Scotland) and at the beach where it was fictionally set (Broadstairs, Kent, in the south of England).

speaking, Abrahams and Liddell journeyed in different "chariots of fire"—that is, in their Jewish and Christian traditions, respectively—both have a place of honor in the life of the nation. A closing caption informs us that Liddell went on to work as a missionary in China, dying young in 1945 ("all of Scotland mourned"), while Abrahams lived a long life and became the elder statesman of British athletics.

The producer, David Puttnam, whose mother was Jewish and his father Christian, has spoken intriguingly about the making of *Chariots*. He has said that he felt a kind of divine supervision at various moments in the production, most notably in the scene of the athletes running along the beach. A whole day had been spent recording this footage, but when it was reviewed, a piece of grit was found to have got inside the camera, ruining the entire day's work. The cast and crew had to reassemble and repeat everything, and when they did so, the weather was completely different. There had been a flat calm the first time around. Now, it was a lovely, windy day that tossed the sea into dancing white caps, making the whole scene vastly more vivid and active. The director, Hugh Hudson, thought the new footage so powerful that he eventually decided to use it twice, over both the opening and closing credits.

Puttnam has also spoken about how the film "finds" its audience in unexpected ways. Many sporting movies (*Rudy, Champions, Oxford Blues,* among others) are structured principally as celebrations of victory, of triumphing over the odds.

*Chariots* certainly contains such elements, but the moment that Puttnam regards as the emotional heart of the film is the scene where Liddell, preaching in a Paris church, quotes the following verses from Isaiah 40:

> Behold the nations are as a drop in the bucket and are counted as the small dust in the balance. All nations before Him are as nothing. They are counted to Him less than nothing and vanity. He bringeth the princes to nothing. He maketh the judges of the earth as a vanity. Hast thou not known, hast thou not heard, that the everlasting God, the Lord, the creator the ends of the earth, fainteth not, neither is weary? He giveth power to the faint, and to them that have no strength he increaseth might. But they that wait upon the Lord shall renew their strength, they shall mount up with wings as eagles, they shall run and not be weary, they shall walk and not faint.

As Liddell speaks these words—delivered with a powerful simplicity by Ian Charleson and accompanied by the stirring soundtrack of Vangelis—we see cutaways of runners stumbling and falling, including the likeable Aubrey Montague, made wretched by his own failure. The contrast between word and image strikes deep. We pity the runners, for we know ourselves what it is to fall and fail. But we also know what it is like—or at least, we *long* to know what it is like—to be given new strength, new hope. Indeed, earlier in the story, we have seen the realization of such hope, when Liddell himself falls during a race, yet gets back up on his feet and goes on to win (an authentic historical

*Chariots* won four Oscars, including for Best Picture. David Puttnam also produced another of the movies on the Vatican Film List, *The Mission*.

> LORD CADOGAN: That's a matter for the committee.
> LORD BIRKENHEAD: We are the committee.

detail, as it happens). Puttnam is right to say that the Paris sermon catches viewers unawares. It pries open an emotional recognition that all of us, athletes or not, are running a race, the race of this life, and hope to finish it well. The metaphor suddenly becomes potent and inescapable, cutting deep into the heart.

To describe *Chariots of Fire* as a testimony to the virtue of hope might make it seem intolerably stodgy and moralizing. The brilliance of screenwriter Colin Welland (himself an atheist, by the way) is to show us what hope is like and to make us experience, if only with our imagination, its reality.

*MW*

## DISCUSSION QUESTIONS

- When Liddell and his sister debate the relative urgency of missionary work versus other activities, who is right?

- Was Liddell correct not to run on a Sunday? Would it have mattered? If so, why?

- Of the two protagonists, Abrahams and Liddell, do you sympathize with one more than the other?

# *Dekalog*

## 1988

*Ten modern tales set in Soviet-era Warsaw loosely inspired by the Ten Commandments.*

D*ekalog* has been described as a secular look at the Ten Commandments by an agnostic and skeptic, and among the several curious choices included on the Vatican List, this is one of the most perplexing. It is not a stand-alone movie but a ten-part series of films (each about an hour in length) made for television. It is unusually drab and dreary, even among the other "realist" entries. And for a selection included in the "Values" category of the list, it is often difficult to interpret what morals it means to convey, given that the characters, as a rule, seem more intent on defying God's laws than observing them. Is it meant to show us how difficult it is to live up to Judeo-Christian ideals in the contemporary world? Are its episodes intended as so many exercises in compassion, often for outsiders, creeps, and oddballs? Whatever it is, *Dekalog* is certainly ambiguous and leaves plenty of room for interpretation as it raises open-ended ethical questions without supplying tidy answers.

Made for Polish television a year before the fall of the Berlin Wall, these partially overlapping stories are shot in a documentary-like fashion that takes no pains to romanticize their characters' stark, dispiriting late-Soviet surroundings. The characters are inhabitants of a single Warsaw apartment block, mostly lonely, isolated individuals who, in director Krzysztof Kieslowski's terms, "can't quite find their bearings." Generally, the drama of each episode turns on some kind of ethical dilemma, loosely inspired by the corresponding commandment. But the correspondence is often quite loose; in fact, only in a minority of cases (episodes 5, 8, 10, and to a lesser extent 1) is the connection straightforward. Not coincidentally, perhaps, these are also the only episodes where the main character is not caught up in complications brought about by unchastity, such as how to manage an extra-marital affair or what to do about a child conceived out of wedlock.

How much easier and brighter life would be if folks simply *followed* the commandments, these stories seem to suggest. But "everyone has their reasons," Kieslowski has remarked, including these wan, unhappy people who are acting badly. "You have to understand why they're like that."

Kieslowski, whose film career started with documentaries, argued that the reality in Poland needed to be described before it could be changed.

One way to watch *Dekalog*, then, is as a series of snapshots of human behavior that invite

Kieslowski originally meant to hire a different director for each of the ten episodes, but finally directed all of them himself. However, he did collaborate with a different cinematographer each time, except episodes three and nine, where Piotr Sobociński was director of photography.

sympathy even as they deny us grounds for approval. Another is as convoluted moral test cases, where unmixed good and evil are difficult to discern owing to the characters' previous moral compromises. A third approach, less a lens for watching than a method for reflecting afterward, is to try to reconstruct various facets of the great *positive* fact underlying these violated prohibitions. The commandments say, "You shall not murder," "You shall not steal," "You shall not commit adultery," etc. (Exod. 20:2–17); these stories quietly invite us to consider what would happen if these commandments were *not* broken. What goodness would then emerge— or at least stand a chance of emerging? The answer appears to be: love, joy, and community—all of which, as *Dekalog* shows again and again, are weakened, obscured, or prevented by the soul-isolating, misery-causing, and apathy-inducing choices traditionally referred to as "sins."

Granted, it will take some work to reach this kind of insight from these meditations, which are mostly preoccupied with human beings' frailties and failures. But some viewers might find a sort of solace, even an indirect kind of encouragement, precisely in such portraits of messy human lives, which affirm that no matter how difficult making good choices may prove, there are others out there having a hard time too.

*DPB*

> Living is the joy of being able to help others. Of being there. When you do something for someone, no matter how small, you feel needed. And life seems brighter.
> —AUNT IRENA, EPISODE ONE

### EPISODE ONE

A university professor who only believes in what can be empirically measured gives lectures about programming computers to replicate human personalities. He also does math problems for fun on a personal computer with his young son, and together they work out a formula that determines whether the pond outside their apartment complex is safe for skating. But when the ice breaks—an outcome he continues to insist is "impossible"—this father is forced to reconsider the ultimate source of his confidence.

Do forms of idolatry still exist even among persons who recognize no "gods"?

### EPISODE TWO

A woman knocks at a doctor's apartment and insists she must know whether her husband, a patient in his ward, will live. The doctor says he does not know. She explains that she is three months pregnant with another man's child, and that she wants to keep the baby but will abort it if her husband recovers. The doctor begs her not to kill the child and pronounces her husband's case hopeless. She cancels the abortion. Then her husband recovers and rejoices that he and his wife will be parents.

What connection, if any, do you see between the drama of this episode and the second commandment, "You shall not make wrongful use of the name of the LORD your God"? What would you do in this woman's situation? The doctor's? The husband's?

## EPISODE THREE

A man enters an apartment complex on Christmas Eve dressed as Santa, and his wife imagines their children will remember the night like "the old times," before his affair. He then spends the rest of the evening with "the other woman" on the pretext of looking for her husband who has gone missing. After visiting a hospital, morgue, and a drunk tank, she admits that her husband moved away and remarried years ago. "It's hard being alone on a night like this," she says.

Which of our holidays, if any, are truly "holy days"? Is there a "sacred" reason for setting them apart?

Stanley Kubrick, director of another film on the Vatican List–*2001: A Space Odyssey*–has commended *Dekalog*'s stories for the powerful way they dramatize their ideas rather than simply talk about them. "They do this with such dazzling skill, you never see the ideas coming and don't realize until much later how profoundly they have reached your heart."

*(Content advisory: contains nudity)*

## EPISODE FOUR

A young woman finds an envelope that reads, "To be opened after my death." It contains a letter her mother wrote from her deathbed, which states that the man the young woman lives with is not her father. Things get weird, as they

> Do the innocent truly make the laws?
> —LAWYER, EPISODE FIVE

entertain erotic feelings for each other, but in the end he remains fatherly toward her. Then she admits that she never actually read the letter but made up its contents.

Have you ever acted as a spiritual father or mother to someone who is not your natural child? Or have you been treated in this way by someone else? How is this like and unlike your other relationships?

### EPISODE FIVE

In this episode, which is the *Dekalog*'s most artistically and philosophically accomplished set piece, a lawyer questions the justice of punitive legal statutes while reviewing the details of a brutal murder committed by a disaffected young man.

"Punishment is a form of revenge. Especially when it aims to inflict harm and doesn't prevent crime. But in whose name does the law exact revenge? Is it really in the name of the innocent?" How would you respond to these, the lawyer's questions?

> Everyone wonders if what they do has any meaning. I'm afraid that meaning gets harder and harder to find. . . . I believe it's a decline in our criteria, or worse, our values.
> —LAWYER, EPISODE FIVE

> VISITOR: Interesting building.
> PROFESSOR: Like any other.
> —EPISODE EIGHT

### EPISODE SIX

A young man uses a telescope to spy on a woman through the windows of her apartment. He also concocts elaborate excuses to interact with her in person, like slipping her fake mail and taking a job delivering milk to her door. When she finds out, she gets angry but later toys with him, cynically undermining his belief in love. He despairs, and when she apologizes, he coldly responds, "I don't watch you anymore."

Do you sympathize with one of these characters more than the other? How is each mistaken about the real nature of love?

*(Content advisory: contains partial nudity and erotic content)*

### EPISODE SEVEN

A young woman steals away into the woods with a little girl, apparently her sister. But she is actually the little girl's mother, impregnated as a teenager and compelled to misrepresent the situation by her own parents. She begs the girl to call her "Mommy," but the little girl continues to address her as a sister. Over the phone, as in a ransom call, the young woman laments to her parents, "You robbed me of my baby, of the fact that I'm a mother. Of love. You robbed me of myself, of the two of you, of everything."

Who is the thief here? Or whose theft is worse, in your opinion? Why?

**EPISODE EIGHT**

An elderly ethics professor entertains a scenario involving a Catholic couple during World War II who agree to pretend a Jewish child is theirs to save her from the Nazis, but at the last moment change their minds, citing the commandment to bear no false witness. The professor then clarifies that the real reason they turned her away was to save numerous Resistance fighters from being betrayed to the Gestapo, and that the excuse about refusing to bear false witness was itself, ironically, an act of false witness.

Did the couple do the right thing? What would you have done in the situation: refused to shelter a child from evil or sacrificed the lives of many adults actively combating the same evil?

**EPISODE NINE**

A man is diagnosed with impotence and worries this will spell the end of his marriage. His wife reassures him of her love and commitment, but he begins secretly observing her and soon enough discovers evidence of her infidelity. She repents and proposes they adopt, but he says they need some

> PROFESSOR: Goodness. It exists. I believe it's there in every human being.
> VISITOR: And who's the judge of that?
> PROFESSOR: The one who lives inside each of us.
> —EPISODE EIGHT

time apart and deliberately rides his bicycle off the ledge of a construction site. She visits him at the hospital, laid out in a plaster cast on an operating table, and tells him, "I didn't realize it would hurt you so much."

Why does betrayal hurt? Is it wrong to be possessive of another person?

### EPISODE TEN

A rock star and a businessman examine the extensive stamp collection left behind by their recently deceased father. "What drives people to covet stuff, to possess something at any cost?" one brother asks. But when they discover the collection is worth a sizeable fortune, they obsess over it. One brother even agrees to sell a kidney to procure another exceedingly rare stamp. While he is recovering from the operation, though, thieves break into the apartment and steal the entire collection. The brothers each suspect the other, call in the police, then share a laugh over their combined foolishness.

When does appreciating or admiring something cross over into coveting?

# *Dersu Uzala*

## 1975

*A simple story about the wisdom of a hunter living in admirable harmony with nature and his fellow man.*

Enjoyable at one level simply as an adventure story of man versus nature, this cinematic adaptation of the travel journals of Russian explorer Vladimir Arsenyev by Japanese director Akira Kurosawa takes on an added layer of richness when viewed in the context of the historical circumstances surrounding its release. After the destruction of much of its infrastructure during the Second World War, Japanese society was rebuilt and modernized at an astonishing pace. It became, in only a few years, one of the twentieth century's most industrially advanced and urbanized societies. Glass,

> Me can't live in town. . . . Me go back to mountains.
> —DERSU UZALA

concrete, steel, traffic jams, automated machines, and the spasms of international financial markets—these were, for the first time, the backdrop of everyday life. As a side effect, many persons—including numerous artists and storytellers—felt a keen sense of lost contact with nature and a longing for a simpler, more organically grounded way of being in the world. And into this situation stepped *Dersu Uzala.*

It opens in a foggy wood over Korfovskaya, a region of southeast Russia near the Chinese border, with the sounds of birds chirping and the vigorous hammering of nails. The camera tilts down to show a ragged strip of cleared away forest, which turns out to be a construction site where a visitor asks after the grave of a friend he buried there under a tall cedar and fir. "You remember those trees?" he asks a passerby. "I guess we cut them down to build the village," the man responds, and points toward some piles of split wood and sawdust, presumably piled over the top of the grave.

The film flashes back to the same site almost a decade earlier, where uninterrupted virgin forest stretches to the horizon. Some soldiers march and sing, while in a voiceover this same visitor—Vladimir Arsenyev, the captain of the company—describes their mission to make a topographical survey of the region. He gives voice to humanity's complex relationship to the wilderness: "Sometimes the mountains

> "People have forgotten that man is part of nature. They injuriously exploit it. We must cry about it at every corner. As for me, I'm speaking out with my films."
> —Akira Kurosawa

Probably most famous for *Seven Samurai* and *Yojimbo*, Kurosawa shot *Dersu Uzala*, his twenty-seventh and only non-Japanese language film, with state sponsorship by Mosfilm and a Russian crew in the same region the film depicts.

and the forest look pleasant, welcoming. Sometimes though, they can be silent and forbidding. This wasn't just a personal feeling; every man in the survey group felt the same way." They set up camp under the declaration "He whom God helps nobody can harm," and as Arsenyev journals that the woods remind him of a painting of the witches' sabbath, a branch snaps beyond the ring of campfire light. The entire company jumps up, rifles to the ready, but a voice calls out, "Shoot not! Me a man!"—and then from the darkness emerges the square-shaped, bow-legged, mustachioed local woodsman who lends this film its name.

Dersu joins them at the fire, and Arsenyev asks, "What are you? Chinese? Korean?" His people are called "Gold," he replies, and goes on to describe how he hunts all the time, has no permanent home, and sleeps in a little hut in the mountains. It is good enough for him, he shrugs. The fire crackles, and Dersu reprimands it like it is a person, ordering it to stop chattering at them. A soldier exchanges a surprised look with Arsenyev—is this woodsman not quite all there, perhaps from spending too much time alone? Or is he a St. Francis sort of figure, living in unusually close communion with nature?

Perhaps suspecting the latter, Arsenyev asks this unusual man to be their guide, and "the next day, without saying a word, Dersu took his place at the head of the group." He points out a trail of boot prints left a few days before by Chinese soldiers, and the infantrymen he now leads ask how he knows. "You all like little children. Got eyes but don't see. When you live in wilds, real soon you be dead."

> He had a deep knowledge born of a lifetime
> spent in the wild.
> —CAPTAIN VLADIMIR ARSENYEV

Dersu goes on to demonstrate his prowess as a marksman and natural conservator in a charming episode of target practice. When the soldiers invite him to compete with them shooting at a bottle hung from a branch, Dersu instead shoots the string and pockets the unbroken glass, which, for him, amounts to a precious limited resource. He also displays an extraordinary sense of humanity when, coming across an empty shack, he asks Arsenyev for salt, rice, and matches to leave behind there, just in case a lost man should stumble upon it and by these meager provisions be kept alive. "I couldn't help admiring him," Arsenyev reflects. "He was so wise. He had a deep knowledge born of a lifetime spent in the wild. He was good hearted, generous minded. He could think of a man he'd never met, and that he probably would never meet." They journey on, and Dersu proves himself an invaluable guide time and again. "I'd have died many times if it hadn't been for him," the captain journals. "He doesn't think it something to talk about. There are lots of others who would brag about such things."

As they near the end of their mission, Arsenyev invites Dersu to accompany him back to town, but Dersu declines and explains the reason: he can't hunt there. Arsenyev offers him money, but Dersu says he has no need for it, so Arsenyev orders his men to give him all their remaining ammunition. When they part ways, one of the infantrymen comments, "He's a good man, isn't he? I never met anyone like him before."

By happy chance, Arsenyev and Dersu meet again on a subsequent expedition, and Dersu recounts how he made a lot of money since they last met trapping sable, only to have

> I'd have died many times if it hadn't been for him. . . .
> He doesn't think it something to talk about. There are
> lots of others who would brag about such things.
> —CAPTAIN VLADIMIR ARSENYEV

it all swindled by a rich merchant. "Why he that way? Me not understand." They encounter further evidence of "civilized humanity" in a string of neglected traps full of dead animals, and a similar lot of men who were robbed and left tied up in a stream to be eaten alive by mosquitos. When Dersu's eyesight begins to fail, he reluctantly accepts Arsenyev's invitation to move into his home in Khabarovsk, and there the previously fur-clad woodsman sits on the floor for hours on end, dressed in a cardigan and slacks, simply staring into the flames of the furnace. "Town life is no good for him," Arsenyev's wife observes, and eventually the captain concurs, agreeing to send Dersu back into the mountains equipped with a rifle of the latest model.

Sometime thereafter Arsenyev receives a telegram: "Your visiting card found on the body of a dead Gold. Please come and identify the corpse." The official at the scene registers Dersu's name and occupation, but finds it strange that a hunter would be found with no rifle. Arsenyev replies that he should have had the weapon he himself gave him. "Oh, that explains everything," the official realizes. "The killer wanted his rifle and killed him for

> If *Dersu Uzala* expresses nostalgia for a simpler, more natural way of life, similar sentiments might be detected in the films of another Japanese director, Hayao Miyazaki—for instance, the animated features *Princess Mononoke* and *Nausicaa of the Valley of the Wind*.

it." It is a bitter discovery for Arsenyev, finding he is implicated indirectly in the old man's death, but in the wider context of the film the moment resounds as an indictment of a whole civilization whose members value material gain more than the life of such a man. As Arsenyev stands watching the civil employees who fill Dersu's grave, questions arise concerning the "advances" of modern society, whether the "civilized world" is not somehow more wild and less hospitable to the soul of man than Dersu's woods, and, ultimately, what it profits any of us to leave all that behind for a world of soldiers, cities, and thieves.

*DPB*

## DISCUSSION QUESTIONS

- Does the overall perspective of *Dersu Uzala* suggest that there is nothing good that comes from modern society or that civilization is intrinsically corrupting? Or does it offer a more complex assessment? Do you agree with its diagnosis?

- From a Christian point of view, is the sense of lost contact with the natural world a uniquely modern problem? Would it be solved if we all chose to leave the cities and live closer to the wilds?

- According to Genesis 1:27–28, "God created humankind in his image" and ordered us to "be fruitful and multiply, and fill the earth and subdue it." Does this "cultural commission," as it is sometimes called, involve "civilizing" the natural world? Are we ourselves part of the nature we are commissioned to master, and if so, what does that mastery look like?

# *Gandhi*

## 1982

*A stirring portrayal of the "great soul" at the center of the movement for India's political independence.*

Shot on a scale that has scarce been replicated in cinema, this film opens with a recreation of the funeral of the man whose life it depicts, a scene attended by over four hundred thousand extras—probably the largest crowd ever assembled for a motion picture. Such magnificence says a lot about the impact of the man, who, despite the pomp and ceremony of this monumental commemoration, lived, among other things, with an extraordinary simplicity. The comments of a radio reporter on the scene offer a précis of a life that may not have been one of a confessing Christian in any conventional

In this cause, I too am prepared to die. But, my friends, there is no cause for which I am willing to kill.
—GANDHI

sense, yet comes just about as close to anything on the screen to communicating the real stature and significance of a saint:

> The object of this massive tribute died as he had always lived, a private man without wealth, without property, without official title or office. Mahatma Gandhi was not the commander of armies nor a ruler of vast lands. He could not boast any scientific achievement or artistic gift. Yet men, governments, dignitaries from all over the world have joined hands today to pay homage to this little brown man in the loincloth who led his country to freedom. In the words of General George C. Marshall, the American Secretary of State, "Mahatma Gandhi has become the spokesman for the conscience of all mankind. He was a man who made humility and simple truth more powerful than empires." And Albert Einstein added, "Generations to come will scarce believe that such a one as this ever in flesh and blood walked upon this earth."

The film cuts to South Africa 1892, where a dapper Edwardian gentleman, Mohandas Karamchand Gandhi, sits reading a book in a train carriage. Played by Ben Kingsley (born Krishna Pandit Bhanji to an Indian father and English mother), Gandhi attempts to engage the porter in civilized discussion on the subject of hell, only to be told "there are no colored lawyers in South Africa" and to find himself thrown off the train. He resolves to resist racial injustice in that country and organizes an act of civil disobedience that is met by police brutality. Newspapers across the British Empire hail it as the most

This film was a passion project for many of those involved: from conception to release it took director Richard Attenborough twenty years to produce the film, and he drew no income from the project. Similarly, when Martin Sheen saw first-hand the condition of the poor in Kolkata, he donated his entire salary to look after them.

significant colonial event since the Declaration of Independence.

When he is released from prison, Gandhi meets a Christian minister named Charley Andrews (played by Ian Charleson, who stars as Eric Liddell in *Chariots of Fire*), and Vince Walker (played by Martin Sheen), an American reporter from the *New York Times*. They talk about Gandhi's principles-based agricultural initiative, the *ashram*, where Muslims, Hindus, and "even Christians" live side by side and share all duties equally. When Walker questions Gandhi's resolve to face down the combined might of the South African government and larger British Empire, Gandhi's response is simple. "There are unjust laws, as there are unjust men," he maintains, but "if you are a minority of one, the truth is the truth."

As momentum builds, he addresses growing crowds and begins to develop the principles of nonviolent noncooperation he will espouse across his career. With explicit admiration for Jesus Christ and his doctrine of "turning the other cheek," Gandhi exhorts an angry assembly, saying, "We will not strike a blow, but we will receive them. . . . You must make the injustice visible and be prepared to die like a soldier to do so." Asked why he does not believe in fighting, he counters, "Where there's injustice, I always believed in fighting. The question is, do you fight to change things or do you fight to punish? . . . I want to change their minds, not kill them for weaknesses we all possess."

> The only devils in the world are those running round
> in our own hearts, and that is where all our battles
> ought to be fought.
> —GANDHI

After the successful repeal of racially discriminatory laws in South Africa, Gandhi returns to India dressed in an Indian fashion and hailed as a national hero. He meets with leaders from various factions seeking national independence, among them an aged professor who promises to find funding for Gandhi's mission in the country. "When I saw you in that tunic, I knew I could die in peace," he utters in a kind of *nunc dimittis.* "Make India proud of herself."

As the reach of his public activity extends from national to international news, people start calling him *Mahatma,* Sanskrit for "great soul." He sets off on an epic journey to find the true India and assimilates native ways of eating and farming. (For weeks leading up to filming, to prepare for the role, Kingsley ate only vegetarian food, drank goat's milk, and slept on the floor.) After meeting with villagers all but starving as a result of British land-holding policies, he strips the last vestiges of the genteel London-trained lawyer and assumes the vesture of Gandhi as we know him. "If I want to be one with them," he says, now shirtless in a loin cloth, "I have to live like them."

He calls for prayer and fasting (which,

The salt march sequence was filmed in a coastal region of India whose population was largely Catholic. A member of the production team asked the local Catholic priest to help gather five thousand extras, and he agreed on condition that, instead of paying these people, the production would create two new classrooms for the local school.

incidentally, also amount to national strikes), boycotts, and a march of over two hundred miles to make salt at the Indian Ocean in defiance of the British government's monopoly on its sale and production. The British respond by making tens of thousands of arrests, including most of the members of Congress and

> *Gandhi* won eight Academy Awards in 1982, more than any other British film up to that point, including Best Picture, Best Director, Best Actor, Best Screenplay, and Best Original Score.

their families. Later, sitting down at a table with representatives of His Majesty's government headed by Viceroy Lord Irwin (played by John Gielgud), Gandhi states quite simply that it is time for them to leave. The representatives of the Crown can hardly believe it: surely he does not expect them simply to walk out? He does. "In the end, you will walk out because one hundred thousand Englishmen simply cannot control three hundred fifty million Indians if those Indians refuse to cooperate. And that is what we intend to achieve. Peaceful, nonviolent, noncooperation till you yourselves see the wisdom of leaving. Your Excellency."

There is much more that could be recounted from such a sweeping, stirring, beautiful film. But by way of conclusion, it is worth simply pausing to observe how *good* human beings can be. Made in the image of God, an image that has not been expunged even amidst the devastation of sin, Gandhi demonstrates the genuine greatness that all men and women are still capable of in an imperfect world. Portraying the potential power of one life wholly dedicated to a common cause, this film offers an astonishing witness to how a self-described soldier of peace, armed with only simplicity and honesty, overcame history's largest empire. It might be unbelievable if it had not actually happened.

> An eye for an eye only ends up
> making the whole world blind.
> —GANDHI

What might this tell us about the persons we can become and the work we can do in this world? What does it suggest about the ultimate outcome we might expect to the conflicts and violence of history? A paraphrased answer would not say it better than the man this movie grants us the privilege to meet:

> When I despair, I remember that all through history the way of truth and love has always won. There have been tyrants and murderers, and, for a time, they can seem invincible. But in the end they always fall. . . . Whenever you are in doubt that this is God's way, the way the world is meant to be, think of that. And then try to do it his way.

*DPB*

## DISCUSSION QUESTIONS

- Under the shadow of Nazi takeover of Europe, the *Time Magazine* reporter Margaret Bourke-White (played by Candice Bergen) visits Gandhi in prison and asks if he really believes nonviolence would stop someone like Hitler. He responds, "Not without defeats." Are love and peace more powerful than evil and violence? Could a Gandhi stop a Hitler?

- In the context of arguing that Hindus and Muslims are the right and left eyes of India, Gandhi as portrayed in this film declares, "I am a Muslim. And a Hindu. And a Christian. And a Jew. And so are all of you." What does he mean? Is there any sense of truth in this?

- "Those also can attain to salvation who through no fault of their own do not know the Gospel of Christ or His Church, yet sincerely seek God and moved by grace strive by their deeds to do His will as it is known to them through the dictates of conscience" (*Lumen Gentium* 16). Is it possible to be good, even saintly, without being a Christian?

# *Intolerance*

## 1916

*A sprawling superspectacle that attempts to show, in its own words, "how hatred and intolerance, through all the ages, have battled against love and charity."*

Astonishing in scale and at times breathtaking in ambition, this experimental epic of the silent era is most remarkable for the sheer eye-popping immensity of what it sets out to do. Intercutting four loosely relatedly stories from different historical epochs, which together are meant to encompass the entire sweep of human experience, it dramatizes "love's struggle throughout the ages," from the earliest written records to the "today" of the film's early twentieth-century context. With a special ire directed

> Today as yesterday . . . the same human passions,
> the same joys and sorrows.
> —INTERTITLE

against puritanical scruples and holier-than-thou moralism of all kinds, *Intolerance* might be faulted for overshooting its mark and indulging in a less-than-explicit yet nonetheless disorderly sensuality. But even so, it does this on a cinematic scale that is all but unimaginable today, and for this alone it demands admiration on grounds of simple bravado.

It starts out with a modern story of sanctimonious upper class social reformers, "the vestal virgins of uplift," who endeavor "to make people good" by placing bans on dancing and drinking in public houses. The tone is incisive yet comical: after several unflattering closeups of these well-dressed but less-than-stunning middle-aged marms, an intertitle reads, "When women cease to attract men they often turn to Reform as a second choice." The story then jumps to first-century Palestine, where the Pharisees thank God that they are better than the tradesmen in the marketplace, and peer disapprovingly through a window on the festivities at the Wedding of Cana, insisting, "There is too much revelry and pleasure-seeking among the people." In a third story line set in early Reformation-era Paris, Catholic royals and Huguenot courtiers cast sideways glances at each other, whispering, "What wonderful persons, if only they thought as we do." And in the final and most lavish of the narrative threads, the Babylonian story, the advancers of

The palace of Belshazzar in this film was the largest set ever constructed for a movie, and until its removal in 2021, a full-scale replica appeared on the site of the Dolby Theatre, home of the annual Academy Awards.

At a cost of one hundred thousand dollars, Griffith's previous film, *The Birth of a Nation*, was the longest and most expensive American film to date. *Intolerance* cost several times as much, and, in an era when most movies ran for a mere ten to twenty minutes and used just one or two reels of film, its first cut was over eight hours in length with raw footage occupying more than four hundred reels.

intolerance are once again the keepers of the era's established religion, this time the priests of Bel, who betray the king and his ideal representation of a sensually uninhibited pre-Christian civilization.

In contrast to all of this stands the carpenter of Nazareth, introduced in the film as "the greatest enemy of intolerance." He turns water into wine and refuses to condemn the woman caught in adultery, as intertitles quote Sacred Scripture: "To everything there is a season . . . a time to mourn and a time to dance. . . . He hath made everything beautiful in its time" (Eccles. 3:1–11). They also supply ideologically pointed historical context: "Wine was deemed a fit offering to God; the drinking of it a part of the Jewish religion." This is all true, of course, but the film's juxtaposition between love and intolerance, as if these were completely incompatible, is probably too simplistic. How tolerant would the biblical God of love have been toward the scantily clad goings on in Belshazzar's harem, for instance?

But on a more sanguine note, *Intolerance*'s repeated potshots at teetotalers and every kind of moral and religious hypocrisy have much to recommend them. Like the sort of cold-blooded philanthropy devoid of supernatural charity that G.K. Chesterton lampoons in *The Flying Inn*, the misguided do-gooders in this film truly fail when, instead of trusting or training their fellow citizens to discipline their appetites, they try to abolish their pleasures. This not only end ups treating ordinary men and women more like unruly apes than creatures capable of reason, virtue, and the aids of religion. It also misses the gargantuan truth behind the maxim *abusus non tollit usum*, which is, if there is a thing some people abuse, it is because they have discovered something worth abusing—namely, something fundamentally *good*. From this perspective, it is right and just that in *Intolerance*, God himself is depicted as the cheery ally of the common enjoyments of the common man.

The story lines develop, jump back and forth one to the others, and eventually race toward the film's finale: a rapid montage of accelerated crosscutting between the St. Bartholomew's Day Massacre, the sack of ancient Babylon, a modern man on his way to public execution for a murder he didn't commit, and the condemnation and Crucifixion of our Lord. The sequence is visually gripping, even thrilling, whether or not the allegedly parallel events ultimately succeed at blending into a transtemporal portrait of "intolerance, burning, and slaying." Then it ends with a bang when, with only two and a half minutes to go, it suddenly introduces a fifth story line. A fleeting image of industrialized warfare familiar from the Great War (which was still being waged at the time of this film's release) gets interrupted by angelic armies who, instead of hurling bombs onto cities, drop flowers from celestial dirigibles. Cannons grow over with vines, fields of flowers spring up in place of prisons, and laughing children exchange kisses in stark contrast to the adults who, only

> Now for a time the little love god works his small but mighty way, in other days and the same as now.
> —INTERTITLE

moments before, had been exchanging bayonet thrusts and artillery shells.

This eschatological imagery culminates with a cruciform beam of light that appears over the halted battle (evocative of the Second Coming of Christ), then gives way to the film's final visual: a glimpse, for the first time, inside "the cradle endlessly rocking." In a surprising reversal, this recurring mythic image is shown to contain the same flowers dropped by the angels as signs of reconciliation and peace. The symbol of fatalistic resignation transfigures into a sign of perennially blossoming hope. The film then concludes with an echo of the biblical prophecy of beating swords into plowshares (Isa. 2:4), anticipating a time "when cannon and prison bars wrought in the fires of intolerance shall cease—And perfect love shall bring peace forevermore."

Monumental, grandiose, and vaultingly ambitious, *Intolerance* continues to impress as much by the power of its anti-war message as by the consistent sense, conveyed across its more than three-hour running time, that its images and energy are almost ready to burst from the screen—but it is certainly not above reproach. Whereas one early reviewer called it "the most stupendous thing that has ever been presented," many others have denounced it as incoherent. Sergei Eisenstein called it a magnificent failure, and it certainly proved a commercial disaster from which it took director

When Griffith innovated with *Intolerance*, experimenting with combinations of long shot, mid shot, and close shot that have become standards in cinematic representation today, studio producers at the time seriously protested, fearing audiences would think the film amateurish and that the camera had cut off the actors' legs by mistake.

D.W. Griffith years to recover. Allegedly made without a script, it is in many ways a hodgepodge. Much of what we see on screen does not seem to be included for the sake of advancing the story or even as a contribution to the film's main themes: it is simply there for the spectacle—but what a spectacle!

In the end, *Intolerance* might be best enjoyed like many other silent features: less as a piece of coherent narrative or philosophy, and more like a piece of music that makes an impression but defies attempts to get one's head fully around it. It might be enough just to get our heads in, and marvel.

*DPB*

(*Content advisory: contains some nudity*)

### DISCUSSION QUESTIONS

- The Crucifixion of Christ operates as an explicit subtext and consistent touchpoint throughout *Intolerance*, as if to say, "What men once did to Man they have done in all ages, before, during, and after the time of Christ." How similar are human beings across time and different cultures? Has humanity changed since the Crucifixion?

- Is intolerance the opposite of love? Are there things love should not (or cannot) tolerate?

- The infighting of Christians in the French Story suggests that a tendency toward other-fearing, persecutory self-righteousness can be found among human beings in every age, under the banner of any creed. Do you agree? Given that the slaughter of the St. Bartholomew's Day Massacre is obviously *not* the best way to reconcile Christians of different professions, what are some better, more constructive ways to address the issues that divide us?

# It's a Wonderful Life

## 1946

*A Christmas classic in which George Bailey of Bedford Falls,
New York, is shown by an angel what the world would be like if
he had never been born.*

Directed by Frank Capra and starring James Stewart and
Donna Reed, *It's a Wonderful Life* is a Christmas movie
about individual human dignity, demonstrating that every
life matters and that one person's sacrifices can make a world
of difference. It is also a story about the divine gift of life in
community and the transforming power of human solidarity.
*It's a Wonderful Life* speaks to us about putting the common
good above individual greed, reminding us of an America of
the not-so-distant past where everything a person needed was

> All you can take with you is that which
> you've given away.
> —PA BAILEY

right on his doorstep. And it all begins with a cacophony of voices praying for a man named George Bailey.

*It's a Wonderful Life* is also a movie about the ministry of angels, albeit coming from a fanciful and somewhat unorthodox perspective. The particular angel at the heart of the story is the loveable loser Clarence Odbody, a human who has died but has not yet achieved the necessary merit to receive his angelic wings. To prove his mettle, Clarence is sent at Christmastime as an answer to the petitions of the people of Bedford Falls on behalf of Mr. George Bailey—husband, father, and local businessman, whose associate and kinsman Uncle Billy has made an absent-minded banking blunder. George believes he is financially ruined, and in a panic, he imagines he may be more valuable to his family dead than alive. George's last option in these direst of circumstances is to give God a try, adding his voice to the chorus of his loved ones' prayers. "I'm not a praying man," he confesses. He then pleads, "Show me the way." Clarence arrives in time to put himself in danger, forcing George to jump into freezing water for altruistic purposes instead of despair—to save another instead of destroying himself. We then see the pivotal moments of George's life, and Clarence reveals an alternate reality in which George has never lived at all. In a journey that evokes Dickens' *A Christmas Carol*, Clarence gives George countless examples of his special purpose in the world and poses the possibility of countless tragedies that would have resulted from his absence. Eventually, Clarence asks plainly, "Strange, isn't it? Each man's life touches so many other lives. When he isn't around he leaves an awful hole, doesn't he?"

*It's a Wonderful Life* is a powerful tale about the inherent dignity of the individual. In biblical terms, we may say that the film shows us how the Body of Christ, like the body politic, has no spare parts. The world needs George, but it needs everyone else too. For example, George saved his brother Harry's life when they were boys. If Harry had died, a large group of soldiers at war would have died too, because Harry would not have been present years after his boyhood accident to save them. The chain goes on as far as one can imagine. In perhaps the most emotionally raw scene in the film, young George discovers that his boss, the druggist Mr. Gower, has accidentally put poison in a batch of capsules destined for the home of a family sick with diphtheria. Gower is drunk and near the brink of despair grieving the loss of his son. He slaps George violently when he discovers George has not delivered the pills. In tears, George shows Mr. Gower what he has done, swearing never to tell a soul while also comforting Mr. Gower in his misery. In this moment, we see how a single act of courage and compassion has the potential for exponential goodness. Mr. Gower gets through his difficult time, and he is afforded the opportunity to help others for years to come, including George.

As we watch George's young life unfold, we may identify with his longing to break free from the bonds of small-town life and make a difference "out there." George wants to build new things, not tend to the old ones. And yet, George ultimately finds blessedness in the ache he feels for staying put and improving life for people right where he is. He experiences transformation himself when he decides to marry a beautiful local girl named Mary, with whom he soon renovates an old home, starts a family, and begins to give selflessly to the

> James Stewart was overcome with real emotion and began to cry real tears during the scene where he prays in Martini's bar.

> No man is a failure who has friends.
> —CLARENCE ODBODY

community he had once planned to escape. George and Mary even spend their honeymoon funds to save the old Bailey Building and Loan from a run on the bank.

Here the other great theme of *It's a Wonderful Life* emerges: solidarity, which the *Catechism of the Catholic Church* describes as being "articulated in terms of 'friendship' or 'social charity.'" Solidarity has to do with the spreading of both temporal and spiritual goods in accord with the equality of all people as creatures of God. Capra was well-known for including plots and characters that brought issues of social responsibility to his audience's attention, and *It's a Wonderful Life* provides perhaps the best opportunity of any of Capra's films for a strong ethical message. There are no self-made men, and no one succeeds alone.

George's plight quickly draws us into the interconnected network that has defined existence for humans throughout most of history but that has become rarer in recent decades as people have become more mobile. Sadly, Bedford Falls represents one of the last outposts of localism before the reach of the twentieth-century global economy expanded everywhere, and in the poetic logic of this film, it is the big shot who has left town, Sam Wainwright, with his fancy cars, mistresses, and travel, who becomes the pitiful one—not George. Mr. Potter, played by Lionel Barrymore, represents the heartless reality of valuing the bottom line over the common good. The "Pottersville" of a world without George represents a society without leaders who love their neighbors as themselves. In contrast, we find George and Mary celebrating the purchase of a new house with an immigrant family who could never have dreamed of home ownership without "Bailey Park" and the humane policies of George's bank.

When George returns to real life after experiencing the bleak alternate world Clarence shows him, George wants to remain alive, no matter what. "Isn't it wonderful?" he exclaims. "I'm going to jail!" All his old headaches, including the loose knob on the staircase that always came off in his hand, are suddenly sources of grace. Everything gladdens his heart and makes him grateful to be alive. George and Mary embrace in a gesture of both passion and appreciation, and George discovers a houseful of people, including the men who sought to arrest him, standing in his home singing Christmas carols and emptying their pockets to pay off his debt.

Whether or not Bedford Falls eventually succumbs to the deracination and atomization of today's world, we are given pause to consider that life could be different, even now. The world of *It's a Wonderful Life* is both enchanted and gritty. It is a place where angels come to visit and prayers are answered. It is a place of great need, but it also contains a community of miraculous provision. It is a place where one man's selfless life—however reluctantly chosen—can overcome the darkness of greed, and where, despite all the shams and drudgery of the world, a chain reaction of kindness may start. Bedford Falls is a place of hope, and George Bailey is its ambassador.

Although Bedford Falls looks like a real northeastern American town, it was actually an enormous set constructed at RKO's Encino Ranch in California. The town's Main Street was the equivalent size of three real city blocks, complete with stores and businesses.

*It's a Wonderful Life* ends with the ringing of a bell on a Christmas tree and a cute but theologically incorrect

> In 2006, the American Film Institute ranked *It's a Wonderful Life* the "Most Inspirational" film of all time.

explanation from little Zuzu, the youngest Bailey child: "Teacher says, every time a bell rings, an angel gets its wings." Christians believe that angels are angels, and humans are humans. Forever. But who is going to make a fuss while experiencing such a beautiful and captivating story? Indeed, amusing and affecting portrayals of the ministry of angels have long been a hallmark of cinema, and we find this welcome theological creativity at its apex here. And *It's a Wonderful Life* even redeems itself theologically by ending in a ruckus of perfect angelology, with a roomful of neighbors belting out one of the great hymns of the Nativity: Charles Wesley's "Hark, the Herald Angels Sing."

As the credits roll, all of Bedford Falls is grateful for George Bailey, for their life together in community, and for the possibility of redemption for everyone. With each Christmas viewing of this classic, we give thanks for the hope offered to us too.

*AP*

## DISCUSSION QUESTIONS

- Can you imagine a few things that would be worse about the world if you had never existed?

- Do you make known your needs with people in your community so that they can show you generosity, or do you hide your problems from them out of fear or pride? Do you share generously with those who express their need, or do you hold back from them out of self-concern or self-indulgence?

- What do you think of the world of Bedford Falls? What have we lost by having a more transient society now in the West?

# *On the Waterfront*

## 1954

*A dock worker and reluctant hoodlum in mid-twentieth-
century New York City fights against the undertow of
the local underworld.*

A film that is very much of its era but has stood the test
of time, *On the Waterfront* tells the story of the moral
awakening of Terry Malloy, a reluctant gangster who starts out
the film inadvertently helping a pair of thugs murder another
young man in the neighborhood. The deceased turns out
to have been one of the few laborers brave enough to speak
out against the corrupt practices of the local mob-run labor
union, and when Terry realizes what he's done, he retires to the
rooftops and tends to the dead man's coop of racing pigeons.

> Did you ever hear of a saint hiding in a church?
> —EDIE, ON THE NEED FOR SOCIAL ACTION

Set against a backdrop of bottom-scraping urban poverty, this simple act of kindness contrasts with the blunt violence of Terry's criminal connections, and together these set the tone and the stakes for the young man's emerging crisis.

Played with tough-knuckled tenderness by Marlon Brando—one of the era's iconic leads who went on to take the titular role in *The Godfather*—Terry turns out to be an ex-boxer who intentionally blew his title shot when pressured by mobster friends to fix the fight. In this respect, Terry is both complicit with and the victim of a wider culture inimical to upright living. His complex position becomes apparent in the daily "shape-up" at the dockyards where laborers crowd together for a chance at a day's wage. Terry receives preferential treatment but is conflicted about it, and he laments his predicament in one of classic cinema's most celebrated lines: "I coulda been a contender." On the surface this is a reference to Terry's squandered potential in sport, but it also suggests a sense of having forfeited the opportunity to live a good, meaningful life. In this regard, Terry stands in for all those persons who feel so enmeshed in inherited patterns of evil that they can only grieve, no longer even imagining how they might escape.

*On the Waterfront* garnered twelve Academy Award nominations and won eight, including Best Picture, Best Screenplay, Best Actor, Best Supporting Actress, and Best Director.

Speaking directly into this situation, *On the Waterfront* also includes one of film's strongest, most impressive priests. After witnessing his parishioners' reticence and resignation in the face of

The film is reported to have attracted the attention of many real-life mobsters: an observer at the time noted that if somebody tied a rope around the first two hundred people in the ticket line at the New York premiere and then dragged all of them off to prison, organized crime in the city would virtually cease to exist.

organized crime, Father Barry resolves to stand beside anyone courageous enough to stand up and speak out. A solitary dock worker responds to the call, and when he gets killed in a workplace "accident," Father Barry reacts with one of cinema's greatest sermons on social action.

"Some people think the Crucifixion only took place on Calvary," he preaches to a mixed audience of mobsters and taciturn day laborers from the belly of a whiskey freighter. "They better wise up." Every time the mob exploits, abuses, or murders a worker, he proclaims, that's a crucifixion. And every time somebody keeps quiet about it, that's like the Roman soldiers who stood by and watched it happen.

Christ is down here on the waterfront, Father Barry continues. He sees honest folks getting passed over, and crooked folks caring more about an easy dollar than about their fellow man. Yet—and here Father Barry directly quotes Jesus Christ in the Gospels—"if you did it to the least of mine, you did it to me" (Matt. 25:40). Speak the truth, stand together, and trust God, he concludes, because this is the only way that you are going to improve your situation.

Like the words of many an Old Testament prophet or even Christ himself, Father Barry's preaching is not noticeably very effective straight away: in the moment, the only responses he elicits are the derision of the thugs and the averted eyes of their victims. But his words do throw a gauntlet at the feet of the criminal element and indicate the direction heroic

> Some people think the Crucifixion only took place
> on Calvary. They better wise up.
> —FATHER BARRY

sanctity must take under the circumstances. This is compelling cinema, but it takes on an even weightier significance from the fact that Father Barry is based upon a real priest.

In the years immediately preceding *On the Waterfront*, the rampant corruption of the New York dockyards had been brought to the forefront of public consciousness through a series of sensational news articles. But when *Waterfront's* scriptwriter, Budd Schulberg, began his own research into the matter, he found (much like in the film) very few longshoremen willing to talk. Then he met Father John Corridan.

A Jesuit known locally as "the waterfront priest," Father Corridan ran a school that taught the wharf workers basic principles of economics and strategies for organizing a trade union. His instruction in that context was not explicitly theological but offered practical guidance based upon fundamental Christian convictions about the dignity of man—rather than, for instance, principles borrowed from dog-eat-dog capitalism or communist ideology. The shipyard sermon in the film draws much of its content from Father Corridan's actual preaching on the docks.

If Father Barry shares in Christ's prophetic ministry by proclaiming the Good News at the level of principle, Terry is a kingly figure whose task is to translate this into practical action. Prepared for a violent confrontation by his background in boxing, Terry's toe-to-toe with the mob boss and his goons is an opportunity

Several of the film's actors, including many of the mobsters, were former professional heavyweight boxers in real life.

> Isn't everybody a part of everybody else?
> —EDIE

for poetic justice—dusting off his buried talents against the very persons who convinced him to bury them—but also for something like redemption. This time around, Terry does not fight for individual glory but takes a beating on behalf of his community. He turns his back on the moral compromises of his youth and faces the painful consequences, but his suffering also accomplishes good that ripples far beyond his individual life. It does not overstate the case to say that, in his own little corner of things, Terry's suffering changes the world.

Like many other great works of art, *On the Waterfront* reflects both its time and a humanity that transcends it. It is a piece of fiction based upon particular historical events, yet it is also a timeless story about a social outsider who struggles to carve out a place for good in a morally perilous world. Caught between the enticements of this-worldly compromise and a conscience he cannot silence, Terry's plight offers a parable of the universal human struggle in a place where "we have no lasting city" (Heb. 13:14). Like him, we almost inevitably discover ourselves complicit in patterns of evil. Like him, we must sacrifice to help put things right. But also like him, we may always feel a little bit like this world is not our home. Yet this need not stop us from fighting the odds to make it a little more like one.

*DPB*

## DISCUSSION QUESTIONS

- Do you know of any Father Barry figures? How do they challenge the status quo?

- If Terry were a Christian, would his struggle look any different?

- Is there some area in your life in which you are going with the flow rather than taking a needed stand?

# *Rome, Open City*

## 1945

*An epoch-making portrayal of a short-lived historical moment
when Italian Catholics and communists banded together
against Nazi occupation of the Eternal City.*

The first major film produced in Italy after the Second
World War, *Rome, Open City* is consistently listed
alongside *Bicycle Thieves* as one of the most influential films
in modern cinema. A deliberate departure from the kind of
film that invites audiences to escape into a more exotic or
glamorous world, it confronts viewers with a hard look at
some of the seedier, less attractive sides of its contemporary
historical moment. Shot and released in early 1945 only
months after the Nazi occupation of Rome, its documentary-

> I believe that anyone fighting for justice and liberty walks in the way of the Lord, and the ways of the Lord are infinite.
>
> —DON PIETRO

flavored dramatization of harsh living conditions still prevalent at the time made it one of the seminal films in the rise of Italian neorealism—an *avant-garde* cinematic movement that emphasized the lives of ordinary, often impoverished persons in a style typically characterized by location shooting, natural light, nonprofessional actors, and extended shots that give the impression of real life captured whole cloth. In dramatic terms it might be a less than wholly riveting experience for some viewers, but a lasting interest might be found in its portrait of a heroism conceived in terms of humanity's natural nobility, the universal imperative to neighborly love, and a brotherhood of all men of good will united in opposition to egregious evil and in anticipation of a common hope.

It is difficult to recapture the feeling of what must have been this film's startling novelty at its release in 1945, but a few comparisons might help. Set side by side with other films on the Vatican List, such as the grand spectacle of *Intolerance* or the technicolored fantasy of *The Wizard of Oz*, what is immediately striking about *Rome, Open City* is the way it plunges audiences directly into the everyday world of regular folks just barely scraping by. The film's leading lady, for instance, is the pregnant, outwardly plain Pina (played by Anna Magnani), the sort of person in whom viewers might recognize the likeness of a neighbor or someone encountered on the street. In an age when the typical American import was shot at a studio with a headlining diva like Rita Hayworth or Ingrid Bergman, the appearance of real city streets and unfamiliar, relatively unglamorous faces would have hit the silver screen with the gritty immediacy of headline news.

The film opens with a shot of St. Peter's Basilica nestled amongst the rooftops of Rome, and then quickly cuts to a platoon of Nazi soldiers marching through the streets on a nighttime raid on the apartment of Giorgio Manfredi (played by Marcello Pagliero), a military leader of the underground resistance movement. Manfredi escapes out a window and over the rooftops, then, at the apartment of his fellow revolutionaries, Francesco and Pina, makes an appointment with a sympathetic Catholic priest, Don Pietro (played by Aldo Fabrizi). This cleric, whom we meet in a cassock and biretta playing a rowdy game of playground soccer, agrees to deliver a sum of money for Manfredi, and after a series of twists and turns (that includes his students deliberately blowing up a tank car of German gasoline), Don Pietro and Manfredi get picked up for questioning by the SS.

It is worth noting how already in its first half, *Rome, Open City* noticeably departs in many ways from those traits typically considered hallmarks of the neorealist style—a great irony, considering how often the film is hailed as the movement's urtext and its director, Roberto Rossellini, the patriarch and pioneer. Rather than employing nonprofessionals, for example, several of the film's leading roles were filled by seasoned actors from Italian vaudeville theater, and while many scenes were indeed shot on location, much of the movie's second half was filmed on a studio soundstage. Additionally, with its emotional theme music, unambiguously malevolent Nazis, various

Following the fall of Benito Mussolini's fascist government in 1943, the German army temporarily occupied Rome before declaring it an "open city," a military term for a city left undefended.

> Spring will come again, more beautiful than ever,
> because we will be free.
> —FRANCESCO

twists, surprises, and sudden reversals of fortune, *Rome, Open City* amounts to something closer to traditional melodrama than to any realistic documentary. Its claim to innovative realism, then, comes not from a simple transcription of "the world as it is" but from a novel fusion of artistic and documentary conventions. Despite obvious contrivances, the film achieves an aura of authenticity largely by introducing many things into fiction that up to that point had not been deemed cinematic material.

In its second half, the film's major themes come to fruition and its vision of true heroism emerges, as each of the co-protagonists, partisan and priest, faces his final ordeal of interrogation, torture, and, ultimately, execution. When Don Pietro refuses to make a deal—"What little I know I learned in the confessional, and those secrets must die with me"—the Nazi officer questioning him points to a packet of counterfeit papers picked up from his rooms, citing them as indisputable evidence of Don Pietro's intention to harm the Reich. Don Pietro counters that this was not exactly his aim. "Then what would you call a man who not only provides refuge and forged documents to Italians planning attacks on our soldiers, but even shelters German deserters?" "A man who humbly seeks to practice Christian charity," Don Pietro replies.

Later, the same officer drags Don Pietro face to face with a bloodied and physically broken Manfredi (who has, like his clerical counterpart, refused to capitulate), insisting, "Look, priest! Satisfied now? This is your Christian charity, your love for your brother in Christ." A profound and darkly ironic *ecce homo*, this moment draws attention to the devastating effects

of moral evil (Manfredi's ruined body) as well as the fundamental creaturely integrity (his resolute will) that persists despite it. Also recalling in its visual style many depictions of the Crucifixion in Western art, the scene implicitly asks whether Don Pietro (and we with him) might recognize even in a communist atheist like Manfredi some residual semblance of the self-sacrificing God.

When shooting started for *Rome, Open City* in January 1945, the war was still going on in other parts of Italy. Amidst the ongoing shortages, director Roberto Rossellini had to cobble together abandoned scraps of filmstock and whatever he could find on the black market, which is one reason for the grainy texture and inconsistent quality of parts of the final film.

Such a deeply charitable challenge to discover in our neighbors the common humanity of a person made in the *imago dei*—even those whose philosophies oppose our own—converges with *Rome, Open City*'s consistent emphasis upon the everyday heroism of loving one's neighbor. The real test of this value comes at Manfredi's death, when Don Pietro, momentarily overwhelmed by the immensity of humanity's capacity for evil, spontaneously cries out against his Nazi tormentors, "You tried to destroy his soul, but you only destroyed his body! Curse you all! Curse you all! You'll be trampled in the dust like worms!" For a

NAZI OFFICER: Then what would you call a man who not only provides refuge and forged documents to Italians planning attacks on our soldiers, but even shelters German deserters?
DON PIETRO: A man who humbly seeks to practice Christian charity.

A young Federico Fellini (director of Vatican List films *La Strada* and *8½*) contributed significantly to the script *Rome, Open City*, which he claims was written in a week at his kitchen table.

moment, the ordinarily affable, down-to-earth priest towers in judgment over the assembled Nazis like an outraged Old Testament prophet. He quickly shrinks back down to size, though—"My God, what have I said? Forgive me, Lord"—suggesting that even a legitimate desire for justice does not do away with Christianity's deeper logic of love that extends even to one's enemies.

The film's optimism about a human brotherhood founded on neighborly love is most forcefully—and, perhaps, controversially—expressed in the repeated way it emphasizes a convergence between communist and Christian hopes for the future. United by the expectation that this world will one day turn into a utopian place of perfection, good-willed persons agree on what is essential, *Rome, Open City* seems to tell us, even when they remain divided over who and what will bring this about. "We mustn't be afraid, now or in the future, because we're on the just path," Francesco, a communist, tells Pina, a Catholic, whom he is preparing to marry. "Spring will come again, more beautiful than ever, because we will be free." All roads lead to Rome, as the expression goes, and in this film the morally upright—beginning from whichever corner on the confessional map—can expect to converge eventually on the common ground of a liberated Italy.

From our standpoint in history, of course, we know that the end of the Nazi occupation did not usher in an Italian paradise—social conflicts, squalor, and existential anxieties persisted (as we see chronicled in other Vatican List films like *Bicycle Thieves*, *La Strada*, and *8½*). Nonetheless, the film's suggestive image of an Eternal City abloom in springtime, the meeting place of reconciled friends and lovers-to-be-wed, might continue to inform the Christian expectation for eventual, permanent deliverance, not only from passing political oppressors, but from all evil in this world. This vision is rendered all the more striking as set against the wintry backdrop of Nazi-occupied Europe, and the revolutionary aesthetic and ideals in *Rome, Open City* continue to impress critics and filmmakers around the world. With its bold suggestion of what warrants representation on the screen, this film set the stage for an age of grittier, more down-to-earth cinema. But its most enduring impact might turn out to be as old as the golden rule: a vivid encouragement to love our neighbors as ourselves, however inimical they at first appear to be.

*DPB*

## DISCUSSION QUESTIONS

• "My enemy's enemy is my friend," as the saying goes. Does it require a Nazi takeover for Christians to find common ground with communist atheists, or are there convictions we share even now?

• Is it appropriate to represent the torture of an atheist like Manfredi as an echo of the sufferings of Jesus Christ? How are the passions of these men alike and different?

• In light of his Christian commitment to brotherly love, was Don Pietro wrong to curse the Nazi torturers? Or was there something just about this spontaneous outburst? Is it possible, somehow, that the truth includes both?

# Schindler's List

## 1993

*The true story of a profit-minded industrialist torn between colluding with the Nazis and his desire to rescue Jews working in his factory.*

Steven Spielberg's *Schindler's List* is one of the best-known films about the persecution and murder of millions of Jews at the hands of the Nazis during World War II. Adapted for the screen by Steven Zaillian from Thomas Keneally's novel *Schindler's Ark*, the film tells the story of Oskar Schindler, a Czech-born Nazi who eventually uses his wealth and position to shield his Jewish employees from extermination. Starring Liam Neeson as Schindler and Ben Kingsley as the humble, heroic accountant Itzhak Stern, Spielberg's film is

Missing for decades, the original typed list of Schindler's Jewish workers was found in 1999 in the attic of his former residence in Hildesheim, Germany.

a devastating examination of human depravity, resilience, and hope.

In real life, Oskar Schindler spent his younger years carousing, philandering, and serving as a spy for Nazi intelligence in his native Czechoslovakia before moving to Kraków, Poland, to follow in his father's footsteps as a businessman. The film initially depicts Schindler's obsession with wealth, image, and status, as he ingratiates himself with the German command in Poland in order to ensure lucrative financial favors. Schindler is a lapsed Catholic, and he wants to be remembered not for Christian charity or even basic human decency but for success in business. He imagines others saying of him, "He came with nothing . . . and left with . . . all the riches of the world."

But Schindler's ability to navigate complex bureaucracy to secure his own success proves to be a gift with far more important effects than his personal enrichment. As Polish Jews are dispossessed of their land and crammed into urban ghettos, Schindler seizes the opportunity to employ a cheap work force whose skills make him wealthy and whose survival is therefore in his best interest. He trusts Stern with the day-to-day operation, and before long "Schindler Jews" are partly shielded from the worst-case scenario at the hands of their tormentors. Schindler eventually comes to value the people in his care for their own inherent dignity instead of their productivity, finally impoverishing himself to keep the Nazis away from them for good.

Throughout the film, Spielberg presents the brutality of Nazi oppression, depicting point-blank executions and beatings as well as gruesome survival tactics, including children hiding in a latrine full of human waste. The cruel power of

> This list is an absolute good. The list is life.
> All around its margins lies the gulf.
> —ITZHAK STERN

Hitler's war machine is embodied by the Austrian SS officer Amon Göth, played by Ralph Fiennes. Tasked with liquidating the Kraków ghetto and overseeing the Płaszów concentration camp, Göth kills prisoners at random, picking off defenseless victims with a rifle from his balcony. He espouses the official Nazi position of the inferiority of Jewish people, but he loathes himself and acts out in sadistic violence when he experiences sexual attraction to his beautiful and graceful Jewish maid.

In contrast, Schindler begins to lose whatever weak attachment he may have had to Nazi beliefs, and he even faces criminal charges for spontaneously kissing a Jewish woman as a gesture of gratitude for a birthday cake. As Schindler begins to wake up to the need to help and defend the Jews, he temporarily gets through to Göth's humanity, which has been almost annihilated by decades of diabolical ideology and the brutalizing effects of his own wicked behavior. Schindler tells him that true power comes from showing mercy, and the next day Göth restrains his usual rage, looking in the mirror and tenderly saying to himself, "I pardon you," before erupting in violence again. Unwilling to change, Göth enriches himself by participating in Schindler's plan to move the workers from Poland to a safer environment in Czechoslovakia, but he ridicules Schindler for daring to give Jews hope of survival. In the end, Göth goes to the gallows, stuck in his murderous delusions.

*Schindler's List* depicts the suspension of virtue required to participate in the Nazis' system of injustice, and shows the Jews to be the moral superiors of their oppressors. In one troubling scene, Germans look for Jews hiding in the Kraków ghetto as a soldier plays a piano. While machine guns spray bullets into walls and ceilings in order to kill any remaining Jews, two soldiers debate whether the music they are hearing is by Bach or Mozart. The Nazis prove themselves depraved, callous, and totally unworthy of the beauty of their cultural patrimony.

Toward the end of the film, Schindler appears in a church, reverencing the altar before reassuring his wife that he will never be unfaithful to her again. He also has his factory workers sabotage the munitions they produce so that they cannot harm anyone on the battlefield. When the war ends, Schindler encourages the German guards to go home "as men" rather than murderers, but since he is a Nazi war profiteer himself, he must flee as the liberating forces approach. Schindler's workers present him with the gift of a gold ring, and he breaks down in tears, lamenting that he wasted so much money that could have been spent to save more lives.

The eponymous Schindler's list is not only an important item in the plot, but it also has a metaphorical significance that resonates with the biblical worldview of both Jews and Christians. In order to save his Jewish workers from being sent to Auschwitz, Schindler and Stern compose a register of names, each of which requires a fee Schindler will have to pay to the Germans to take them away to work for him in Czechoslovakia. Schindler is repeatedly told not to entangle himself in bureaucracy for the sake of specific people. "You shouldn't get stuck on names," an officer tells him. And indeed, if Schindler had picked a different set of Jews than the ones who

As producer, Steven Spielberg asked fellow director Roman Polanski if he would direct the film. Polanski, who was a child in the Kraków ghetto and whose mother died at Auschwitz, declined, but later directed *The Pianist* (2002), which contains many autobiographical elements from this time period.

> ## What's a person worth to you?
> —OSKAR SCHINDLER

had worked for him all along, he would still be celebrated today. But Schindler has a strong attachment to *his* Jews, just as the God of the Bible shows tender love to *his* people and calls them by their names: first the people of Israel, then everyone in the world redeemed by the Messiah of Israel. Schindler loves specific people, not abstract humanity. And in this way, Schindler's list may call to mind the biblical Book of Life, which is described in the Old Testament books of Ezekiel, Daniel, and the Psalms, and also in the New Testament (St. Paul's Letter to the Philippians and the book of Revelation). There, each individual appears by name, and it is the individual that Schindler comes to reverence and to regret not saving in greater numbers: "I could have got one more person, and I didn't."

*Schindler's List* evokes deep emotion from viewers throughout its run time of three hours and fifteen minutes. The film is full of elements that rend the heart, including a recurring image of a little girl in a red dress and the orange-blue glow of Sabbath candles on the factory floor—bursts of color that shatter the gloom of the dominant black-and-white photography. And as a master popular storyteller, Spielberg has a unique way of building tension from

> In 1962, Oskar Schindler and his wife Emilie were included among the "Righteous Among the Nations" at Yad Vashem, Israel's official memorial of the Shoah located on the Mount of Remembrance in western Jerusalem. When he died in 1974, Schindler became the only former member of the Nazi Party to be buried in Mount Zion.

> It's Hebrew, it's from the Talmud. It says, "Whoever saves one life, saves the world entire."
> —ITZHAK STERN

one scene to the next. His tale finally reaches a cathartic ending that brings the action up to the (then) present day, as the real-world "Schindler Jews" file past their benefactor's resting place in Jerusalem, placing stones of remembrance on his grave.

Words on the screen at the end of the film inform the audience that "there are fewer than four thousand Jews left alive in Poland today" (in 1993, the year the film came out), revealing the scope of devastation Hitler wrought on a multi-million-person community that had thrived there for hundreds of years. But despite the unparalleled atrocity, Stern reminds Schindler, "There will be generations because of what you did," and a caption confirms that there are now "more than six thousand descendants of the Schindler Jews." In his real life, Oskar Schindler did not have much worldly success after the war, and although he showed heroic virtue when put to the test, he was an obviously flawed man at other times. His sacrificial philanthropy, however, bears witness to the reversal of fortune Jesus describes as belonging to members of the kingdom of heaven: "Those who find their life will lose it, and those who lose their life for my sake will find it" (Matt. 10:39).

Indeed, even as we agree "never again," *Schindler's List* reminds us to stop and give thanks that not all was lost, and to cherish this tale as a small token of the ultimate victory of God for his people.

*AP*

*(Content advisory: contains some nudity and violence)*

## DISCUSSION QUESTIONS

- How essential do you consider the Jewish roots of Christianity or of Jesus, the Messiah of Israel?

- The Second Vatican Council's document *Nostra Aetate* condemns all forms of anti-Semitism. Have you ever witnessed this form of hatred in the world or even in the Church? What is an appropriate Christian response?

- Have you ever had to repent from selfishness or greed in order to help someone in need? Are there opportunities in your life right now to sacrifice in ways that would benefit other people?

# The Seventh Seal

## 1957

*A knight returning from the Crusades plumbs the meaning of existence while crossing a landscape gripped by the Black Death.*

**"W**hen I was young, I lived in great fear of death. It was really through *The Seventh Seal* that I somehow came to terms with that." So reflects Ingmar Bergman, celebrated auteur of this film that many critics place among the chief accomplishments of artistic cinema. A profound piece of work whose philosophical vision amounts to a kind of cheery nihilism, *The Seventh Seal*'s enduring impact seems at least partly tied to the impressive way it questions the meaning of life while gazing unshrinkingly into the eyes of death.

> What will become of us who want to believe and cannot?
> —THE KNIGHT

It opens with one of film criticism's most talked about sequences: an image of a Knight (played by Max von Sydow) playing chess with a personification of Death (played by Bengt Ekerot). On one level, the scene replicates the real-life frescoes of fifteenth-century Swedish church muralist Albertus Pictor. On another level, this symbolic and somewhat unsettling image summarizes the film's overarching aesthetic strategy— namely, to engage head on with the specter of death in the hope of discovering some route to victory over it.

Among the possible routes entertained, two dominate. On the one hand, there is the idealistic approach represented by the Knight, who intrepidly seeks answers to life's big questions despite the terrifying possibility that he might not like what he finds. On the other, there is the pragmatic approach represented by the Squire (Gunnar Björnstrand) as well as a troupe of traveling actors, who, neither aspiring so high nor taking the risk of sinking so low as the Knight, attempt merely to keep up a sense of humor and cultivate a blithe simplicity while skimming across the surface of things.

We witness the Knight, for example, resolutely seek some sort of ultimate certainty as he airs his doubts to a hooded confessor in a country church. Recognizing his own anguish in the tormented Christ of the crucifix, the Knight admits that what he really wants, rather than faith or conjecture, is sure knowledge. "Must it be so cruelly inconceivable to know God through one's senses? Why must he hide in a fog of half-spoken promises and unseen miracles?" The confessor, who turns out to be Death in disguise, suggests that God might not exist. "Then life is just senseless horror," the Knight responds. "No man can live facing death knowing that everything is nothingness."

Bergman was outspoken about his lack of Christian conviction, despite having been raised in a religious household. His father—by all accounts a hard, domineering figure—had been a prominent Lutheran minister in Stockholm and, at one point, even chaplain to the Swedish royal court. Reacting strongly against his father and distancing himself from his childhood faith, Bergman nonetheless retained a lifelong preoccupation with religious questions that can be detected across much of his work. We hear in the Knight's plaintive searching, for instance, sentiments that may well reflect Bergman's own. "Why can I not kill off this God within me? Why must he live on inside me in this painful, humiliating way when I want to tear him out of my heart?" Like the Knight who wishes for "God to reach out his hand, show his face, speak to me," Bergman's writing often evinces the anxiety and perplexity of someone who would like to believe, but feels the absence of some necessary proof.

> The title of the film is an allusion to the book of Revelation and its vision of the cataclysmic events leading up to the Final Judgment, excerpts from which are recited at the film's opening and closing: "When the Lamb opened the seventh seal, there was silence in heaven for about half an hour. . . . Then the angel took the censer and filled it with fire from the altar and threw it on the earth; and there were peals of thunder, rumblings, flashes of lightning, and an earthquake" (Rev. 8:1, 5).

By contrast, the Squire strikes a very different posture toward the world. Seated elsewhere in the same country church as the Knight apprehensively wrings his soul, the Squire drinks copiously and paints a caricature of himself on a wooden shingle. "Here's Squire Jöns," he jests. "He grins at Death, scoffs at the Lord, laughs at himself, and smiles at the girls. . . . Ridiculous to all, including himself, meaningless to heaven, and of no interest to hell." With his witty, bawdy, and rough-hewn largesse, the Squire represents an accurate portrayal of how, according to those who knew him, Bergman conducted himself in his intimate relationships.

Another expression of this less existentially beleaguered side of Bergman's sensibility is evident in the family of traveling actors who reiterate amongst themselves a softer version of the tension between Knight and Squire. Whereas the husband (played by Nils Poppe) is a clownish figure prone to periodic religious visions, his cheerfully earthbound wife (played by Bibi Andersson) consistently recalls him to the concrete simplicities of domestic life with her and their toddling son.

If, on the one hand, this family of actors suggests a rather idealized portrait of pastoral existence unburdened by metaphysical doubts, they also serve as part of the film's refreshingly down-to-earth, tongue-in-cheek commentary on the artist's profession. We see part of the player's performance on the village square, for instance, and it is a simple slapstick affair whose whole goal seems to be to introduce some levity into the everyday lives of ordinary folk. The artist's task is certainly not treated with overblown solemnity; when later a villager at the local inn expresses his wish to murder an actor, the leader of the troupe buoyantly lauds the prospect as a service to society.

> Why can I not kill off this God within me? Why must he live on inside me in this painful, humiliating way when I want to tear him out of my heart?
> —THE KNIGHT

As a professional dramatist himself, Bergman is famous for the practical attitude he took toward his own work, likening it to that of a craftsman whose job is to make a good table or comfortable chair. "Nobody today knows the names of those who built Chartres Cathedral," he has remarked, adding that what upsets him most is not the possibility of his own name being forgotten but of making films that nobody wants to watch.

Despite this desire to make accessible and useful art, a widely recognized (and often lamented) characteristic of Bergman's work is its consistently ponderous and portentous air. No doubt this has something to do with the nihilistic bent of his philosophy. Bergman once related how during a routine surgical procedure he was given too much anesthetic and nearly did not wake up. "For me those eight hours were no hours at all, not a minute, not a second. I was completely gone." That experience, he continues, gave him extraordinary comfort when it came to thinking about death. "First you're something, and then you're no longer anything. You're nonexistent."

Such an attitude comes through near *The Seventh Seal's* conclusion in the fate of a girl condemned to burn as a witch. The pyre is lit, and as the girl's expression twists in terror, the Squire attributes this to her realization that neither God nor Satan are, in fact, watching over her—only emptiness. The Knight recoils at this verdict but is clearly deeply shaken, as perhaps it strikes the same chord as his earlier observation: "Faith is a heavy burden, you know? It's like loving someone out in the darkness who

The internal debate between religious doubt and a wish to believe, so prominent in this film and common in the modern world, can be detected elsewhere in Bergman's work—for instance, in the argument between the minister- and doctor-to-be in *Wild Strawberries*.

never comes, no matter how loud you call."

Significantly, *The Seventh Seal* gives the final word neither to the melancholic Knight nor cynical Squire, but to the clownish players. After the remainder of the main cast meet their earthly demise, the husband describes a vision of seeing these departed stretched out in a line across a sunny hilltop, reminiscent of medieval depictions of the dance with death. "You and your visions," his wife replies. Unfazed by the weightier matters of metaphysics or any hint of existential dread, hers is a voice of simple, family-begetting vitality, which, here at the film's end, calls the visionary back to the simple matter-of-fact necessities in the practical world. Thematically, it is as if her role in the drama is to say, now that we have had our brief bout with Death, we can return our attention to the merry business of living. Death, on this reckoning, is neither answered nor conquered; it is acknowledged, then left to one side.

> Reflecting upon the fifty plus films of his career, Bergman felt there were about ten he could really stand behind, among them *The Seventh Seal*.

If this does not amount to a very integrated outlook, Bergman was candid about the unresolved tensions of his own interior life. He describes himself, for instance, as a single composition within which "there are enormously strong oppositions and an enormous amount of chaos and enormously complicated situations." Indeed, Bergman's own complex sensibility toward the subjects raised in his own films is well summarized in the exchange between the Squire and the church muralist he discovers painting his own rendition of a man playing chess with Death.

Squire: "Why paint such nonsense?"
Muralist: "To remind people they are going to die."

> A skull is more interesting than a naked woman.
> —THE MURALIST

Squire: "That won't cheer them up any."
Muralist: "Why always cheer them up, damn it? Why not scare them a bit?"
Squire: "Then they won't look at your paintings."
Muralist: "Oh, yes, they will. A skull is more interesting than a naked woman."

Between the Knight and Squire, the clown and the clown-maid, Bergman puts his inner conflicts, hopes, fears, and desires onto the screen for the world to see, regardless of how it lays his insides bare in the process. It may not be entirely satisfactory as a piece of philosophy, but *The Seventh Seal* is undoubtedly a courageous work of art.

*DPB*

## DISCUSSION QUESTIONS

- What do you think about death? Is it something to be faced head on, laughed at, or ignored?

- How do you feel about Bergman's suggestion, "First you're something, and then you're no longer anything. You're nonexistent"?

- "No man can live facing death knowing that everything is nothingness." Do you agree? Is there an alternative?

# The Tree of Wooden Clogs

## 1978

*A deeply reverent depiction of pre-industrial Italian peasant life.*

This film accomplishes what some would call impossible: it is an Italian neorealist drama that is genuinely enjoyable to watch. Carrying on in the tradition of *Rome, Open City* and *Bicycle Thieves,* it offers a naturally lit, nonprofessionally acted, documentary-like chronicle of the plight of the poor— and it does so like one untimely born, several decades after the influential style fell from fashion. To be sure, from a bald summary of its action, *The Tree of Wooden Clogs* has no right to be even a quarter as interesting as it is. A struggling single mother does the wash; an old man finds a coin; a young man walks across cornfields and sings aloud to bolster his courage as dark falls; and so on, across over three hours of screen time. But the overarching miracle of a film that is filled with commonplace miracles is how it imbues such outwardly simple occurrences with a profound, even majestic sense of the sacred.

This is certainly thanks at least in part to the deep Christian faith of director Ermanno Olmi, a practicing Catholic born into a working-class family in

Filmed as a three-part miniseries for public television, *The Tree of Wooden Clogs'* original dialogue was in the Bergamasque dialect so that even most Italians required subtitles in order to understand it. It only gained a theatrical release after winning the 1978 Cannes Palme d'Or.

the same region that the film depicts. Set on "a typical tenant farm in Lombardy at the end of the nineteenth century housing four or five families," the sublime music of J.S. Bach rolls in the background as men and women work alongside each other plowing fields and scattering seed; they uproot spent plants and husk corn; their children play in a hayloft as others beneath shovel fodder from a wooden cart. It might sound utterly mundane or sickly sweet, but *The Tree of Wooden Clogs* is no airbrushed, sentimental piece of rural nostalgia. This becomes obvious when the film's introductory sequence comes to an abrupt climax with a farmer who unceremoniously chops the head off a goose (clearly not a special effect).

Such gritty, authentic realism anticipates an even more graphic scene later in the film, when a pig is slaughtered in a kind of communal celebration. The parish priest, Don Carlo, happens to be present for this moment and compliments the big animal. "I raised it myself with tender, loving care," the farmer beams, as the carcass is hacked in half behind him. Don Carlo laughs, "See that you love God, or you'll come to the same end." "What have I done wrong? I've never killed anyone," the man says. "That's not enough," the priest replies. Like the children standing by whose mothers turn their faces towards the scene, we, too, are invited to face without flinching this fact of life, which serves not as a gratuitous act of violence but as a springboard to higher truths.

In a more intimate mood, later that night the folk of the compound sit and sing together, husk more corn, knit, and chat about the day. It is one of several such evening assemblies in the film, whose entertainments alternate seamlessly between grisly ghost stories, silly burlesques of ecclesial chant, and unironically pious recitations of the Rosary. The juxtaposition of sacred and profane initially comes as a jolt, but little by little we grow more accustomed to the way these people incorporate the faith into the rough and tumble rhythms of their agricultural and domestic lives. One minute they poke fun at a thing—their folk traditions, religious conventions, and most of all, each other—only to treat it completely in earnest the next. It is a hearty, humble, and humorous approach to the world that seems utterly natural. These imperfect Christians till the soil and pray together; shout at and steal from each other; and interweave acts of profound belief with the little dishonesties of people just trying to scrape by.

There is no getting around the fact that they are poor, even desperately so. Circumstances are so straitened that minor serendipities and accidents like the discovery of a gold coin or the busting of a child's wooden shoe take on momentous significance. When the cow of an especially destitute family is diagnosed as terminally ill, the mother grabs an empty wine bottle and walks out of the house, peppering her rote

> Dear friends, we wouldn't be here without miracles.
> —DON CARLO

Most of the vignettes in the film come from stories that director Ermanno Olmi's grandmother told him about growing up on a communal farm. As a consequence, he did not need to do much research in advance of filming, but simply, in his words, "made a treasure chest of all those emotions, all those memories of what life was like in those times, and I turned them into my narrative."

prayers with personal pleas: "I do what I can. You can see that. But without your grace, I'll never be able to go on." Kneeling before the altar at a creekside chapel, she asks for a miraculous cure for the animal, then fills the bottle at the stream and returns home, still pleading, to drain the draught down the creature's throat. When the cow recovers, the family gives heartfelt thanks to God for what, to them, amounts to nothing short of a miracle.

Is this legitimate piety, superstition, or merely an expedience of raw desperation? One of the strengths of the film is that it provides no unequivocal answer to this question, nor to others raised by the numerous small miracles that punctuate its homespun dramas.

One such occurrence comes when this same woman elects, even at the lowest point of their poverty, to share a slice of her family's polenta and milk with a homeless simpleton who pushes through the door. "Poor souls like that who have nothing are closer to God," she reminds her giggling children, with a semi-miraculous disregard for their own precarious situation. Later in the film, a young man and woman from the farm get married in a subdued ceremony, and they travel by barge that very day to sleep in a convent and adopt a child from the orphanage there. "All he needs to be truly happy are real parents," one of the sisters tells them, then goes on to describe how the child comes with a stipend twice a year.

> Poor souls like that who have nothing are closer to God.
> —PEASANT WOMAN

"For a poor family, that can be a true gift of providence. . . . We must help each other in this world. He can be of help to you, and you can be of great help to him."

The significance of the film's title comes into play when, back at the communal farm, the landlord notices the stump of a tree that a tenant had chopped down to replace the split sole of his son's shoe. He immediately evicts the guilty party, his wife, and his children, only allowing them a day to gather their limited belongings and find somewhere else to live. "That's taking the bread right out of their mouths," a neighbor observes. "Poor people. They have nothing now."

That the film ends on such a tragic note—rather than, say, with the marriage and start of a new family—reinforces the neorealistic concern at the heart of *Tree of Wooden Clogs*: it does not aim to entertain or console its viewers so much as to unsettle us through a confrontation with the material wretchedness of the poor. For a man to have a claim on so little—not even the trees that line the fields—that he cannot even supply primitive shoes for his child calls into question an economic status quo that

"As soon as the word got around that I was about to make a film on their world," Olmi recalls, "everyone brought something for me. Someone brought an old farming tool, someone else brought a shawl, someone else some kitchen utensils. So that farmhouse came back to life. So much so, that when we were not shooting on Sundays, the old people brought the children because they wanted the kids to see what their old world was like."

many take for granted. In terms of Catholic social teaching, such a deeply unjust distribution of earthly goods suggests that the right to private property has been taken too far and eclipsed the complementary principle—that is, a duty to respect the universal destination of goods. God has given creation to provide for the legitimate needs of all his creatures.

Granting this quietly revolutionary point of view, it might come as a surprise that a number of communist critics chastised *The Tree of Wooden Clogs* at its release, claiming that it idealizes resignation in the face of oppressive power: the only acts of rebellion in the film, they argue, come from the animals. In response, Olmi points out that the film begins and ends with rebellions of a sort: a family sends a child to school, which would have been scandalous among peasants at the time; and the families stand witness and offer a rosary for their evicted neighbors. In neither case, he admits, are there shouts from the city squares, but the relative voicelessness of these people in this-worldly terms does not prevent them from invoking supernatural intervention, nor from doing the little things that might obtain for them, "even slowly, step by step, a more tranquil space for living that will be more in harmony with the rest of society."

The impoverished farmers in *The Tree of Wooden Clogs* may be denied the means to obtain their desires by force, but, in the spirit of the Beatitudes, such "wretchedness" also converts into counterintuitive blessings. Often desperate, they are often at prayer, and, stripped of any illusion of self-sufficiency, they are predisposed to recognize divine assistance when it arrives. A large part of the purpose of

> Paradise begins with the love that we show each other here on earth.
>
> —DON CARLO

*The Tree of Wooden Clogs* is to encourage just this kind of perspective that does not overlook the small miracles in our daily lives. As Don Carlo tells us, "Miracles are the power man doesn't have, the power of God's love. We need that love as much as the air we breathe, the land that feeds us, and the water and light that give us life." Later in the film, he says, "And remember that paradise begins with the love that we show each other here on earth."

*DPB*

*(Content advisory: contains some brief nudity and violence toward animals.)*

### DISCUSSION QUESTIONS

- How do you feel about the way animals are treated in this film?

- Was it just or unjust for the landowner to evict the tenants who chopped down the tree?

- Have you experienced any "little miracles" like the ones portrayed here?

# *Wild Strawberries*

## 1957

*A retired professor undertakes a symbolically charged car ride during which he reflects nostalgically on his legacy, failed relationships, and overall outlook on life.*

Less well known than *The Seventh Seal*, director Ingmar Bergman's other film on the Vatican Film List, *Wild Strawberries*, was written, produced, and released later the same year. Wrestling with comparable existentialist questions in a more contemporary context, it is a beautifully constructed film whose old-fashioned gait and seemingly loose episodic structure are almost enough to conceal its profound simplicity of vision, which is one of the marks of great art.

On the surface, the story is simple. An elderly professor, Isak Borg (played by Victor Sjöström), wakes up on the day he is being bestowed with an honorary degree in another city, then drives to receive

> Bergman often worked with the same actors. For example, Max von Sydow, who plays the wandering knight in *The Seventh Seal,* appears briefly here as a gas station attendant.

it. The journey, though, proves fraught with momentous encounters, each stop along the way supplying revelations of self-knowledge and hints at the reasons underlying Isak's quietly angst-riddled state of mind.

The introspective and symbolic tenor of the film is established early when, after a brief introduction of the key players, the drama cuts to an extended surrealist dream sequence. In it, Isak finds himself eerily alone and outside of time. He finds a coffin abandoned in a city square, pulls back the lid, and discovers himself inside—a fitting introduction, as we shall see, to Isak's central preoccupation with a sense of somehow being alive and dead at the same time. The dreamlike quality of what follows, not only in the explicit dream sequences but the film as a whole, probably derives at least in part from the fact that most of Bergman's films have their origins in his own minutely recalled dreams.

Bergman reflects upon the deeply personal character of *Wild Strawberries* in his memoir, *Images,* where he describes the film's protagonist as "a figure who on the outside looked like my father, but was me through and through." Isak Borg has the same initials, we note, as the director, and apparently his names are cognates with the Swedish words for *ice* and *fortress,* suggesting a frigid, self-protecting personality.

Isak embarks on his drive accompanied by his pregnant daughter-in-law, Marianne (played by Ingrid Thulin), but stops on the way at a house where his family vacationed when

> Recently I've had the weirdest dreams . . .
> that I'm dead. Although I'm alive.
> —ISAK BORG

he was a child. There, the sight of some wild strawberries sparks a melancholic reverie about a lost love from his youth, and the symbolic significance of this location—the film's title in Swedish actually means "wild strawberry patch"—is twofold. On the one hand, strawberries emblematize the bright days of summer and the happy, fruitful days of life. On the other, the rarity and ephemerality of such days in a country like Sweden adds an intensity and tinge of melancholy to such cheerfulness.

Before departing this place of reminiscence, the travelers pick up a trio of young hitchhikers, and then, back on the road, nearly crash head-on into a veering vehicle commanded by a married couple in the thick of a violent spat. When the car of this new pair ends up in a ditch and unserviceable, they, too, clamber into Isak's car, but they prove so incapable of civility toward each other that Marianne insists they be left behind. The couple voices no objection; they confess their actions have been intolerable, yet they cannot help themselves and beg those still in the car to forgive them, if they can. Their surname, not coincidentally, is Alman—the equivalent of "every man" in other languages—and Isak later admits how they brought to mind his own marriage.

Isak, Marianne, and the young trio later stop for a leisurely lunch. The trio turn out to be a medical student, a minister-to-be, and a female companion admired by them both (she also stands for Isak's lost love: the same actress plays both roles). The minister, who plays the guitar, sings some bars of a celebrated Swedish hymn whose beauty merits quoting it in full.

*Where is that friend, whom everywhere I seek?*
*When the day dawns, my longing only grows;*
*When the day flees, I still cannot find Him*
*Though my heart burns.*

*I see his traces, wherever power moves,*
*a flower blooms, or a leaf bends.*
*In the breath I draw, the air I breathe*
*His love is mixed.*

*I hear his voice, where summer winds whisper,*
*where groves sing and where rivers roar*
*I hear it best in my heart speaking,*
*and me keeping.*

*O! When so much beauty in every vein*
*of Creation and life fail,*
*How beautiful must the source be,*
*The eternally True!*

This song sparks a debate: the doctor does not understand how any serious person can become a minister these days, whereas the minister accuses him of lacking all imagination. The argument between these representative intellectuals pulls the young woman back and forth between them. "How sweet they *both* are!" she remarks. "I always agree with the one I spoke with last."

Their disagreement also seems to articulate an interior struggle that has marked the professor's

*Wild Strawberries* won the 1960 Golden Globe Award for Best Foreign Film. It was also nominated for an Academy Award for Best Original Screenplay, but Bergman refused the nomination.

> Ah, when creation shows so much beauty,
> how radiant must be its source!
> —THE STUDENT MINISTER

entire life. As a young man, he had been preoccupied with questions about sin and the afterlife, and in his middle years had enjoyed a successful career as a man of science. Now, as an old man, Isak allows the argument to go unresolved; when asked for his opinion he simply recites poetry, then sits with the young woman in the car as the squabbling younger men trade kicks and punches up a hill.

As the company nears its destination, the film's various thematic strands draw together in a sequence that features an extended conversation between Isak and his daughter-in-law. After a short visit to the professor's nonagenarian mother, whom Marianne describes as "cold as ice, more forbidding than death," she then articulates terror at the prospect of her own shortly expected child reaching the same conclusion about her. The fear stems back to her own deteriorating relationship with her husband, Isak's son, whom we learn through a flashback had once refused even to entertain the prospect of becoming a father. "It's absurd to bring children into this world," he insists, and alludes to his own experience as "an unwanted child in a hellish marriage."

Bergman himself described his own parents' relationship as a cold and dead partnership, and apparently for years quarreled with his parents and hated his father. It seems plausible, then, that this relational breakdown at least partly informs the feeling described by Isak Borg—the "ice fortress" who represents Bergman "through and through"—that he himself is a living corpse.

This is where the film comes to a climax, but it is not where it ends. Professor Borg travels on to receive his

Former film director Victor Sjöström, who plays the lead role of Isak Borg, was at the time of shooting an ailing, querulous man whose wife was deceased. He often forgot his lines, but he began performing much better once he was permitted to return home each day by 5:15 p.m. for his punctual evening whiskey.

honorary degree and re-unites Marianne with his son, who awaits them at the ceremony. (Evidently the younger man has followed in his father's footsteps not only personally but professionally.) Isak then concludes the eventful day in bed, slipping into another dream where the sun shines, he is young again, and his parents are together, the whole family enjoying a return to the fleeting, happy days of wild strawberries.

This final flash of brilliance in a film whose mood ever darkens raises a last hope against hope, that maybe even after a lifetime of failures, disappointments, and corpse-like experiences, there can be a return to life as it was known in its most beautiful moments. The philosophical vision of *Wild Strawberries* can certainly not be characterized as simply uplifting, embroiled as it is in fatally unhappy marriages, intractable psychological quandaries, and an inability to resolve doubts about the existence of God. However, there is something cumulatively bittersweet in the intrepid way its characters trace their existential discontent all the way back to philosophical first principles. In this closing visionary return to an earlier innocence, *Wild Strawberries* can also tell us something about, if not *what* to believe, then *how* to believe: with utter honesty, attentiveness to beauty, and, above all, a love that invokes the entirety of our humanity.

*DPB*

## DISCUSSION QUESTIONS

- How would you describe the feeling at the end of *Wild Strawberries?* Hopeful? Regretful? Something else? Do you sympathize with Isak Borg?

- "Ah, when creation shows so much beauty, how radiant must be its source!" Do you find this kind of reasoning compelling? Why or why not?

- Isak Borg's sensation of being alive and dead at the same time parallels a similar description in the biblical parable of the prodigal son: "For this son of mine was dead and is alive again; he was lost and is found!" (Luke 15:24). What connection, if any, do you perceive between these two fictional characters?

# PART III

# Art

# 8½

## 1963

*A freewheeling, self-referential foray into the manic day-to-day of a movie director trying to figure out what film he is making.*

By turns confusing and luminous, chaotic and assiduously crafted, self-indulgent and self-accusatory, Federico Fellini's *8½* is one of the great films about making a film. A tragedy that charges intrepidly upon the barricades of farce, it is also a kind of lament for lost love, purity, and innocence that offers a privileged look both into an artist's creative process and a disordered soul's existential predicament. Intriguing in its mixture of beauty and ugliness, such a virtuoso portrayal of a morally reprehensible life would probably be unbearably pretentious if it were not so disarmingly self-exposing. It

> This confusion is ... me.
> Not as I'd like to be, but as I am.
> —GUIDO ANSELMI

is cynical and silly and brazen and lost, and yet this does not stop it from being a heartfelt appeal for forgiveness and understanding, as well as a masterful piece of art.

An opening dream sequence establishes the film's highly subjective, fantastical tone. This continues even after Guido Anselmi (played by Marcello Mastroianni), a film director, wakes to find himself ensconced in a hotel and spa, where he is poked and probed and prodded in equal measure by medical and movie people from the moment he opens his eyes. Lost at the center of a world of fame, privilege, and easy access to pleasure, Guido cannot cross the lobby without being bombarded by questions from an aging actress chasing a role in his latest film; a cynical critic who ruthlessly pulls apart his script; producers, casting directors, and talent agents, all with their own interests and agendas; even a gossip columnist enquiring into his love life. Everyone wants to know what he is doing with his film-in-progress. What they do not guess is that he does not know.

He presses forward anyway, as the film we watch jumps restlessly between his sensory experiences, memories, and fantasies. Along the way he meets an elderly cardinal whose conversation triggers Guido's conflicted attitude toward Catholic faith and morality. When it is suggested that his art mixes profane and sacred love too casually, Guido replies that the film is religious "in a way," in that the protagonist had a Catholic upbringing "like all of us. . . . So, he has certain complexes, certain needs he can no longer repress." As an illustration of this, Guido's mind wanders to a schoolboy encounter with "la Saraghina," a massive woman holed up in an abandoned beachside artillery turret whom he and some schoolmates hire to dance for them. Her sensual Rumba is an act of grotesque titillation she undertakes with gusto, until it is interrupted by the school's clerical supervisors, who rain down shame and public ridicule on Guido's youthful brush with sexuality.

Following the associative logic of the film, the action then cuts to the critic who offers an analysis of the scene we have just watched, arguing that it is merely a self-indulgent childhood memory that does not amount to a general critique of the Italian Catholic conscience. "Your intention was to denounce, but you end up supporting it like an accomplice. See? What confusion . . . what ambiguity!" Such self-commentary runs throughout *8½*, anticipating and incorporating many of the actual criticisms later leveled against the film. In this case (and in many others), the criticism is astute. The film *does* try to have it both ways: it is self-indulgent but also self-reproaching about this; its central character is petty and dishonest, but also nobly tells the truth about being so. This complex mix of dissemblance and sincerity is summarized by the producer who hounds Guido throughout most of the story, when he relays that he's figured out what the film is really about: man's inner confusion. "But you've got to be clearer," he concludes with a flourish of self-contradiction.

As the plot progresses, there is an increasing sense that *8½* is at least partly autobiographical, and for good reason. By Fellini's own admission, the "inspiration" for the film, ironically, was a void he calls "director's block." "I had a producer, a contract . . . everybody was ready. . . . There were sets already up, but I couldn't find that sentimental feeling." So, what he eventually resolved to do

> Once asked about his early influences, director Federico Fellini replied, "Sex, circus, cinema, and spaghetti."

> How do you benefit from stringing together the
> tattered pieces of your life? Your vague memories,
> the faces of people that you were never able to love?
> —THE CRITIC

was recount his feelings at that time, his insecurities about making the film, the uncertainties over what it was even about, the complexities of his own marital infidelities, etc.

The divide between fact and fiction becomes thinnest with the appearance of Claudia Cardinale (playing herself), who arrives to play a part in Guido's film. (Viewers will also recognize her in another film from the Vatican List, playing the role of Angelica in *The Leopard*.) Guido slips away with her, and she admits to not getting much from the screenplay. "A guy like your character, who doesn't love anybody, is not very sympathetic you know." She asks why, for example, he pushes away even the girl in the script whose love could offer him a new lease on life, to which Guido offers a trio of answers: "Because he no longer believes in it. . . . Because it isn't true that a woman can change a man. . . . And above all because I don't feel like telling another pile of lies." But each time in response, Claudia offers an alternate explanation: "Because he doesn't know how to love." In this triple call and response, we might hear an echo of our Lord's questioning and restoration of St. Peter after his infidelity (John 21:15–17). In Guido's case, the exchange beckons him toward a renewed innocence, simplicity, and faithfulness that might be his only chance for deliverance from the confused mess of his life.

This confusion comes to a climax in the manic, cacophonous press junket at the site of a half-completed rocket pad Guido has had built for his movie. The purpose of the event is ostensibly to promote his as yet unfinished film, but it also doubles as an inquisition into Guido's lingering uncertainties about it, his marital infidelity, and his general attitude toward art, life, and love. It is a chaotic hubbub of aggressive questions and invective, whose only relief comes when Guido crawls under a table and shoots himself. Surrealistically, he then reappears and converses with the critic who commends the suicide: "You've made the right choice. Believe me, today is a good day for you." He rambles on, congratulating Guido for also opting, incidentally, to abort the film: "Such a monstrous presumption to think that others could benefit from the squalid catalogue of your mistakes! . . . And how do you benefit from stringing together the tattered pieces of your life? Your vague memories, the faces of people that you were never able to love?"

Somehow in the midst of this apparently abstracted (albeit in fact quite penetrating) prattling, Guido undergoes a kind of epiphany, and expresses a sudden surging desire for life, forgiveness, and the clarity that comes from a simple love.

Fellini was involved in various ways with other projects on the Vatican Film List. In his memoir, he recalls how, after collaborating with Roberto Rossellini on *Rome, Open City*, the director asked him to rewrite another script. "After reading the script, I said no. Absolutely no. He said, 'Would you like to be assistant director?' I said yes. Then he gave me the script to rewrite. It was to be called *The Flowers of St. Francis*."

"I'm not afraid anymore of telling the truth, of the things I don't know, what I'm looking for and haven't found. . . . Life is a celebration. Let's live it together!"

The tone then shifts as a motley marching band of clowns appears, trailed by a boy flautist in pristine white. To their lively tune, Guido shouts directions for an increasingly surrealist promenade that includes many of *8½*'s main characters. Spa-goers wrapped in towels, members of the production team, the cardinal, Saraghina, Guido's parents, his mistress and his wife—these all get reprise appearances and join hands in a merry dance around the skeletal base of the unfinished rocket pad. As the procession winds down, the last to exit is the boy in white, still playing his beguiling tune.

The original title of the film was *La Bella Confusione* ("The Beautiful Confusion"), but was changed to *8½* to reflect the fact that it was Fellini's eighth directorial feature—plus one shared director's credit, hence the half.

An image of lost—or perhaps not quite lost—innocence and purity buried at the back of a morass of riotous, incoherent sensuality, this final note strikes a similar chord to the ending of Fellini's most celebrated film, *La Dolce Vita*, whose protagonist seeks absolution for a dissipated lifestyle in a climactic vision of inaccessible childhood beauty. It also recalls an earlier scene in *8½* where Guido as a boy recites an incantation in the half-serious hope of bringing a painted portrait on the wall to life. The formula "Asa Nisi Masa"—a kind of Italian pig Latin for the word *anima*, doubling each syllable with an interposed "s"—anticipates in a confused, oblique way exactly what he is still earnestly looking for as an adult: a principle of spiritual vitality, order, and simplicity; in other words, the soul.

Effectively amounting to the portrait of a man helplessly trapped in a mess of his own making, *8½* testifies to the way impurity darkens our insight into the meaning of life. Layered, swirling, self-involved, the film itself might be likened to that dance of Saraghina writ large: a jiggling bulk of tantalizing flesh, equal parts burlesque and enticement—a raucous, unblushing indulgence in distaste.

Yet the fact that it ends on a note of celebration suggests, rightly, that there are beauties and hints of hope to be found

> Life is a celebration. Let's live it together!
> —GUIDO ANSELMI

even amidst such lostness. In Guido's case, there remains the residue of a conviction concerning the power of faithful love that persists even in the heart of an infidel, like the abiding grandeur of a cathedral in ruins—or a half-built platform for launching man into the heavens. Masterful as a work of art and reprehensible as a template for actual living, *8½* is ultimately tragic in the best sense: a scintillating, sympathetic look at a life no one ought aspire to live.

*DPB*

## DISCUSSION QUESTIONS

- Is it legitimate, as the inclusion of this film on the Vatican Film List suggests, to admire as art the portrait of an existence we would not wish to commend or emulate in life?

- "Blessed are the pure in heart, for they will see God" (Matt. 5:8). To what extent is Guido's confusion about life linked to illicit sensuality and a failure to love? What is the purity Guido seems to long for but not to be able to attain?

- "Accept me for what I am, if you want me. It's the only way we might be able to find each other," Guido concludes. Is there any truth to this? What, if anything, would you add?

# 2001: A Space Odyssey

## 1968

*A groundbreaking science fiction story that begins at the dawn of humanity, depicts an expeditionary crew on a spaceflight to Jupiter with a sentient computer, and concludes with a mystical exploration of human destiny.*

Watching *2001: A Space Odyssey* today, it can be easy to overlook how important it is. Whether or not we like the film, we must give credit to its visionary director, Stanley Kubrick, for inventing an aesthetic, if not a whole cinematic sub-genre, built to explore some of the most inscrutable philosophical questions. When *2001* was released in 1968, it was still more than a year before humans walked on the moon; but then, as now, there was no better setting than outer space to ask big questions about humanity's origins and purpose.

Each of the three parts of the film raises a major issue. The first act, "The Dawn of Man," depicts the prehistoric past to consider the compatibility of faith and science, and particularly evolutionary biology and divine providence. The long second section travels through space and considers the benefits and dangers of modern technology. The baffling finale takes us on a mystical journey that reckons with the question of eternity, both for the individual soul and for the universe writ large. Throughout *2001*, Kubrick offers some of the most iconic images in cinematic history to explore questions that are as relevant today as when the film was released. For hundreds of generations, humanity has moved from one frontier to the next. But what have we been looking for? And where do we go from here?

At the beginning of the film, Kubrick depicts a group of apes who take an evolutionary leap forward with the appearance of a large black monolith near their caves. The apes are drawn to the foreign object; they touch it, dance around it, and shout out in ecstatic worship. They then begin using bones as tools and weapons, eating meat, and competing for domination in new ways. Today's viewer may be too distracted by the ape costumes to take note of how the film weighs in on a centuries-old debate between scientists and theologians. In Kubrick's vision, the apes only become humans in response to an active intelligence that intervenes from outside.

When the film jumps forward from prehistoric

Stanley Kubrick formulated the idea for *2001* after reading the 1951 short story "The Sentinel" by Arthur C. Clarke, who cowrote the screenplay for *2001* and published a novelization of the film after its release.

> I've got a bad feeling about him.
> —FRANK POOLE

times to the twenty-first century, we learn about a second monolith buried on the moon, where humans have begun forming colonies. Scientists examine the artifact, touching it with reverence like the apes in the opening section of the film. Then, in response to a related radio signal emanating from the planet Jupiter, an expeditionary team sets out on a quest for the origin and meaning of the monolith—and everything else in the universe. Here Kubrick includes one of several shots in the film where celestial bodies align, implying a deliberate, divine ordering of the created realm—a feature that many theologians discuss under the category of "natural theology." In the Psalms we read, "The heavens are telling the glory of God" (Ps. 19:1). Likewise, St. Paul teaches, "Ever since the creation of the world his eternal power and divine nature, invisible though they are, have been understood and seen through the things he has made" (Rom. 1:20).

Kubrick's research on the physics of people and objects in motion was impeccable, creating the film's elegant look that paved the way for *Star Wars* and a whole new generation of cinematic sci-fi. There is a real beauty to some elements of *2001*'s vision of technological innovations, and the airy, dance-like scenes depicting a rotating space station and passengers aboard a ship practically cry out for classical music, famously provided by Johann Strauss' *Blue Danube Waltz*. Even today, it is amazing just how slowly and dramatically the Jupiter-bound Discovery One spacecraft moves through the frame before the whole thing is visible on screen. On board the vessel is a large hibernating crew overseen by just two waking men, Dr. David "Dave" Bowman and Dr. Frank Poole, played respectively by little-known actors, Keir Dullea

and Gary Lockwood. Kubrick at first depicts space travel as banal and lonely; but as the mission goes wrong, the audience experiences the terror of Dave's complete disconnection from the rest of existence, expressed by his heavy breathing inside his space suit.

The film's prologue, "Dawn of Man," ends with an ape throwing a bone into the air, representing humanity's first weapon, then jump cuts to a future space scene of a nuclear missile orbiting earth, representing what Kubrick considered humanity's final weapon.

And then there is HAL, the artificially intelligent onboard computer system, whose soothing voice belies paranoia about his own survival. His red eye sees all, and he inexplicably sabotages the mission to Jupiter, killing everyone on the crew except for Dave. When Dave eventually disconnects HAL, whose voice wobbles and finally fades out as he recounts his origins in a lab in Illinois decades earlier, the viewer is left to wonder about the meaning of HAL's demise and Dave's survival. Is humanity experiencing judgment for developing artificial intelligence and transgressing unbreakable natural laws? Or has a malevolent spirit infected and overtaken an otherwise neutral technology? Is this whole episode of betrayal and violence instigated by the same intelligence that introduced the monoliths? Is it simply a means of spurring on the next phase of human evolution?

In two iconic moments in the film, we hear Richard Strauss' dramatic *Also sprach Zarathustra*, based on Friedrich

I am putting myself to the fullest possible use, which is all I think that any conscious entity can ever hope to do.
—HAL

Nietzsche's philosophical novel in which he wrote "God is dead." Dave's climactic victory over HAL is not true deicide, but rather the death of an idol of technological innovation in which humans increasingly place their hope. Even more now than in Kubrick's day, as we trust in computers for so many of our daily tasks, we may sometimes wish to take back control from a force that seems more powerful than we are. What would happen if we just switched off all the "smart" speakers, devices, and appliances in the world?

If *2001* had not been weird and confusing enough leading up to the final act, here it takes an even sharper turn. A third monolith appears and leads Dave through a stargate, depicted in hallucinogenic colors and set to the ethereal, avant-garde composition *Atmosphères* by the Hungarian-Austrian composer György Sándor Ligeti. As Dave travels into the lights, at first wide-eyed, then with his face contorted, we wonder where he is headed and what he will become. Is pure energy the future of fully evolved humanity? Or is it pure spirit? In a confusing set of images, Dave then sees himself as an old man eating alone at a table, followed by a glimpse of himself on his own deathbed. Is Dave experiencing a Platonic recollection, coming into a deeper knowledge of his origins and end? Is he about to have an Eastern-style reincarnation?

The final shot of *2001* is of a giant baby approaching the earth, suggesting that Dave may be a representation of the *Übermensch*, whom Nietzsche describes as breaking the cycle of eternal recurrence by being reborn as an innocent child. But Dave's journey toward death

> The film features no dialogue either during the opening twenty-five-minute sequence or during the final twenty-three minutes: of the total run time of one-hundred-forty-eight minutes, eighty-eight minutes feature no talking.

> As to whether he has real feelings is something I don't think anyone can truthfully answer.
>
> —DAVE BOWMAN

and new life may also represent the prospect of Christian resurrection, both on an individual and a cosmic scale. With rare exceptions in cinema, babies always mean good tidings, and in a symbolic way, this might suggest not only the renewal of the world through the birth of the Christ child, but also the biblical promise of a new heaven and a new earth: "See, I am making all things new," the Lord declares (Rev. 21:5).

The ending of *2001* raises more questions than answers, and some viewers will find this frustrating. Many fans of the film, however, respond with an increased desire to seek the truth about the things that matter most: where we have come from, how we cope in the alienating, hyper-technological world of today, and what we are doing to prepare for the life to come. Faced with the weird visual stimulus of a trip beyond the world, it is only natural to wonder where our own bodies and souls may one day be headed too.

For good reason, *2001: A Space Odyssey* is in the "Art" category of the Vatican Film List rather than "Religion" or "Values." Like looking at a painting or listening to a piece of music, it suggests deep meaning without offering any obvious conclusions. And in an instance like this, we may do well to step back from the core principles and firm answers upon which we normally base our lives of faith, and let a bigger mystery wash over us. By the end of *2001*, we have had quite a bath.

*AP*

## DISCUSSION QUESTIONS

- How does *2001: A Space Odyssey* make you feel about modern technology? Are we transgressing boundaries we should avoid, or are we progressing toward a more humane, enlightened future?

- Are faith and science ultimately reconcilable? Can we articulate a good account of evolution, for example, while at the same time understanding ourselves to be created by an all-powerful and all-knowing God with a specific design and for a specific end?

- There is very little dialogue and very few characters in this very long movie. What do you think this lack of normal film elements is meant to achieve? Does *2001: A Space Odyssey* prompt you to look inward and think deeply, or does it produce a different kind of reaction in you?

# *Citizen Kane*

## 1941

*A riveting, unsettling tale of massive wealth, titanic ambition, and the seemingly inevitable unhappiness they bring.*

Amasterpiece of filmcraft that is undeniably old school yet somehow not at all out of date, *Citizen Kane* consistently appears at the very top of lists of the best films ever made. Loosely based upon the actual lives of several business tycoons at the time, *Citizen Kane* particularly drew the ire of yellow journalist William Randolph Hearst, whose sensationalist (and at times only loosely factual) news stories instigated, among other things, the Spanish-American War. Outraged in particular by the way the film outlines an unflattering portrait of his mistress, Hearst did everything in his power to keep audiences away; this included offering to buy every existing copy with the express intent to destroy them. It is one of the great ironies of film history, then, that the work many consider the best ever made very nearly never saw the light of day.

It opens with the aura of a horror film. Ominous music plays over a no trespassing sign tied to a chain-link fence, through which a gloomy estate leads up to a castle lit at only one gothic window. The light suddenly blinks out, a man whispers the word "Rosebud," and then, in an abrupt sequence of staccato, high-energy news headlines, we learn that the "master of Xanadu palace . . . America's Kubla Khan, Charles Foster Kane . . . the greatest newspaper tycoon of this or any other generation," has died. Not satisfied by this newsreel account of a man who had parlayed with world leaders, constructed an entire opera house for his mistress, and ended his days "alone in his never finished, already decaying pleasure palace . . . aloof, seldom visited, never photographed," a room full of reporters reviewing the footage resolve to follow the trail of Kane's final utterance and get to the bottom of his "essence as a man."

The story that follows dramatizes their findings across a string of flashbacks punctuated by rapid-fire, overlapping, early-talkie-style dialogue. The young Kane inherits a gold

William Randolph Hearst, the real-world newspaper mogul who partly inspired the central character in *Citizen Kane*, was once asked by filmmaker Douglas Fairbanks why he did not get into movies, which exert a worldwide audience, rather than newsprint, which only has a citywide or nationwide readership. Hearst thought for a second before replying, "Because you can crush a man with journalism, and you can't with motion pictures."

> If I hadn't been very rich, I might have been
> a really great man.
> —CHARLES FOSTER KANE

mine (and the world's sixth largest private fortune), grows up to take over the day-to-day management of a struggling newspaper, then massively grows its circulation. He leverages this success into a nationwide news empire and marries the niece of the sitting U.S. president. The mood of these early scenes is upbeat, at time almost slapstick, putting to effective use classic comedic gags like mistaken identities, pratfalls, and characters who try to maintain a meaningful conversation around the corners of men moving too much large furniture into a room.

The tone shifts, though, as year by year Kane drifts away from his youthful principles and becomes increasingly defiant, distant from those nearest him, and disconnected from reality. He starts an affair with a giggling girl on the street, runs for political office and loses, and then pours himself into pushing his mistress' ill-fated singing career. Roundly panned by the critics—except those working for Kane-controlled papers, whose headlines resound with superlative praise—she wants to quit, but he refuses to let her until sitting at her bedside after her attempted suicide. When she leaves him, he spends his remaining years filling the halls of his echoing palace with foreign-acquired curios.

When the team of journalists investigating his life finally arrive to photocatalogue the overwhelming collection of headless Venus statues, Spanish ceilings, and stones from a disassembled Scottish castle never unboxed, one journalist suggests that if they had only found out the meaning of Rosebud, they might have solved the puzzle of Kane's life. Another disagrees: "Mr. Kane was a man who got everything

After the commercially calamitous reception of *Citizen Kane*, Orson Welles never again received a contract with complete control over a major studio film. Nonetheless, he went on to direct various minor projects and continued to act—for example, as Cardinal Wolsey in *A Man for All Seasons*.

he wanted, and then lost it. Maybe Rosebud was something he couldn't get or something he lost. Anyway, it wouldn't have explained anything. I don't think any word can explain a man's life. No. I guess Rosebud is just a piece in a jigsaw puzzle. A missing piece."

They leave, and as the camera glides over the virtually endless expanse of crates, boxes, and artifacts in the former businessman's private vault, a worker picks up a child's sled. On it is written the name "Rosebud." He throws it into a furnace, as outside Xanadu, black smoke belches from the chimney, and we return beyond the chain-link fence and its no trespassing sign.

What should we make of Rosebud? Various theories have been advanced over the years: it is a symbol of Kane's lost innocence; merely the meaningless doddering of an ailing egomaniac; an intimate, real-life nickname shared between William Randolph Hearst and his mistress, Marion Davies. Perhaps it offers something less like an explanation and more like a lingering question: Can anything we pick up and hold in our hands in the end really make sense of the mystery of living in this world? In the end it may be hard to say.

Something less hard to say is that *Citizen Kane*'s interest as a piece of fiction is not quite, but nearly, overshadowed

I am, have been, and will be only one thing: an American.
—CHARLES FOSTER KANE

> He was disappointed in the world so he built one of his own, an absolute monarchy.
>
> —JEDIDIAH LELAND

by the real-life drama that surrounded its highly contested release. As chronicled in the Oscar-nominated documentary *The Battle Over Citizen Kane*, the heavyweight public bout that erupted between the youthful genius who made the film and the proto-billionaire who wanted it obliterated is the stuff of movie-making legend. In one corner was a twenty-four-year-old Orson Welles, fresh off dazzling successes on Broadway and a sensational radio theater broadcast of *The War of the Worlds* that reportedly caused people to run screaming from their homes. Newly arrived into Hollywood with the most lucrative studio film contract to date, Welles had unprecedented control to write, direct, produce, star in, edit, and release a film just the way he wanted.

*Citizen Kane* did for the sound period what *Birth of a Nation* did for the silent period, according to critic Roger Ebert. It brought together the cinematic techniques developed up to that point and put them "all together in one place at one time so that every picture after that, in some way or another, would be informed by the breakthrough of *Citizen Kane*."

In the other corner was William Randolph Hearst, aged seventy-six, the owner of newspapers read by one in every five Americans. Perched north of Los Angeles in his private estate of San Simeon half the size of Rhode Island—George Bernard Shaw once quipped that it was the place God would have built, if he had the money—Hearst mobilized his stupendous fortune to

Citizen Kane was nominated for nine Academy Awards but only won one, Best Screenplay, a credit shared between director Orson Welles and the script's principal writer Herman Mankiewicz.

crush the project, directing his papers to run a smear campaign on Welles' personal life, reject all advertisements and reviews of Citizen Kane, and deny placement of any other ads from cinemas that showed it.

When theaters began pulling screenings, Welles fired off a telegram to RKO Pictures: "Show it in tents, it'll make millions—'The Film Your Theater Won't Let You See.'" But the damage had been done. It took years for Citizen Kane to trickle out from the independent and arthouse circuit to find a general audience, by which time it had already been written off as a commercial disaster that effectively blacklisted Welles for life. He lived out much of the rest of his life in professional isolation, not so different from the character at the center of this film. As his long-time collaborator John Houseman observed, it was as if with Citizen Kane Welles had directed his own autobiography.

So, what is it about this story that inspired a rising star in his prime to risk everything to tell it, a man three times his age to do everything he could to suppress it, and critics down the decades to garland it with such superlative accolades?

A definitive answer is probably as elusive as the final meaning of the film itself. But it might have something to do with the beguiling overlap of these on- and off-screen dramas—the way Citizen Kane as a work of fiction both reflects and anticipates actual history. It might have to do with the spellbinding contrast, as critic Peter Bogdanovich observes, between the bright, world-striding panache of its storytelling and the dark, deeply cynical view of success in the story. Or it might have to do with the sheer overawing way it transposes the American dream into a tragedy and offers a troubling spectacle, equal parts glamorous and gruesome, of what it could look like to gain all there is in the world and still lose everything that matters most.

*DPB*

## DISCUSSION QUESTIONS

- "There's only one person in the world who is going to decide what I'm going to do, and that's me," declares Charles Foster Kane. What do you make of this as an approach to life?

- If the reporters *had* found out the meaning of Rosebud, would it have explained the essence of Kane as a man? If not, what (if anything) could?

- The fourth-century Church Father John Chrysostom once preached that relatively few lives are ruined by poverty, obscurity, or social failure compared to the many that founder upon the rocks of fortune, worldly honors, and success. Do you agree? Is it possible to love God but also power, prosperity, or prestige?

# *Fantasia*

## 1940

*A unique film experience in which a series of classical
masterworks played by a symphony orchestra accompany
vivid sequences of Disney animation.*

With the advent of radio and later with motion pictures and television, people in the twentieth century suddenly had access to cultural offerings that their
ancestors would not have so easily experienced. It was no
longer necessary to get dressed up and go to a concert hall
in a big city in order to hear classical music; an industry
developed to popularize it through mass media. Audiences
could now tune in to listen to Arturo Toscanini's famous
broadcasts with the NBC Symphony Orchestra, and the

Walt Disney Company began to offer whimsical exposure to orchestral music through their *Silly Symphony* cartoons. Warner Brothers followed suit with *Merrie Melodies* and, later, *Looney Tunes*.

In the late 1930s, Walt Disney began developing the idea that would become *Fantasia*, a film in which music does not merely accompany a story but serves as its star. With Leopold Stokowski conducting the Philadelphia Orchestra, *Fantasia* is a celebration of music augmented by visual accompaniments from the early golden age of animation. Divided into seven segments and hosted by the composer and critic Deems Taylor, then known as the "dean of American music," *Fantasia* opened in 1940 at the Broadway Theatre in New York City, with an innovative sound design called "Fantasound" meant to give the sense of an orchestra actually playing in the theater.

Taylor introduces the film with an explanation of three different types of orchestral pieces that Disney animators chose to depict. The first, he tells the audience, is a piece of music that tells a definite story, like the famous "Sorcerer's Apprentice" sequence in the film. The second is a composition that may not tell a specific story but paints definite pictures—for example, Beethoven's *Pastoral Symphony*, which enraptures the listener with a sense of the natural landscape and weather. The third type, Taylor explains, is "absolute music" that exists for its own sake, and a prime example is Johann Sebastian Bach's "Toccata and Fugue in D," which opens the film.

> What you're going to see are the designs and pictures and stories that music inspired in the minds and imaginations of a group of artists.
> —DEEMS TAYLOR

"The Sorcerer's Apprentice" is the first appearance of Mickey Mouse in a Disney animated feature film.

In this first sequence, the audience is invited to pay attention to the musicians, their instruments, and the act of creating melody and harmony, as the animators put colorful abstractions on the screen to spur the intellect to contemplation and stir the soul to inspiration. The timpani drums seem to bubble up with fire, and the violin bows soar up to heaven, while the bows of the double basses dip down to the underworld. At the end of the piece, light bursts through the darkness, foreshadowing a theme that will come back in the final sequence of the film. The conductor stands in front of a glowing orange orb, having ordered thousands of independent notes played on a variety of instruments into a mysterious unity.

The second sequence is a collection of music from Tchaikovsky's *Nutcracker Suite* ballet, eschewing the normal Christmas story for a journey through an enchanted natural world. Beginning from the ground up, the audience encounters a lively collection of mushrooms on the forest floor, with fairies dashing around revealing the hidden force of life teeming everywhere. The animators depict what theologians call "natural theology," which sees God's presence manifested in created things in the world. Although a common view in pagan antiquity and revived by the Romantic movement in Europe in the nineteenth century, various forms of natural theology are found in Judaism and Christianity as well. For example, in the "Prayer of Azariah" from the book of Daniel, there is a long list of created things depicted as not only being dependent on God but also glorifying God by their mere existence: "Bless the Lord, all that grows in the ground; sing praise to him

> He was a little bit too bright, because he started
> practicing some of the boss' best magic tricks before
> learning how to control them.
> —DEEMS TAYLOR

and highly exalt him forever" (Dan. 3:76). As the sequence progresses, the natural world appears to be a beautiful and complex dance, with exotic and dangerous elements alongside the simple delights of the outdoors.

The third piece is perhaps the best known: "The Sorcerer's Apprentice" by the French composer Paul Dukas, based on a German poem by Johann Wolfgang von Goethe. Emphasizing the potential for awful outcomes when spiritual power is wielded by amateurs, Mickey Mouse steals a wizard's hat and unintentionally generates an out-of-control watery chaos and a legion of violent broomsticks.

The fourth piece is Igor Stravinsky's dissonant masterpiece *The Rite of Spring*, which may sound random and confusing to an unfamiliar listener but is actually intricately designed. Stravinsky was a devout Russian Orthodox Christian who believed that music had a unique ability to give glory to God and inspire the faithful. *Fantasia* uses Stravinsky's landmark work to illustrate the development of life on earth, from its cosmic origin through the time of the dinosaurs. The sequence was originally intended to continue up to the dawn of man, but Disney pulled back for worry of offending Christians who disapproved of theories of human evolution. Nowadays, many Christians may set aside the debates on the topic and simply enjoy the music with its accompanying images of bubbling primeval lava and primitive reptile combat in the knowledge that God is ultimately behind it all.

After an intermission, *Fantasia* resumes with Beethoven's *Pastoral Symphony*, imagined as a mythological day in

In the final sequence, "Night on Bald Mountain," the movements of the demon Chernabog are based on the acting of Bela Lugosi, who modeled for animators at Disney studios. Lugosi is famous for portraying Dracula and other horror characters in films, mostly in the 1930s.

the countryside, featuring centaurs, fawns, a family of winged horses, and a Bacchanalia ruined by the thunderbolts of a capricious Zeus. Although the gods of this world are selfish and unpredictable, the natural world is beautiful and abundant, and the audience may come away with an appreciation of the rhythm of life on earth in relation to divine activity in heaven. The sixth selection is the familiar "Dance of the Hours" from Amilcare Ponchielli's opera *La Gioconda*, here featuring hilarious dance routines by ostriches, hippos, elephants, and crocodiles. Gracefulness, apparently, comes in many shapes and sizes.

The final sequence of *Fantasia* is equal parts terrifying and edifying, and it is by far the most religiously and spiritually significant part of the movie. Taylor introduces the piece by noting that it is designed to show how darkness and evil finally give way to light and hope, and it is the only instance in the film where two musical pieces have been combined to achieve the desired effect. First, there is Modest Mussorgsky's "A Night on Bald Mountain," which was written to evoke the Slavic legend of a satanic "Witches' Sabbath," an event rumored to occur every year on the Eve of the Feast of St. John. For *Fantasia*, Stokowski modified a previous arrangement of the piece by Rimsky-Korsakov, and the animators chose to depict a powerful demon from Slavic lore named Chernabog, described in the film as akin to Satan himself. Waking up and spreading his enormous wings on a mountaintop, Chernabog

> Ave Maria! Heaven's bride. The bells ring out in solemn praise, for you, the anguish and the pride.
> —FRANZ SCHUBERT'S "AVE MARIA,"
> SUNG IN THE FILM'S FINAL SEQUENCE

summons restless ghosts and minor demons, only to cast them into a fire, which illuminates him as he rises toward the sky in malice and arrogance.

Brass instruments blare loudly and drums rumble ominously to heighten the sense of horror before the sequence shifts to its second phase, when the Angelus bell suddenly begins chiming from the church in the shadowy town below. At this sound, the demonic creatures cower and disperse, and Chernabog diminishes and folds himself back onto the mountaintop. Over a chorus of Franz Schubert's *Ave Maria*, a long procession of haloed travelers moves along a river's edge towards a bridge of vaulted arches. As the English text of the Marian hymn begins, the camera pans through a cathedral-like forest—a move that retrospectively seems to Christianize both the enchanted nature of the *Nutcracker* section of the film and the mythological pagan religion of the *Pastoral Symphony* sequence. Finally, in a breathtaking affirmation of Christians' resurrection hope, the scene ends with the opening of a curtain and entrance into paradise, where the dawn breaks just before the credits roll.

Disney's original intention was to refresh and rerelease *Fantasia* every few years with new musical pieces. This plan never materialized, but in the early 1940s, animators did storyboard work on several pieces by composers including Wagner, Sibelius, Chopin, Debussy, Rimsky-Korsakov, and Strauss.

*Fantasia* is thought-provoking and aesthetically

marvelous, using sight and sound to invite a mass audience not only into the world of classical music but into a deep spiritual reality that the best musical compositions explore. It is the only animated film on the Vatican List, but it stands tall among the other masterpieces of cinema in terms of its lasting influence. And in a world where many of the most popular entertainment offerings deliberately aim at the lowest common denominator, *Fantasia* stands out all the more in the way it draws everyone up, perhaps even as high as the things of heaven.

*AP*

### DISCUSSION QUESTIONS

- What part does classical music play in your life? Do you value music as part of your religious devotion? Do you ever play classical music at home or in the car for specific purposes (e.g., to relax, to contemplate, to pray)?

- Are you primarily a visual or auditory learner, or something else? What does the interplay of sound, image, and text do to your mind and soul?

- When you think of Disney, what comes to mind first? Over the years, have Disney's films and other cultural offerings been good or bad for you and your family and for the world? How does *Fantasia* compare to your favorite Disney films or programs?

# The Grand Illusion

## 1937

*A World War I drama about French officers in German prison camps, which contrasts the senselessness of war with the unlikely blessings that develop among people in difficult circumstances.*

Jean Renoir's *The Grand Illusion* centers on a group of French officers imprisoned in two different camps at the height of the Great War, now called World War I, which promised at the time to be "the war to end all wars." Exploring class, religion, and nationality, the film highlights how needless much modern warfare is and proposes that Europeans—and, by extension, people all over the world—have much more in common than what divides them.

> A golf course is for golf. A tennis court is for tennis.
> A prison camp is for escaping.
> —CAPTAIN DE BOËLDIEU

From the opening scenes of the film, Renoir, himself a veteran, impresses upon the audience that no one involved in the Great War really wanted to fight, least of all the gentlemen leaders on each national side who had more in common with one another than with many of their own countrymen. The working-class Lieutenant Maréchal (played by "France's everyman," Jean Gabin), is shot down during a reconnaissance mission with the high-born Captain de Boëldieu (played by Pierre Fresnay); but after receiving medical attention, the two men are invited to dine with their German counterparts, led by Captain—later Major—von Rauffenstein, played by the inimitable Austro-American actor Erich von Stroheim. The Germans warmly welcome their French prisoners as lunch guests, and as Rauffenstein and Boëldieu discuss the goings-on of their mutual friends in high society, one of the German officers cuts the meat for Maréchal, whose arm is in a sling. On both sides, violence is an unfortunate matter of duty that disturbs the normal, more desirable state of camaraderie.

Soon Maréchal and Boëldieu are sent to an officers' prison camp, where they join a lively community that cuts across the usual worldly distinctions. Early on in their confinement, Boëldieu washes the feet of the still-injured Maréchal—a gesture of solidarity and an example of sacrificial love taken directly from Christ's ministry to his Apostles in the upper room. Also in the camp is Lieutenant Rosenthal, a rich Jewish soldier who receives lavish care packages from home and shares the contents with the other prisoners. Another man, Cartier, is a larger-than-life former vaudevillian who organizes entertainment options that are as enjoyable for the

German guards to watch as for the inmates to perform. When word comes through of a French victory, Maréchal leads the men in singing "La Marseillaise"—an act that requires the Germans to punish him with solitary confinement. When Maréchal laments his loneliness behind bars, the German guard shows him compassion just as if he were a family member or friend. The French soldiers make it almost a game to dig a tunnel under the camp, and Boëldieu states it plainly: "A golf course is for golf. A tennis court is for tennis. A prison camp is for escaping." Ironically, the war outside the walls is utterly barbaric and unnatural, while life inside the prison possesses a semblance of civility ordered toward the common good. Why, one wonders, cannot such peace and fraternity simply replace the gore and strife of the trenches?

Just as the rag-tag group of French officers finish digging their tunnel and hatch an escape plan, they are split up and shipped off to different prisons, with Maréchal, Boëldieu, and Rosenthal ending up together at Wintersborn, presided over by Rauffenstein, now seriously disabled after a plane crash. The Frenchmen are warned that escape from Wintersborn is impossible, but they begin planning their exit anyway. Rauffenstein's quarters are in the chapel of an old castle, where an enormous crucifix hangs suspended overhead, representing suffering and death, but suffering and death in which God himself, in the person of his Son, participates.

Director Jean Renoir was the son of the French impressionist painter Pierre-Auguste Renoir and a subject of the painting *Gabrielle Renard and infant son, Jean* (1895-1896).

Bored of patriotic duty and disconnected from the urbane existence he once enjoyed, Rauffenstein now must wear a constricting neck brace and cover his burns with gloves. He tends to a geranium so as not to forget the beauty of life, and in one of the most

When the Nazis invaded France in 1942, Joseph Goebbels confiscated the print of this film and referred to Renoir as "Cinematic Public Enemy Number One."

memorable scenes in the film, he invites Boëldieu for an intimate, gentlemanly chat. The men agree that the world has changed; the privilege of their class has come to an end, but they wonder what will follow next in the long wake of the French Revolution. Back with the other inmates, Boëldieu humorously remarks that one of the consequences of egalitarian trends is that the poor will soon suffer from rich men's diseases like gout.

When the Frenchmen finally make their escape attempt, Boëldieu parades around the camp playing a flute, creating a distraction so that Maréchal and Rosenthal can make their getaway. Again in Christ-like fashion, Boëldieu lays aside his privilege and sacrifices himself for his friends, as Rauffenstein tries to reason with him in the dignified, neutral language of English before being forced to shoot. In perhaps the tenderest scene in the film, Boëldieu receives Last Rites from a German priest, offers Rauffenstein a bleak word of farewell, and reminds him of the sacrifice required of people placed in positions of honor and power. "I am not the one to be pitied. . . . You'll have to carry on," Boëldieu mutters. "For a commoner, dying in war is a tragedy. But for you and me, it's a good way out."

The final sequence of the film depicts Maréchal and Rosenthal on the run, finally taking refuge in the home of a young German war widow, Elsa, who is happy to receive them as a respite from her own loneliness. Elsa's home is full

May the earth lie lightly upon our valiant enemy.
—LIEUTENANT ROSENTHAL

of domestic comforts like glasses of milk, loaves of bread, a hot stove, beds, and prominent Catholic symbols including a statue of Our Lady, a crucifix, and a prayer desk. But Elsa also points out the portrait of her husband, killed at Verdun, and other family members killed at Liège, Charleroi, and Tannenberg, which she ironically describes as "our biggest victories."

Elsa and Maréchal do not speak the same language, but they make an immediate connection that develops into romance, even though they both know it cannot last. Rosenthal's injured leg heals over several days as he plays with Elsa's young daughter, Lotte, before they celebrate Christmas. In stark contrast to Rauffenstein's enormous crucifix in a cold and almost lifeless prison, Elsa's warm living room contains a crèche scene that includes a baby Jesus made from a potato, which (appropriately for Catholics) Lotte wants to eat. It is a celebration of an intimate, incarnational, and joyous faith, which even has a place of honor for Rosenthal, who half-jokingly mentions that Jesus' family may have been his distant ancestors. When it is finally time for the men to leave Elsa's farm, they look out on the landscape and ponder the unnaturalness of human greed and conflict. Once Maréchal and Rosenthal step over the invisible border into Switzerland, the German soldiers pursuing them are relieved to stop their hunt and put away their weapons. Again, no one really wants to fight this war.

In the final scene, Maréchal declares, "We've got to end this damn war and make it the last!" Rosenthal replies, "What an illusion!" Sadly, Europe was pitched into a new war just two years after Renoir's film came out, making the "Great War" the first of two great bloodbaths. After World War II, the nations of Europe tried again to make

> *The Grand Illusion* was nominated for the Best Picture Academy Award in 1938, the first foreign language film nominated in that category.

> Frontiers are an invention of men.
> Nature doesn't give a hoot.
> —CAPTAIN DE BOËLDIEU

lasting peace a reality rather than an illusion. Christian statesmen like Konrad Adenauer in Germany and Charles de Gaulle in France focused on Europe's common Christian identity while making arrangements to bind different nations' economies and governments closer together so that future violence would become unlikely if not impossible.

The commercial and political unions have largely succeeded in keeping the peace in western Europe, but a renewal of the Christian identity that once characterized "Christendom" has largely failed. Instead, the new grand illusion these days is of progress toward worldly utopia. Nonetheless, the reality of human sin and brokenness persists, and opportunities for an other-worldly peace of God, which passes all understanding, remains deep in the hearts of most people. The guiding Christian principles of "old" Europe, therefore, may still be the answer to today's problems. As Pope Pius XI said to the German people the same year Renoir's film was released, "Charity is the apostle's indispensable weapon in a world torn by hatred." Accordingly, one of the biggest lessons of *The Grand Illusion* is that no matter what statesmen and generals may do, everyone can cherish the gift of virtuous human interaction when it comes, even in the darkest depths.

*AP*

## DISCUSSION QUESTIONS

- World War I was supposed to be "the war to end all wars." Are there any grounds for hope for a sustained peace among different peoples and nations?

- The film explores relationships between people of very diverse backgrounds. Where have you found common ground with people whose life experiences have differed from yours? What role has your faith played in such relationships?

- What do you make of a principled rejection of all warfare? Catholics, for example, are not required to embrace pacifism nor forbidden from embracing it. Is there anything worth fighting for?

# *La Strada*

## 1954

*A simple parable about callousness, compassion, and the cost of redemption that follows a pair of knockabout circus performers.*

Simply signifying "the street" in Italian, *La Strada* plunges its audience into a gritty world familiar from other Italian neorealist films, but in a way that marks a transition away from the overriding social and political concerns of the style. Focusing more on the suffering of individuals caused by emotional, relational, and spiritual problems, it obviously struck a chord at the time: it won a silver lion at the Venice film festival, sharing the prize with Kurosawa's *Seven Samurai* and Kazan's *On the Waterfront* (another film on the Vatican List), and made international celebrities of director Federico

Fellini and his wife, Giulietta Masina, who plays the lead role. Millions of copies of its soundtrack—scored by Nino Rota, best known in the United States for writing the music for Francis Ford Coppola's *The Godfather*—sold across the world, and Fellini was pursued by figures such as Walt Disney, who wanted to make an animated movie about the lead character Gelsomina. So, what is it about this outwardly unostentatious story that has made it one of the most popular exports of Italian cinema?

It begins with a barefoot young woman, Gelsomina, who has a bundle of sticks strapped to her back and returns to her impoverished home to find she has been sold into indentured servitude to a vagabond circus performer. Attempting to plaster a smile on the situation, Gelsomina's mother speaks about how she will travel the world and learn a trade, to which the man, Zampanò—whose name in Italian suggests the word for an animal's paw, *la zampa*—adds, "Of course. I can even teach dogs." Gelsomina, whose simple-minded yet tender disposition is already on display in these early moments, climbs into Zampanò's motorized gypsy cart, wipes away tears, and waves goodbye to her family as they set off down *la strada*.

Zampanò is nothing if not a brute, a fact reflected in his main act, which involves breaking the link of a chain wrapped around his chest. He trains Gelsomina as a clown in a lame skit where she pretends to be the duck he hunts with a rifle; offstage, he brings her "training" to a ghastly climax when he forces himself upon her in the back of the van. Shortly thereafter he spends the night with a prostitute, and at their reunion, Gelsomina summons the courage to ask if this has long been a habit. He replies, "If you want to stay with me, you've got

> If you don't stay with him, who will?
> —THE ACROBAT

> When the Best Foreign Language Film award became a regular feature of the Academy Awards in 1956, *La Strada* was its first recipient.

to learn one thing—to keep your mouth shut!"

The yoking of violent strong man and innocent simpleton is difficult to watch, but there are flashes of silver lining—for instance, in how close these characters often come to burlesques. Fellini remarked that if he hadn't become a film director, he would have wanted to be a comic-strip artist, and this is evident in the droll, pantomime demeanor of Gelsomina, whom critics immediately dubbed the female Charlie Chaplin. "When I was in the States with her after *La Strada*, people didn't know whether to smile at her or to kiss the hem of her garment," Fellini once commented. "They saw her as someone halfway between St. Rita and Mickey Mouse."

She dances in bells alongside Zampanò at a wedding, the budding happiness of the newlyweds standing in stark contrast to their unhappy arrangement. When Zampanò slips away to betray Gelsomina again with the mother-in-law of the wedding party, Gelsomina declares that she no longer wishes to be mistreated and leaves. Alone on *la strada*, she walks, pokes at bugs, and joins a religious procession where she kneels before images of the crucified Christ and Madonna with Child. Then she bumps back into Zampanò. "Get in," he tells her, and when she resists, he slaps her around until she reluctantly climbs back into the caravan.

Feeling trapped, Gelsomina eventually laments her fate to a high-wire actor in a new troupe she and Zampanò join. She breaks down, laments being of no interest to anyone, and asks plaintively why she was even born. The acrobat picks up a small stone, insisting that it, like everything in the world, has a purpose, even if only God knows what. But it must be

> You follow your husband and I follow mine.
> —THE RELIGIOUS SISTER

*something*, he shrugs, or else everything is pointless. "If you don't stay with him, who will?" She nods, apparently taking the sermon on the stone to heart, only to erupt in an apparent *non sequitur*: "One of these days, I'll take a match and set fire to everything. . . . That'll show him. . . . I'll put poison in his soup, too. I'll set fire to it all!"

Gelsomina and Zampanò return to the road and pick up a religious sister whom they agree to drive back to her convent. In a sequence that provides an interpretative key for the whole film, the sister draws a parallel between the circus performers' way of life and her own: "We travel around, too. We change convents every two years . . . so we don't get too attached to the things of this world." She then looks at Gelsomina. "You follow your husband and I follow mine." This is a bitterly ironic suggestion—could Gelsomina's relationship be any more different from a sacramental marriage to Jesus Christ?—but one that also adds a deeper dimension to the film's title. The street, by this light, becomes a symbol of a human predicament always *in via*, marked by a kind of homelessness but not without hope for something more to come.

Abuse piles on abuse, painful to watch, as Gelsomina appeals to Zampanò once again and attempts to elicit any kind of tender emotion. She asks if Zampanò likes her even a little, but he does not respond, instead beating her brutally for refusing to help him steal silver votive offerings from the sisters' chapel. At their departure the next morning, one of the sisters notices Gelsomina's tears and asks whether she might prefer to stay. But Gelsomina sticks with Zampanò despite everything, her beaming farewell melting into resignation as she leaves behind what might have been her last chance at a state approaching peace and happiness in this life.

Back on the road, Zampanò and Gelsomina pass the broken-down car of the high-wire actor, and, resuming an old rivalry, Zampanò strikes him on the head and kills him. Zampanò hides the body, rolls the car off a bridge, and flees the scene, but Gelsomina, unhinged by the murder, whimpers about it continually. Her agony takes its toll on the otherwise insensitive Zampanò—we watch it etch ever deeper into his astonishingly transformed face—until, pushed to wits' end, he abandons her at the side of the road.

The story then cuts to several years later, picking up with Zampanò involved with yet another circus and another woman. When he hears a washerwoman humming Gelsomina's tune, he discovers it came from "a homeless woman" who died nearby some time ago. Shaken by the reminder, Zampanò undertakes his strong man routine one last time—by this point clearly an act in a deeper sense—then gets drunk. After being thrown out of a bar, he winds up staggering through the surf alone on a beach. There he collapses, rolls his eyes towards heaven, and seems suddenly struck by a kind of epiphany. Looking back around him, he appears to be utterly lost and to feel, perhaps for the first time in his life, loneliness and spiritual desolation. He breaks down and weeps—and that's the end.

> Bulldog advocates of documentary empiricism criticized *La Strada* as a betrayal of neorealism, and Marxist critics decried it as a work of sentimentalism and mysticism. Fellini defended the film by insisting that there are more Zampanòs in the world than bicycle thieves, and that the story of a man who discovers his neighbor is just as important—and as real—as a story drawn from the headlines.

> "I know little about Catholic dogma, and I may even be a heretic. My Christianity is rough and ready. I don't go to the sacraments, but I think that prayer can be thought of as an exercise to bring us closer and closer to the supernatural."
> —FEDERICO FELLINI

It is a rough conclusion to a difficult watch, and perhaps raises more questions than answers. Is *La Strada* simply a historical chronicle of man's inhumanity to woman? Or a fairy tale about how the love of a good woman can change a bad man? Is its grinding unkindness and unrelenting harshness an elaborate metaphor for the ongoing impact of the Second World War, whose hatred and violence stamped out so much innocence and life? Or, taking a step further back, is Gelsomina's endurance an allegory of the kind of vulnerability and unvindictive suffering with which heavenly love draws humanity back into relationship, love, and spiritual life? Perhaps encompassing each of these possibilities and more, the open-endedness of *La Strada* is very likely part of its perennial appeal.

Whatever else *La Strada* may be, it is certainly no stroll down easy street. But we can take heart, at least, from where it leaves us: at the end of one long road yet the start of another, at that moment when a one-time merely strong man takes his first, tentative steps toward real humanity.

*DPB*

## DISCUSSION QUESTIONS

- The director Martin Scorsese, whose films *Taxi Driver* and *Raging Bull* feature characters inspired by Zampanò in *La Strada*, speaks of "the Franciscan element in neorealism" and a compassion for every living being, the good and the bad alike, on display in the film. Do you detect this?

- Fellini once commented, "*La Strada* is about loneliness and how solitude can be ended when one person makes a profound link to another." Does this capture the essence of the film, in your view? Once a film is released into the world, do its makers have the final say on what it means?

- Where is the line between rightly forgiving sins and wrongly tolerating abuse?

# The Lavender Hill Mob

## 1951

*One of the best of the celebrated comedies from Britain's Ealing Studios, in which a modest London bank clerk conspires with three other men to steal a shipment of gold bullion and convert it into models of the Eiffel Tower.*

At the comedic heart of *The Lavender Hill Mob* is a character as little like a mobster as might be imagined. He is Henry Holland (played by Alec Guinness), a diffident and law-abiding bank clerk from that suburb of London known as Lavender Hill, where he lives in shabby-genteel hotel lodgings. Pudding-faced and bowler-hatted, Holland is "a non-entity," just one drone among thousands pouring into the city every morning on an underground train (the

> PENDLEBURY: Edgar.
> HOLLAND: I beg your pardon?
> PENDLEBURY: Isn't one supposed to say that when one's being briefed? On my rare visits to the cinema . . .
> HOLLAND: The word is 'roger.'

Waterloo Line) so he can work from nine to five in a boring job. These identikit commuters entering the capital from their bland dormitory towns look much like the flocking sheep at the start of *Modern Times*.

And just as Charlie Chaplin's monotonous existence causes a mental breakdown that is frenetically hilarious, Henry Holland's dull life brings about a moral collapse that is—it cannot be denied—delightfully entertaining. He realizes that after having led a blameless career for nearly twenty years, supervising deliveries of bullion to the Bank of England, he will be the last person suspected of stealing the same. Those decades of scrupulously unimaginative honesty will have their reward.

The incongruity between character and crime is what makes for much of the humor in the story. And it would appear from the opening scene—set in a stylish restaurant in Brazil, where the expat Holland relates his history to an attentive luncheon companion, occasionally interrupted by glamorous fellow diners (including Audrey Hepburn in a brief cameo)—that he has indeed got away with it. Holland is smiling, confident, generous, well dressed. Can he really have pulled off this sensational act of larceny? The answer to that question is given only when we return to the restaurant at the very end.

The intervening story is one long flashback, showing how he got into this improbable position. All his working life, Holland has had fortune literally within his grasp. Stray specks of gold at the refinery offend his probity, for how much money would the Bank of England lose over the years if such specks were allowed to accumulate? His rectitude is as unimpeachable as his tightly furled umbrella. His sober three-piece suit fits perfectly the middle-class mores to which he has bound himself.

But there is another Henry Holland struggling to get out, an alter ego who doesn't have to wipe his feet on the mat when entering his lodgings or remember to switch off the hallway light at night. Those lodgings in Lavender Hill are located at the "Balmoral Private Hotel." *Balmoral*. The allusion to the royal residence in Scotland is no accident. What if the cards had been dealt differently and Holland was possessed of a king's ransom? Each evening, he reads a chapter from a racy adventure story (*You'd Look Swell in a Shroud*) to his fellow lodger, Mrs. Chalk. He and she together revel in the alternative reality to which it gives them access. But it's fantasy, mere fantasy. There's no point in having ideas above one's station.

Then, out of the blue, a new lodger turns up. Mr. Alfred Pendlebury is a genial middle-aged man, a would-be artist with a penchant for quoting the English poets and stuck in a dead-end job that he despises, making die-cast souvenirs for tourists. Yet that very skill—making metal models—is what brings him to Holland's attention as

Alec Guinness earned an Academy Award nomination for his performance in this film, the first of six Oscar nods he received during his career. He won Best Actor for *The Bridge on the River Kwai* (1957) and an Honorary Award for lifetime achievement (1980), but his fame rests on playing Obi-Wan Kenobi in the *Star Wars* franchise. Guinness became a Catholic in 1956, a conversion he wrote about in his memoir, *Blessings in Disguise*.

a potential accomplice. Stolen bullion is hard to hide, but bullion melted down and recast as miniature Eiffel Towers—who would ever suspect it? With masterfully subtle moral probing, Holland suborns Pendlebury and, *voilà*, Burke has his Hare, Butch Cassidy his Sundance Kid.

But the film is not called *The Lavender Hill Duo*, so where does the mob come in? Once the two men have become partners in (theoretical) crime, they realize their woeful inexperience as lawbreakers. They will need help from real criminals. Their nighttime entrapment of two professional burglars, Shorty and Lackery, brims with social comedy based on class distinctions and moral dubieties. The "mob" thus formed is no organized mafia but an ill-assorted quartet of naïve dreamers and practiced ruffians—the ruffians cleverly controlled by the dreamers. However unlikely they may be as a team, with however remote a chance of success, the conspirators proceed to enact their nefarious plan.

It immediately goes wrong, of course, and in all sorts of unexpected ways. Complication leads to complication, and the gathering ironies revolve upon themselves dizzyingly. Pendlebury, the art-lover, would never betray good taste by pinching a Landseer, and although he's robbing the national bank, he cannot bring himself to rob a child. In one especially farcical scene, Holland is paraded from room to room in the Bank of England in order to be praised by various superiors for his fortitude in resisting a robbery he planned himself: "plucky little Holland" (as opposed to plucky little Belgium). Previously a nobody, he is now hailed as a hero; only by defrauding his masters does he gain their recognition.

> Gold is the sovereign o'er all sovereigns.
> —PENDLEBURY

*The Lavender Hill Mob* scooped the 1953 Academy Award for Best Screenplay, written by Tibby Clarke. It is ranked seventeen in the British Film Institute's list of the hundred greatest British films of the twentieth century.

The climax of the caper occurs at the Robert Peel Centenary Exhibition—Robert Peel being the founder of the London police force (hence "bobbies" as the term for British cops). Policemen dressed in Victorian costume join modern-day officers in a madcap chase, first in cars, then on foot. Finally, Holland's conventional appearance comes to his rescue as he darts down the steps of an underground station (again, the Waterloo Line) only to reemerge moments later, blending into the throng of indistinguishable city gents.

"Instead of changing as usual at Charing Cross, I came straight on to Rio de Janeiro." So Holland tells his attentive luncheon companion back in the Brazilian restaurant, at which point the two men rise from the table and leave together, revealing themselves to be handcuffed at the wrist. The companion is a plain-clothes detective, and Holland's whole story turns out to have been his confession following upon a discreet arrest. His plot did fail: he has met his Waterloo.

It should be no surprise that his crime was detected, for *The Lavender Hill Mob* dates from the period of the Hays Code, the film industry's self-regulating set of guidelines concerning moral standards. In the 1950s, it was still taken for granted that even if crime might pay in real life, it shouldn't be shown to pay on screen. One wonders whether the movie would have found a place on the Vatican List if Holland had got away with his heist.

More substantially (from a theological point of view), it is worth considering what it is about heist movies that makes them such a staple. The genre is generally regarded as having begun the year before *Lavender Hill* with John Huston's *The Asphalt Jungle*; it immediately became a popular format and has remained so ever since, some of the more famous examples including *The Thomas Crown Affair*, *The Italian Job*, *Oceans 11*, and *The Usual Suspects*. Though theft is, by definition, a crime, and normally a sin too, somehow cinema audiences still love to watch it being planned and carried out, especially if the means are ingenious and the culprits daring, deserving, or otherwise endearing.

One explanation for our interest in heists is that—as with whodunnits—we like to entertain the possibility of crime in a fictional setting where it can do no real harm. We go through the catharsis of seeing a felony committed and then enjoy order being restored. However, unlike whodunnits, where we are typically on the side of the detective (Holmes, Poirot, Maigret, etc.), heists usually make us root for the would-be criminals. And this indicates that we view theft as less serious than murder.

Why this ranking? The finality of murder is the obvious explanation, but another, more morally intriguing reason might be that we know how randomly fortunes are won and lost and how little they signify moral worth on the part of the winners and losers. Riches are not to men of understanding, says the preacher in the book of Ecclesiastes, "but time and chance happen to them all" (Eccles. 9:11). "Woe to you who are rich," Jesus says (Luke

*The Lavender Hill Mob* was actor Robert Shaw's first film, in which he had a nonspeaking, uncredited bit part as a white-coated chemist. Fifteen years later, he would feature in another movie on the Vatican List, *A Man for All Seasons*, headlining as King Henry VIII. Shaw's best-known role was the shark-hunter Quint in *Jaws* (1975).

> Instead of changing as usual at Charing Cross,
> I came straight on to Rio de Janeiro.
> —HOLLAND

6:24); and again, "It will be hard for a rich person to enter the kingdom of heaven" (Matt. 19:23).

If *we* were rich, of course, we'd manage that hard journey somehow. We'd be the exception. How many of us do, secretly, want to be rich, or at least a little bit richer than we already are? That secret desire presents the most plausible reason both for the popularity of heist movies in general and for the success of *Lavender Hill* in particular. As a comedy, it handles this inner moral equivocation most fittingly. Though we suspect wealth won't make us happy, we still want to give it a try. It *might* just work this time around. With the crisp editing of director Charles Crichton and the sparkling screenplay of Tibby Clarke, we can laugh at Henry Holland's hopes of becoming as rich as Croesus, and thereby laugh quietly at ourselves.

*MW*

## DISCUSSION QUESTIONS

- Bank heist films are popular even though they center on crime. What do you think it is about theft, as opposed to, say, violence or sexual crime, that tends to entertain audiences rather than offending them?

- If you suddenly became very rich, what would you do with your wealth?

- The final reveal shows that Holland has been arrested. If he had got away with his crime, would the film have been better, worse, or no different?

# The Leopard

## 1963

*A sumptuous glance into the final days of an era of European aristocracy set against the backdrop of the* Risorgimento, *or birth of the modern Italian nation.*

Both epic and intimate in scope, *The Leopard* (*Il Gattopardo* in Italian) relays the significance of an epochal transition in Italian history by showing its impact upon a single extraordinary individual: His Excellency Don Fabrizio Corbera, Prince of Salina. Opening with the image of a sun-baked Mediterranean country palace, the film's first spoken words are those of the Rosary, which drift languorously through its open windows. Recited by the members of the manor's upper-crust household assembled in an ornately

> For things to remain the same, everything must change.
> —TANCREDI

painted room before a private altar, the family's prayers are shortly interrupted by the discovery of a dead soldier in the garden and the arrival of a letter announcing the landing of revolutionary military forces on Sicilian shores. Major changes are afoot.

Don Fabrizio, played with regal panache by an elegantly middle-aged Burt Lancaster, wishes to treat the developments with equanimity, but his impetuous nephew Tancredi insists on taking a more active role. He rushes off to join the revolutionaries, discerning in them a counterintuitive set of allies against the bourgeois politicians who would democratize the civil state. "Unless we take a hand, they'll foist a republic upon us," Tancredi insists. "For things to remain the same, everything must change."

This paradox persists across the film's stately, nostalgic immersion in the final days of the Italian *ancien régime.* After meeting Angelica (played by a young Claudia Cardinale), the beautiful daughter of the town's newly elected mayor, Tancredi abandons his pursuit of a matrimonial alliance among the established social elite and instead proposes marriage to this representative of the rising *nouveau riche.* No sooner does the attending priest invoke God's protection on the arrangement than he walks to an old-fashioned barometer mounted on the chamber wall, taps it, and predicts a coming storm.

The disruption and adaptation signaled by this unconventional union sits close to the heart of the story; it is expressed most impressively in the voluptuous and justifiably famous ballroom scene that occupies most of the final third of the film's three hours. Shot over four weeks with nearly five hundred extras arrayed in full period dress, the opulence of this "gold

> Despite his reportedly rakish lifestyle, *The Leopard*'s director, Luchino Visconti, grew up the adoring son of a devout Catholic mother, loved Latin liturgy, and had a Requiem Mass said for him in Rome after his death.

standard of ballroom scenes" is such that *The Leopard* ended up contributing significantly to the bankruptcy of its production company.

Legendary stories abound concerning the lavish expenditure on set. The film's director, Luchino Visconti, an aristocrat born in a palace who could trace his family tree over a dozen centuries back to the Emperor Charlemagne, is reported to have identified deeply with the story, and, according to the film's art director Mario Garbuglia, based the ball upon personal memories of events he witnessed as a child at his family's palazzo in Milan. By all accounts, Visconti was uncompromising in his insistence on historical fidelity in every detail: not only were all the vases filled with real flowers (even those out of focus in a shot) but a florist brought them in from San Remo every two or three days because Visconti did not like the flowers in Sicily. When it came to fabrics for costumes, Visconti would be brought samples without price tags, feel them one by one, and without fail choose the most expensive one. When Burt Lancaster arrived in Sicily early in preparation for his role, he was introduced to a handful of the island's remaining aristocrats so he could study their mannerisms. However, when it came time to shoot, he based his performance principally upon Visconti himself. Apparently, there was no one more aristocratic than him!

At the level of the story, *The Leopard*'s ballroom sequence provides an opportunity for Don Fabrizio to come to terms with "the end"—not only the sweeping sociopolitical recalibrations unfolding before his eyes but also his own mortality. He takes in at a glance the doll-like, homely scions of the elite

jumping on a silk-covered bed, and sinks a little into himself. "These frequent marriages between cousins do not improve the stock," he laments. "They look like monkeys ready to clamber up the chandeliers." The prince then observes the sparkling beauty (and unrefined social bearing) of Tancredi's fiancée, whom he describes as a white swan in a pool of frogs.

Then Don Fabrizio and Angelica waltz. It is a compelling dramatic moment: the last dance of the old and the first dance of the new, as the classes these characters represent take on changing roles in the history of the nation. Don Fabrizio stands for the old regime and its ancient yet fading glory, and circles here in poised, delicate union with the daughter of the wealthy social upstarts presently ushering in a more egalitarian age.

The significance of the film's title comes into play here and recalls a conversation between Don Fabrizio and a visitor to his palazzo from the newly forming parliament in Turin. The visitor is a small man who wears a comb-over and has come to petition the prince to become a senator in the wake of the annexation of—ahem, the unification with, he corrects himself—Sicily. The prince declines. "We were the leopards, the lions. Those who will take our place will be jackals and sheep," he laments. "I belong to an unfortunate generation, straddling two worlds, and ill at ease in both."

Romantic, nostalgic, and poignantly plaintive, Don Fabrizio's withdrawal from public affairs signals the conviction threaded throughout *The Leopard* that no matter how things might appear to change, including the far-reaching innovations of Don Fabrizio's day, such alterations will eventually

> We were the leopards, the lions. Those who will take our place will be jackals and sheep.
> —DON FABRIZIO

circle back and remain more or less the same. Historically speaking, this does seem true of the *Risorgimento*, whose more revolutionary ambitions are considered by many historians to have failed: at its conclusion, the Italian territory we know today was no longer a feudal aristocracy but a constitutional monarchy, yet this apparently momentous shift arguably only transferred power from one group of elites to another. The demise of the movement's more radical goals is indicated in the film when a group of soldiers leaves the ball early to line up a firing squad for the revolutionary hero who landed in the film's opening scene.

Giuseppe di Lampedusa's 1958 novel of the same name remains one of the bestselling Italian novels of all time. However, when it first came out, it was poorly received by representatives of the Church: Cardinal Ernesto Ruffini, the Archbishop of Palermo, cited the book, along with the mafia, as one of the principal contributors to the dishonor of Sicily.

In the same moment, Don Fabrizio exits the ball to stand alone beneath the stars. He quietly appeals for an appointment with something more lasting than the ephemera of his world, just after a child walks past ringing a bell that heralds a priest carrying the Blessed Sacrament to a villager in need of Last Rites.

This juxtaposition of two types of heavenly body—the stars and the consecrated Eucharistic Host—brings to mind an earlier exchange between Don Fabrizio and the Jesuit priest who serves as his *de facto* family chaplain. Standing in the prince's study between a pair of telescopes, the priest makes a half-hearted attempt to rebuke the prince for his moral deficiencies and bleak view of human history, to which the prince responds, "The Church has been promised immortality.

> These frequent marriages between cousins
> do not improve the stock.
> —DON FABRIZIO

We, as a social class, have not. . . . We have no obligations. But the Church has, because she is destined not to die."

An amateur astronomer, the prince treats the stars as symbols of what is immutable, and contrasts them with the social and political turbulence roiling around him. As such, his final appeal to the heavens might be understood as a hope for the kind of revolution that will not overthrow the prevailing political regime but trace back full circle, like the stars revolving in their orbits, and put the ruling class back in its accustomed place.

On the other hand, as Don Fabrizio acknowledges an otherworldly reality embodied by the Church, here and in the film's final scene, his implicit prayer for a good death—for himself and the social class he represents—echoes where the film begins, with the Rosary and supplications to the Blessed Virgin Mary: "Pray for us sinners, now and at the hour of our death." An end must come for all mortal flesh, but such ends may be transfigured into something graceful, this conclusion suggests, when embraced with humility.

When shooting the ballroom scene, wardrobe and makeup would begin at two in the afternoon, rehearsals followed at six in the evening, and shooting continued all through the night, often until sunrise, not unlike the aristocratic revelries it represents.

Why watch *The Leopard*? Quite simply, it is a beautiful film—and no less beautiful for its consistently mixed tonalities of hope and happiness simultaneously realized and deferred. It is an entrancing, almost overwhelmingly baroque farewell to a nearly forgotten age of privilege and refinement. It is also a masterpiece of Italian filmmaking that conveys a sense, however fleeting, of the true gentility and proper princeliness that is fitting to all those who are brothers and sons, sisters and daughters of the Prince of Peace and King of Kings. From the aristocratic prerogatives of a Don Fabrizio, prince of this earth, we might discern a hint of that real regality that reigns everlastingly in heaven—especially when they are admired not simply as ends in themselves but as icons of a more complex and counterintuitive kind of kingship that encompasses, exceeds, and periodically, history suggests, overturns them.

*DPB*

## DISCUSSION QUESTIONS

- "For things to remain the same, everything must change." Is there anything in this world not subject to change?

- The *Catechism of the Catholic Church* teaches, "The Christian faithful are those who, inasmuch as they have been incorporated in Christ through Baptism, have been constituted as the people of God; for this reason, since they have become sharers in Christ's priestly, prophetic, and royal office in their own manner, they are called to exercise the mission which God has entrusted to the Church to fulfill in the world." In what ways are you specifically called to be a prince or princess in the kingdom of God?

- Is it possible to make a good death? What would this involve?

# *Little Women*

## 1933

*An adaptation of the classic Louisa May Alcott novel following the fortunes of the March family's four daughters as they grow up in nineteenth-century New England.*

The Vatican List describes its forty-five titles as "some important films" but does not elaborate on the kind of importance that each possesses. *Little Women* is important for being an early "talkie," and we will have more to say about that subject at the end of this commentary.

Another aspect of its importance pertains to its ensemble female cast; male performers play only supporting roles to Marmee March and her four daughters. Her husband is away

Christopher Columbus!
—JO'S FAVORITE EXCLAMATION

with the Union Army during the American Civil War, and the family's struggles in his absence provide the main action of the story. *Little Women* demonstrated that a movie could foreground female perspectives and succeed both critically and commercially; when it came out in 1933, it was one of film industry's biggest hits to date.

It is also important in being a Katharine Hepburn film (she plays the headstrong second daughter, Jo), for Hepburn would go on to have a phenomenal career as a Hollywood leading lady, headlining movies for over sixty years and receiving four Academy Awards, the most ever won by a performer. In 1999, the American Film Institute named her the greatest female screen legend in cinema history.

*Little Women* is directed by George Cukor, with whom Hepburn made ten films, and who had a directorial role (uncredited) in another title on the Vatican List, *The Wizard of Oz*. The Alcott novel from which the story is adapted has a strong religious tone, and this carries through into the Academy Award–winning screenplay. Marmee's daughters, who as little girls had used rag-bag burdens when playing the part of Christian from Bunyan's *Pilgrim's Progress*, now have "real burdens" of various kinds—professional, relational, medical—but their heaviest burdens are moral. Meg, Jo, Beth, and Amy must learn how to deal with, respectively, envy, wildness, fear, and selfishness. In the opening shot of the movie, a unit of soldiers marches past the United States Christian Commission (a charitable agency doling out clothes and food to needy people) in Concord, Massachusetts. Helping inside the commission, Marmee serves a poor old man who has already lost two sons in the war; a third has been captured, and a fourth is sick in hospital. This quartet of sons (whom we never meet) serves a structural purpose, anticipating Marmee's four daughters, each of whom will soon be setting out to fight her own individual battle. The family name, March, and the place name, Concord, take on new significance.

A letter received from their absent father drives home the point: he charges the girls to do their duty faithfully, fight their bosom enemies bravely, and conquer themselves beautifully. Jo's story dominates in this respect, for she is "rough and wild" and has much to learn about the value of suffering. Jo embarrasses her sisters with her romping, tomboyish ways: she whistles, climbs through windows, hops fences, and loves to expostulate, "Christopher Columbus!" When reproved for her language, she defends it: "I like good strong words that mean something." She'll leave her hair down till she's a hundred if that's the way to avoid becoming a prim and proper lady. She takes the (male) roles of both villain and hero in her own play, *The Witch's Curse*, twirling mustaches one moment and buckling swashes the next.

Jo throws snowballs at the window of the neighboring house to attract the attention of the boy who lives there, Laurie. She and he hit it off—literally—engaging in spirited swordplay that ends only when Jo stumbles and falls. "Are you hurt?" asks Laurie. "Nothing ever hurts me," says Jo, adding that she wishes she could play the part of Hamlet for the fencing scene.

*Little Women* was the third adaptation of Alcott's story for the big screen, following silent versions in 1917 and 1918. It has since been adapted a further three times as a period drama for English-language cinema: in 1949 (with Elizabeth Taylor as Amy), 1994 (with Winona Ryder as Jo), and 2019 (with Emma Watson as Meg).

Hamlet, of course, does not survive his own story, and major challenges are about to beset the happy life of Miss Josephine March. Her older sister Meg has fallen in love with Laurie's tutor, Mr. Brooke. Meg used to tell Jo everything, but now she confides in someone else. Jo has never come across anything so horrid. "Why do things always have to change just when they're perfect?"

Then comes news that Mr. March is ill in Washington and Marmee must go to his hospital bedside. To help pay for the trip, Jo sells her own hair to a wigmaker and stoutly maintains the advantages of a shorn crop: "It's boyish, becoming, and easy to keep in order." Later she cries bitter tears—not over her father's illness or her mother's absence but over the loss of her hair.

Worse is to follow. Beth contracts scarlet fever and teeters on the brink of death. Jo prays earnestly for her sister, and, though she pulls through, she is now a permanent invalid, much to Jo's puzzlement: "Why doesn't she get strong?"

And then Laurie proposes marriage to Jo, ruining their friendship, for "it would be a lie to say I do if I don't." She gives him space to get over her refusal by going off to New York, where she hopes to find fresh material for her writings. She has success with blood-and-thunder melodramas in periodicals such as *The Volcano* and *The Last Sensation*.

Ensconced in the big city, she meets an older man, Professor Bhaer, who is teaching German to the children of the family Jo is lodging with. Clever and fun, he gets the children, including two girls, to play soldiers: "Forward, march!" He can also play the piano and sing romantic songs: "My senses fail;

> I'll take the popovers.
> —AMY, GLOOMILY, AS THE FAMILY CARRY THEIR CHRISTMAS MEAL TO THE HOME OF POOR NEIGHBORS

a burning fire devours me!" He calls Jo "my little friend" and recognizes her ardent spirit. But the Professor is distinctly unimpressed by her stories of villains, murderers, and "such women!" She is devastated by his critique and weeps, but thanks him for his honesty: "If I can't stand the truth, I'm not worth anything." He proffers a stick of peppermint that she takes contentedly.

This moment, though it passes without dramatic emphasis, really marks Jo's conquest of her rough, wild ways. In allowing herself to be treated as a child who needs comforting with candy, she effectively admits that she is not the invulnerable captain of her soul that she had supposed herself to be. She becomes able to relax in ways she hasn't known since her father went off to war, as Professor Bhaer shows her the New York sights and she blossoms under his guidance. At the museum she wants to be a sculptor, at the circus she is amazed by the bareback rider, and at the opera she is entranced by the diva. Wonder and opportunity flood into her life. Her neckline plunges as she learns openheartedness.

Her maturation is confirmed when Beth has a serious relapse. Beth tells Jo, "You mustn't be afraid. . . . I'm not afraid anymore." When Beth dies, Jo shows herself to be no longer like the caged bird that twittered frustratedly in her New York room, but a seagull flying far and wide, as Beth has described her. She understands now that change is part of life. When Laurie and Amy announce their engagement, she is happy for them. Jo knows that she can't return to the happy old playful times she enjoyed with Laurie, and she doesn't expect to: "We never can be boy and girl again. . . . We're

The interior of the March family home was modeled upon the house in Concord, Massachusetts, where Louisa May Alcott grew up with her three sisters.

man and woman now." And having achieved womanhood, she is ready to accept Professor Bhaer's marriage proposal. "Welcome home!" she says (the last words of the movie), as she invites him into the bosom of her family in Concord.

The film's screenplay, by husband and wife writing team Victor Heerman and Sarah Y. Mason, won the 1934 Academy Award for Best Writing, Adaptation.

Jo's acceptance of change in her own life reflects something of the importance of *Little Women* in the history of cinema. It was not the first talkie (that distinction is usually conferred on *The Jazz Singer* from six years earlier), but it is the earliest one on the Vatican List. That talkies should have replaced silent movies now seems as natural and inevitable as adulthood succeeding childhood, but that was not how it was seen at the time. Though technically advanced, the early talkies were artistically a step backward. The first microphones were immovable, meaning that action had to be anchored to their location. Cameras, housed in soundproof booths so that their whirring noise would not be recorded, could no longer range freely. As a result, talkies appeared static and more like filmed stage plays than the grand visual spectacles that audiences had come to admire in works such as *Napoléon*. In 1930, British critic Paul Rotha declared the talkie to be "a degenerate and misguided attempt to destroy the real use of the film and cannot be accepted as coming within the true boundaries of the cinema."

By 1933, however, talkies were triumphant, whatever their drawbacks, and *Little Women* made the most of the new genre. This helps explain its heavy load of dialogue, for in this transitional period audio technology was exploited to excess; the principle "show, don't tell" only gradually took root. It also helps explain the somewhat stagey performances, with cast members at times projecting their voices to the back of

> PROFESSOR BHAER: I have nothing to give, but my heart so full and . . . and these empty hands.
> JO [taking his hands in hers]: Not empty now.

the stalls, not realizing that the microphone would do most of the work for them.

As noted above, Jo asks at one point, "Why do things always have to change just when they're perfect?" The change from silent pictures to talking films is not the subject of Cukor's movie; later titles, such as *The Artist* (2011) and *Downton Abbey: A New Era* (2022), have tackled it well. But *Little Women* does dramatize the perennial tension between change and continuity that is a feature of all human experience, including the unfolding history of cinema, in which it occupies such a significant place. Growing pleasures and growing pains are both exhibited in and exemplified by *Little Women*.

*MW*

## DISCUSSION QUESTIONS

- The artistic principle "show, don't tell" has application in all forms of creative fiction, albeit with certain differences depending on the genre (novel, stage, screen). Do you think the principle is sound? Why or why not?

- Which of the four March daughters do you most sympathize with?

- How do you regard change? Are you keen for novelty or do you desire to maintain the status quo?

# *Metropolis*

## 1927

*A compelling early science fiction dystopia.*

With its gripping visual style and bold use of biblical symbolism, *Metropolis* is one of the most intriguing and enjoyable silent movies on the Vatican Film List. Promoted at the time as "the costliest and most ambitious picture ever," its vividly imagined hypermodern future offers an impassioned argument about the dehumanizing effects of modern industry. It also paints a stirring cinematic portrait of what theologians call *kenosis*, that voluntary self-abandonment which is not content with privilege or superiority but seeks out the lowly to raise them up higher. *Metropolis* thus offers not only one of the great achievements of the silent era

> Into the depths—to be with my brothers.
> —FREDER

of motion pictures but also an insight into that compassionate fellow-feeling that is, on the one hand, indispensable for any stable civil society, and on the other, an essential element in all genuinely God-like love.

Loosely based upon Thea von Harbou's novel of the same name, *Metropolis* opens with images of a modern mechanized city—pumping pistons, spinning cogs, a ticking clock—and then cuts to rows of identically dressed factory workers marching into elevators and descending into the depths like automatons. It then leaps as high as these subterranean laborers are low, to the highest of the city's many skyscrapers, and introduces the film's protagonist, Freder, the pampered only son of the industrialist overseer of the city. He starts out luxuriating in a life of dissipation, but everything changes for him the day a young woman appears at the penthouse and bids him gaze upon a swarm of untidy children she has brought up from the working-class underworld. She names them his unrecognized brothers, and, cut to the heart, Freder spontaneously abandons his pleasure nest and descends into the nether regions to throw in his lot with his fellow citizens.

In 2001, *Metropolis* was the first film to be inscribed on UNESCO's Memory of the World Register, a compendium of documents deemed of "world significance and outstanding universal value."

Shortly upon arrival, Freder witnesses a giant machine overheat and kill many of the operators. Transformed by his feverish imagination into a gargantuan idol—described in the film's intertitles as "Moloch," the

> The character of C-3PO in *Star Wars* was partly inspired by the aesthetic of this film's *Maschinenmensch*.

name of an Old Testament pagan god—the machine gobbles up row after row of workers into its cavernous maw like so much raw material on an infernal assembly line. Freder watches in horror and then tries to relay his distress to his father, but, failing to inspire any system-wide reform, he elects to relieve the distress of at least one tormented worker and takes his place at the machine. The device resembles a kind of torture rack on which he eventually ends up stretched cruciform, crying out in an echo of our Lord's cry of dereliction from the cross: "Father! Father! Will ten hours never end??!!"

Such a deliberate parallel between the hero of this story and the Savior of mankind finds echoes elsewhere in *Metropolis*, as when Freder is explicitly identified as "the mediator" to whom the weary workers can look for deliverance from their wretched circumstances. When their shift concludes, Freder accompanies the other exhausted workers into some catacombs located even deeper than their underground factory. There, backed by a candlelit altar and numerous crosses, the same young woman who brought Freder the message of fraternity (whose name, it turns out, is Maria) conducts a kind of church service featuring a sermon on the "legend" of the Tower of Babel (which is, incidentally, the same name as Freder's father's industrial headquarters). The way she tells it, this biblical episode becomes a cautionary tale about class conflict, as "the hands that built the Tower of Babel knew nothing of the dream of the brain that had conceived it. . . . People spoke the same language but could no longer understand each other." The homily concludes with a forward-looking appeal for someone to reconcile this

discord, and then, spotting Freder in the crowd, Maria greets him with a chaste kiss as this savior-figure "finally come."

You'll have to watch to see how it all plays out, but the twists and turns that follow include a diabolical doppelganger made in Maria's image, variously described as the *Maschinen-mensch* ("Machine Man") or the eschatological "whore of Babylon" who feasts on the blood of the saints. There is an uprising by the workers against their white-collar oppressors and a spectacularly disastrous flood sequence that features a veritable horde of extras (advertisements at the time boasted over thirty-six thousand). And then, in the climactic image of the film, Freder, "the heart," stands hand in hand with both his overlord father, "the head," and the leader of the workers, "the hands," thus fulfilling the epigrammatic imperative that appears at the film's opening and closing: "The mediator between head and hands must be the heart!"

So, in what way does *Metropolis* offer a moving image of the self-emptying love of God? In the character of Freder, we encounter a man who is by origin and birthright ruler over men, yet by conviction and choice becomes brother of all. Rather like the God of Christians who holds back nothing of himself but dives right into our mess and assumes it as his own, so too Freder voluntarily descends from empyreal heights to share in the lot of the grasping mass of unhappy humanity. It is also fitting that Freder is symbolically iden-tified with "the heart" in this fictional dystopia, motivated as he is by a visceral compassion that, like a lover or "a true

> The hands that built the Tower of Babel knew nothing of the dream of the brain that had conceived it. . . . People spoke the same language, but could no longer understand each other.
>
> —MARIA

friend [who] sticks closer than one's nearest kin" (Prov. 18:24), would rather be together and temporarily distressed than remain far off and self-satisfied. When theologians sometimes speak of God's "divine condescension" in becoming man, we might imagine this exact sort of solidarity beating, so to speak, in the Sacred Heart of Jesus over the distress of humanity in the real dystopia of a fallen world.

Even after flopping at the box office, *Metropolis* went on to exert a massive influence on subsequent filmmaking. For example, its perspective on the dehumanizing, even diabolic character of modern industry is repeated in a comic register in *Modern Times*, and a similar insistence on the need for wide-ranging social and economic reform is a subtext in Italian neorealist films like *Rome, Open City* and *Bicycle Thieves*.

Further, it is part of the mystery of the post-baptismal life that the same impulse, Christ's own love, "has been poured into our hearts through the Holy Spirit" (Rom. 5:5). To be sure, no Christian is called to become, like Freder, the heroic-hearted reconciler of all of humanity, and trying to love simply on one's own initiative, "without God, before God, and not in accordance with God," as St. Maximus the Confessor puts it, is a good way to get our hearts to break or, even worse, grow cold. But when we learn the secret of loving from the heart of our hearts—"through him, with him, and in him"—we will have found the only really lasting way to relieve the deficits of

The mediator between head and hands must be the heart!
—INTERTITLE

goodness and justice we discover in the world. We will have also discovered the only really sane reason to leave comfort and satisfaction and seek out suffering and unhappiness: that genuinely supernatural superpower that we are given to share, even in the middle of a this-worldly metropolis, more ordinarily referred to as divine love.

*DPB*

*(Content advisory: contains a few scenes of partial nudity)*

### DISCUSSION QUESTIONS

- According to *Metropolis*, are modern industry and technology intrinsically evil? Why or why not?

- "Though he was in the form of God, [he] did not regard equality with God as something to be exploited, but emptied himself, taking the form of a slave, being born in human likeness. And being found in human form, he humbled himself and became obedient to the point of death—even death on a cross" (Phil. 2:6–8). In what ways does Freder offer a fitting (or unfitting) image of Jesus Christ?

- Inspired by Freder's compassion and solidarity, what might it look like to pursue civic renewal today? Is there any common ground—a "shared heart"— between you and those you most disagree with? What might it look like to love even one's political opponents as Jesus Christ would, who died for us "while we still were sinners"? (Rom. 5:8).

# *Modern Times*

## 1936

*Charlie Chaplin as the Little Tramp struggles to find his way
in the world of modern industry and business, until he finds
friendship and leaves it all behind.*

I t was inevitable—and entirely right—that the Vatican Film
List should include at least one movie by Charlie Chaplin,
the celebrated British actor, director, writer, and producer.
If the cultural legacy of the first century of cinema could be
summed up by a single representative figure, perhaps the
strongest contender would be Chaplin's iconic Little Tramp.
The Tramp made his debut in 1914 and went on to appear in
numerous short films and feature-length titles, becoming
in the process something of a universal folk hero. Like King

> Actions speak louder than words.
> —THE MACHINE

Henry VIII, the only monarch known by his *shape*, the Tramp was immediately identifiable by his silhouette: bowler hat, tight jacket, baggy trousers, big shoes, bendy cane. The "little fellow," as Chaplin called him, was something of a cross between a court jester from a royal household and an Everyman character from a medieval morality play: part innocent clown, part regular guy, endlessly put-upon but utterly irrepressible and subtly subversive. The Tramp dominated Hollywood in the era of silent movies until Chaplin officially retired him in the film we have now to discuss.

*Modern Times* describes itself, in its title card, as "a story of industry, of individual enterprise—humanity crusading in the pursuit of happiness." As "a story of industry," *Modern Times* satirically depicts the working conditions in a large, impersonal, mechanized factory. The Tramp, billed as "a factory worker," spends his days with a wrench in each hand, tightening nuts on pieces of metal that pass him by on the assembly line every few seconds. The endless repetition of this physical movement sends his body into spasm, which leads to much visual comedy, but also makes the Tramp positively hare-brained—the wrenches becoming his ears—and he ends up hospitalized with a nervous breakdown.

On release from the hospital, the factory worker finds himself unemployed and alone. This is where "individual enterprise" comes to the fore. As he tries to make his way in the world, he is tossed up and down on the wheel of fortune, as earlier he had been rotated on the cogs of the factory's massive machines. His adventures and misadventures include unwittingly leading a communist march, inadvertently taking drugs in jail, being hailed as a hero after foiling a prison break, working in a shipyard but accidentally launching a ship, and so on. In the course of these vicissitudes, he encounters another lonely person, a young woman (played by Paulette Goddard) billed simply as "a gamin"—an old-fashioned word for a street urchin—who is also demonstrating her individual enterprise. She is an orphan, desperately hungry, and on the run from the police after stealing bread.

An alternative ending was shot in which the gamin becomes a nun and the Tramp has to live without her. Chaplin eventually abandoned this footage, perhaps feeling that such an ending was too downbeat for the Tramp's final outing, and perhaps also nodding toward his own off-screen relationship with Paulette Goddard, whom he married secretly in the same year that *Modern Times* was released.

The Tramp and the gamin join forces, marking the start of "humanity crusading in the pursuit of happiness." She takes him to share her shack on the edge of town, then helps him land a job as a singing waiter in the café where she works as a dancer. Things are looking up, but when the police get on the gamin's trail again, the couple are forced to flee. In the final scene ("Dawn"), the Tramp urges her to smile despite all their misfortunes, and they walk off together hand in hand along a road leading to the hills.

The Vatican List categorizes *Modern Times* under the heading of "Art" rather than either "Religion" or "Values." It is easy to see why it is not included under "Religion," for there is little or none of that on display. As for "Values," the film implicitly asserts the dignity of the individual by satirizing the dehumanizing effects of machine culture: the opening shot of a flock of sheep blending into a crowd of factory workers makes this point clearly enough. (Readers who want

> Sing!! Never mind the words!
> —THE GAMIN

to explore Catholic teaching on such matters might refer here to *Rerum Novarum*, the encyclical of Pope Leo XIII on capital and labor.)

The fact that there is one black sheep at the center of the otherwise entirely white herd indicates how the Tramp is going to assert his individuality and not allow it to be crushed by the system. And yet even the Tramp cannot flourish entirely on his own. He needs the gamin to help him, and in this respect, we might read the film as promoting also the value of friendship. It is not good for man to be alone.

Notwithstanding these values, *Modern Times* is indeed most interestingly considered under the heading of "Art," for it can be seen as symbolizing the watershed moment in the history of cinema when silent movies finally and fully surrendered, as it were, to the talkies. Talking had first been heard in *The Jazz Singer* (1927), but silent movies continued to be produced throughout the next decade. Chaplin was initially resistant to the new audio technology, not least because early microphones were immovable, which resulted in on-screen action becoming static. But he saw which way the wind was blowing, and in *Modern Times* gives way to the coming medium in an artistically ingenious and thought-provoking fashion.

The music playing under the final scene, composed by Chaplin and David Raksin, was used as the tune for the hit song "Smile," first recorded by Nat King Cole in 1954. The "King of Pop," Michael Jackson, called it his favorite song, and a version of it was performed at his memorial service after his untimely death.

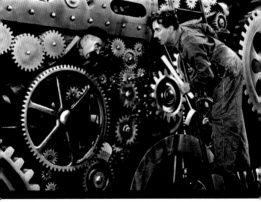

In the course of this mostly silent picture, we actually hear a number of human voices, but they are mechanically mediated. In the factory, we hear (and see) the boss speaking not "live" in his own person but only as an Orwellian Big Brother figure, via a tannoy or a huge screen. This same boss invites a salesman into his office to explain the merits of a new wonder-gadget that will feed workers while they remain at the assembly line. However, the salesman utters not a word and instead starts up a gramophone that emits the sound of a recorded voice proclaiming itself to be "your speaker, the mechanical salesman." Then, with a beautifully involved irony, this same recorded voice says, "Let us demonstrate with one of your workers, for actions speak louder than words." And of course, the guinea pig for this (totally useless) feeding machine will be the Tramp, in one of the funniest scenes of the movie.

All of these moments are leading to the climax when the Tramp will finally speak in his own person. For over two decades, global audiences had seen this character but never heard him. What will he sound like, and what will he say? Chaplin cleverly builds tension as the moment of truth looms. The Tramp prepares himself to deliver not a speech but a song. He will sing it in the café where he works as a waiter. The gamin helps him write the words on his loose cuffs. Then, in the course of his introductory gesticulations, he loses the cuffs and can't remember the lyrics. In an intertitle, the gamin urges, "Sing!! Never mind the words!"

The scene where the Tramp revolves in the cogs of a large machine is recreated in the hit comedy *Paddington 2* (2017). Here the hero is not trapped but released by the gears: Paddington uses the workings of a massive clock to spring himself from prison.

> Buck up—never say die. We'll get along!
> —THE TRAMP

He proceeds to improvise and finds himself singing . . . *non-sense*. It could have been a disaster, but the meaningless words are delivered with such perfect timing and accompanied with so many amusing gestures and grimaces, not to mention such waggishly emphatic music, that the café audience roars with laughter. The movie audience is naturally prompted to do the same.

But who is having the last laugh? Surely it is Chaplin himself, who brilliantly shows that actions do indeed speak louder than words. Even as he capitulates to the talkie genre, he undercuts the ground of its supposed superiority. Audible, intelligible words, he demonstrates, aren't necessary for entertainment. The film thus raises a very telling question about the whole idea of technological progress. Is the latest thing the best thing, or is it just different—better in some ways and worse in others? Which is to be preferred and why: the olden days or modern times?

*MW*

### DISCUSSION QUESTIONS

- What was lost, if anything, when talkies came to dominate cinema?

- Many kinds of labor are menial and repetitive. Is there anything especially dehumanizing about factory work?

- If your heart is aching, should you smile? If so, why?

# *Napoléon*

### 1927

*A silent historical epic portraying—in technically innovative ways and at great length—the early life and career of Napoleon Bonaparte.*

Napoleon Bonaparte, born in 1769, was Emperor of the French and one of the most successful military leaders in human history. He dominated Europe in the early nineteenth century, not only governing his homeland but also gaining extensive control of Italy, Germany, Spain, and Poland. This film, though it bears Napoleon's name as if for a biopic, covers only the first twenty-seven years of his life, before he became head of the French Republic.

> Either I command or I say nothing.
> —NAPOLEON

The story starts in 1781 with the protagonist's extraordinary strategic ability as a schoolboy to organize snowball fights. It proceeds to depict various leaders and episodes of the French Revolution (which began in 1789, involving Napoleon only peripherally). It ends with his marriage to Josephine de Beauharnais and his first Italian campaign. All the better-known episodes from his later years—arresting the pope, invading Russia, losing the Battle of Waterloo, suffering exile in St. Helena (where he died at age fifty-one)—are left out of account.

The title is given on screen as *Napoléon vu par Abel Gance* ("Napoleon as seen by Abel Gance"). Gance, a young French filmmaker who wrote, produced, directed, and acted in the movie, canned about three hundred hours of footage. His initial edit, screened in 1927 at the Apollo Theatre, Paris, clocked in at over nine hours. Subsequently, he made several shorter cuts, and numerous other editions are extant. The two most readily available today are the 1980 edit by Francis Ford Coppola (three hours and forty-three minutes, with music by Carmine Coppola) and the 2016 digitally remastered version by Kevin Brownlow (five hours and thirty-two minutes, with music by Carl Davis).

*Napoléon* appears in the "Art" section of the Vatican List, which is entirely to be expected, for its claim to fame comes from its many innovative techniques, which were hugely influential on other filmmakers, such as the Soviet director Sergei Eisenstein (*Battleship Potemkin*) and the auteurs of the French New Wave in the 1950s. Working at a time when most shots were static, Gance decided to free things up, introducing cameras that were handheld, strapped to the back of a horse, or

Abel Gance acted in his own film, playing the part of the Revolutionary leader Louis Antoine de Saint-Just, who supervised so many sentences of death that he was known as "the Archangel of the Reign of Terror."

even fixed on a swinging pendulum. This process of liberation he continued in the editing suite, where he introduced, or at any rate maximized the use of, extremely fast cutting, superimposition, split screens, and mosaic shots. Not content with novelties in filming and editing, Gance minted a new kind of multi-screen projection named Polyvision. The final section of *Napoléon* folds out into a panoramic triptych, where three panels bear sometimes a single extended image and sometimes three different images at once.

Gance felt he "lacked space in certain scenes. . . . The picture was too small for me. Even a big picture was too small." His boundary-pushing creativity affected the way he regarded the cinema audience itself. Gance didn't want spectators to maintain a critical distance but to be "amazed victims" of what transpired on screen. Indeed, the very distinction between on-screen and off-screen was something he wanted to dissolve as far as possible. He considered extras to be the most important members of his cast because such untrained performers, if they could be sufficiently caught up in the emotion of a scene, would be more easily able to infect the audience with the same emotion. His aim was to have an audience feeling *alongside* the people on screen, not just *for* the people on screen: "Enthusiasm is essential in the cinema. It must be communicated to people like a flame." Thus enflamed, viewers would find their perspective merging with the perspective of the people in the story. The audience would, in a manner of speaking, *become* Napoleon, and the result would be a kind of "reality squared."

The three " Gods " of the Revolution—Marat, Danton and Robespierre—and below, that son of the Revolution who was destined to become all powerful Emperor.

So intense was Gance's belief in the transformative powers of cinema that he viewed it as "a moral religion," and in the 1920s he dreamt of uniting the film industry with the League of Nations in order to promote pacifism across the globe. In *Napoléon*, the protagonist's stated objective is a world at peace: he announces his aim of abolishing borders and creating "a Universal Republic." Gance's grandiose political plans were not entirely unlike those he attributed to the conqueror; the means differed, but the ends were similar—a worldwide empire, led by a true *enthusiast* (literally, "one possessed by a god"). Gance even once described Napoleon as "the world's greatest director." The extent to which he saw himself in his subject or vice versa is unclear, but the parallels are too striking to pass over. Both men appear to be in the grip of insatiable passion: Napoleon for lands to rule, Gance for facts about Napoleon to commit to world-transforming celluloid.

The cast is huge. Here are just some of the historical personages that are put before us: Murat, Marat, Robespierre, Danton, Barras, La Bussiére, Fouché, Couthon. When Napoleon turns up at the headquarters of his Italian army, the intertitle tells us that "present were Sérurier, La Harpe, Victor, Cervoni, Mouret, Doujard, Donmartin, Joubert and, dominating this group of illustrious men, the great Masséna and the invincible Augereau." Groups such as the Girondins, the Hébertists, and the Sectionnaires are identified but not explained. The wealth of factual information, like the storm of visual innovation and the ceaseless musical accompaniment, is designed so to overwhelm us that resistance becomes futile. Conquest is inevitable.

> Bread, olives, and silence!
> —NAPOLEON, PLACING A RESTAURANT ORDER

Other intertitles dotted throughout the movie remind us of the importance of the man whose fate we are following. One reads: "Napoleon's soul, soaring on a fantastic dream, plays with the clouds at destroying and at building worlds." Another: "His eagle eye inscribes in the Italian sky all his desires and victories." A third tells us that Napoleon is "being triumphantly carried to the Heights of History." The unembarrassed magniloquence of these statements is bold, to put it mildly.

> *Napoléon* never had a general release in cinemas. It received numerous special screenings instead, using a variety of different length edits, and there is no official, definitive cut.

There are some attempts at humor—most notably, Napoleon's clumsy wooing of Josephine. An epic film undoubtedly needs comic relief (witness Merry, Pippin, and Gimli in *The Lord of the Rings*), but having the hero's romantic ham-fistedness serve as a pressure valve to his own grandeur is a risky move; it jeopardizes the respect with which we otherwise regard him. Henry V (in Kenneth Branagh's classic film of that title) could get away with bungling his courtship of the French princess because Shakespeare's monarch is a three-dimensional character, and Catherine of Valois has in any case been established as a playful personality. Gance's Josephine, however, is more like a goddess, and Napoleon is portrayed in a mythic, not a realistic, light. His personality is that of "granite heated in a volcano," symbolically one with eagles and fire. He is played (in adulthood) by Albert Dieudonné, whose inexpressive face can take almost any emotion the audience is led by the context to find in it. This works well most of the time: a legendary figure needs a certain impersonality. But when a lady asks, "What's that noise?" and the reply flashes up, "It's Bonaparte entering history again, madame," the snort of laughter it invites imperils the seriousness of the whole project.

Derision is probably a more likely reaction if the film is seen at home, on a small screen, where world-shaking grandeur is harder to receive and accept. *Napoléon* ideally ought to be viewed in a vast, packed auditorium, accompanied by a symphony orchestra under the baton of a conductor whose sincerity is as boundless as his exuberance. Then the monumental nature of the movie, its operatic passion, and its immersive splendor can be felt as intended.

Immersion is key to Gance's directorial purpose. He does not immerse the audience by pulling it quietly into an atmospheric pool, where every tonal shade and flicker of an actor's eyelid is carefully calibrated to mesmerize: he does so by means of an overwhelming tsunami of sensory impressions that have something of a drowning—or, to put it more positively, baptizing—effect. The frenetic cutting, the laying of images over images, the multiple perspectives, the shaky cameras, the musical maelstrom—all of these techniques leave the audience helplessly surrounded and transformed. It is like an early version of virtual reality.

Gance could not contain himself or his art any more than his Napoleon could contain his passion for Josephine and conquest. But is it love or power that is being sought? In one scene, Josephine's face appears superimposed upon an image of the globe; evidently, she means the world to her husband. But is she really a wife, or just a target of his *libido dominandi*, which elsewhere manifests itself in a desire to sweep down masterfully into Europe's fertile plains? One intertitle reads: "And now, turning towards Italy,

Albert Dieudonné acted in four other Gance movies. After his death in Paris in 1976, he was buried, as he had wished, wearing his Napoleon costume.

> When you are silent you are irresistible.
> —NAPOLEON TO JOSEPHINE

the tempter showed the Promised Land to which he would lead them." Napoleon as Satan or as Moses—which is it?

Gance's hero is superhuman, driven, constantly wanting to surpass himself in a quasi-divine manner. He "is everywhere, sees everything." Mirroring that passion, Gance cannot get enough of him and cannot share too much of him. He originally planned a massive six-part treatment of the whole of Bonaparte's life but exhausted the budget for the series in shooting just two-thirds of what was planned to go in the first movie.

*Napoléon* is a genuine landmark in the history of cinema. Landmarks come in many forms, including follies, and this film has something of the *folie de grandeur* about it. Never mind the quality; feel the width! As has been said by others before now, *Napoléon* may not be the greatest movie of all time, but it is certainly the *most* movie of all time.

*MW*

### DISCUSSION QUESTIONS

- If a film is technically interesting, does it matter if the story is overlong or otherwise hard to engage with?

- What are the benefits, if any, of seeing movies in the cinema rather than at home?

- *Napoléon* has a huge cast of characters, many of whom are never fully introduced or explained. Does this matter? Why or why not?

# Nosferatu

## 1922

*An old-timey adaptation of Bram Stoker's novel* Dracula.

Most likely to interest more as a quaint relic from cinematic history than as anything particularly frightening,
this silent and in many ways over-the-top example of the horror genre (the only to appear on the Vatican List) is probably
best enjoyed like a piece of music: at the level of sensation
and suggestion. Many of its images and intertitles—spiders
in cobwebs, rats crawling out of coffins, a random professor
strangely engrossed by carnivorous plants—seem to be included merely for atmospheric effect, and with the characters'
artificial posturing and stagey mug-pulling, *Nosferatu* bears
only a passing resemblance to horror films more familiar to

> Nosferatu. . . . Does this word not sound like the deathbird calling your name at midnight? Beware you never say it—for then the pictures of life will fade to shadows, haunting dreams will climb forth from your heart and feed on your blood.
>
> —INTERTITLE

later audiences. Even so, it offers an enduring testament to humanity's lasting fascination with evil, as well as an indirect insight into what it takes to overcome it.

Opening with a foreboding musical overture—a fitting introduction to a film subtitled "A Symphony of Horror"—the story follows a man called Hutter who works for a rotten-toothed, wild-haired estate agent whose first appearance on screen finds him bent over a document covered in occult-looking symbols. "Count Orlok—His Grace . . . from Transylvania . . . wishes to purchase a nice house in our little town," he relays to Hutter. "You might have to go to a bit of trouble . . . a little sweat and maybe . . . a little blood." Then he gestures out the window with an extended finger: "That house . . . across from yours . . . offer him that one!"

Hutter sets off to conduct the business—a journey that includes some winsome photography out of another era of peasant life in Slovakia and Germany where *Nosferatu* was filmed—and on the way stops to dine at a roadside inn. There he is told that he can't go any further that night because "the werewolf is roaming the forests." Horses bolt and old women cross themselves before the film cuts to crude, almost risible footage of a hyena sniffing around in the grass. After this single appearance, the werewolf, like many of the film's other "terrifying" elements, never resurfaces; apparently, it is just another gag in *Nosferatu*'s overall tactic of piling terror upon terror, often in defiance of any discernible contribution to the plot. Much of what comes next follows the story line of *Dracula*, as Hutter ventures onward, arrives at the creepy castle, and succeeds in drawing its hunched, long-nosed, coffin-dwelling master out into the wider world.

An intriguing deviation from the film's source material is the inclusion of a plague that spreads at each port visited by Nosferatu and his ship loaded with cursed dirt. At one level, this is probably just another turn of the screw of the terror symbolized by the vampire himself, the Black Death a convenient stand-in for the threat of mortality perceived on a massive scale. But at a deeper level, this preternatural contagion also appeals to a sense that there are still things in this world that defy rational explanation, whose causes are unknown and so remain beyond natural redress, even in an age of rapidly advancing science and industry. "Masses of young people are dying," an intertitle reads. "All victims appear to have the same strange wounds on their necks, the origin of which is still a mystery to doctors."

One of the baseline acknowledgements of horror as a genre is that there are forces at work in this world over which humanity is powerless. Certain sicknesses, the decline of age, and ultimately death itself, that "undiscovered country from whose bourn no traveler returns," fall on the dark side of this recognition. Evil, too, exerts a real influence over us, and even in its ugliness and unhealth can be unaccountably alluring in its strangeness, irrationality, and promise of pleasure or power. We see this in *Nosferatu* when

*Nosferatu* explicitly claims to be an adaptation of *Dracula,* even though the producers of the film never purchased the rights to the novel. Bram Stoker's widow sued, and the court ordered every copy of the film destroyed—a verdict that has clearly never been carried out.

Hutter insists that his wife Ellen promise not to go near a book that gives him nightmares, but she does not heed the warning, finding "its strange force irresistible." But Christians acknowledge that an even stronger force operates in reality and that there is a bright side to our recognition of weakness: "the fear of the LORD is the beginning of wisdom" (Prov. 9:10). A certainty about our creaturely inabilities is only a step away from seeking divine illumination, healing, and help.

In a similar way, the fascination with evil that is commonly part of the appeal of horror films *might* often be a morbid fascination, but it need not *always* be so: there are all sorts of unhealthy interest in the things of darkness, but squarely facing a shadow might also be the first move toward stepping into the light. One person captivated by sickness and depravity might be deranged, it is true; another might be a doctor. In *Nosferatu*, Ellen's naïve attraction to evil eventually develops into a more mature knowledge when she discovers by way of a closer examination of the same forbidden text a way to overcome it—"possible by no other means but that an innocent maiden maketh the vampire heed not the first crowing of the cock, this done by the sacrifice of her own blood." She learns that the vampiric plague, which

> "I suspect that the whole obsession of our time with the monstrous in general—with the occult and the demonic, with exorcism and black magic and the great white shark—is at its heart only the shadow side of our longing for the beatific, and we are like the knight in Ingmar Bergman's film *The Seventh Seal*, who tells the young witch about to be burned at the stake that he wants to meet the devil her master, and when she asks him why, he says, 'I want to ask him about God. He, if anyone, must know.'"
> —Frederick Buechner

357

exploits and victimizes people, literally treating them as food, can be defeated by the inverse: a voluntary readiness to become the victim and treat herself as food for others.

The Eucharistic overtones are not a coincidence. Gothic fiction was born in a modern European culture where increasing numbers of people had become strangers to the sacramental practices of ancient and medieval Christianity. Like the unevangelized populations whom St. Paul describes as groping blindly toward God (Acts 17:27), the artists and storytellers working in this genre (as well as the audiences who resonate with their work) might be understood as seeking out, often along dark, sacrilegious passageways, some vestige of the physically accessible supernatural. As scholars of the period like Victoria Nelson have argued, once a person believes that the world is devoid of the real presence of a *good* God, he or she might find at least hints of a similar sensation by imagining incarnate evil.

So, in *Nosferatu*, we find a monstrous, man-shaped embodiment of a nasty spiritual posture. The tangible representation of a deadly parasitism and selfishness, he is almost the exact opposite of the fleshly goodness, generosity, and complete self-gift Christians identify in the Redeemer. More than the equal opposite of this evil, Ellen's Christ-like resolution to give life rather than steal it saves her world from this curse, "and the truth bore witness to the miracle: at that very moment, the Great Death came to an end, and the shadow of the deathbird was gone . . . as if obliterated by the triumphant rays of the living sun."

> You might have to go to a bit of trouble . . .
> a little sweat and maybe . . . a little blood.
> —ESTATE AGENT

Near the conclusion of *Nosferatu*, rows of coffins are shown being carried down the cobblestone streets of Hutter's hometown of Wisborg. It is at

This film was banned in Sweden until 1972 for "excessive horror."

once the literal consequence of a physical plague and an allegorical image of the moral sickness that quietly kills entire communities. If this contagion is associated with the vampire, Ellen's saving action suggests the discovery and spread of an alternative "happy plague." The only way to overcome the spreading sickness of selfish exploitation that pulls so many of our neighbors toward the grave, the film implies, is through the "contagion" of generous, voluntarily surrendered life. From this perspective, we begin to see how horror and the gothic, whose most obvious appeal may be the chance to explore the dark side of reality, might in fact also offer indirect intimations of the opposite. Darkness and light may be antitheses, but there is also a close relationship between them: horror really only exists in the shadow of obstructed awe, and sacrilege could not exist without some residual sense of the sacred.

*DPB*

## DISCUSSION QUESTIONS

- Roger Ebert includes *Nosferatu* on his list of great movies and describes the film as impactful in a different way than later horror films: "It knows none of the later tricks of the trade, like sudden threats that pop in from the side of the screen. But *Nosferatu* remains effective: It doesn't scare us, but it haunts us." What, if anything, in this film do you find frightening? Why?

- "Whatever is true, whatever is honorable, whatever is just, whatever is pure, whatever is pleasing, whatever is commendable, if there is any excellence and if there is anything worthy of praise, think about these things" (Phil. 4:8). Should we necessarily avoid films that have problematic content and themes? What limits should we set for what we watch and why?

- "For the life of the flesh is in the blood; and I have given it to you for making atonement for your lives on the altar" (Lev. 17:11). In what ways is the underlying logic in *Nosferatu* similar to or different from this biblical view?

# *Stagecoach*

## 1939

*A group of strangers traverse treacherous territory in a
defining example of the American Western.*

For those of us steeped in the time-worn trappings of cow-
boy lore, it can be easy to miss the enduring significance
of the Western. Across the years, these tales of seemingly
endless open spaces and "horses and men in all their brute
strength," as French critic Louis Delluc observes, have captured for countless audiences something archetypal about the
American dream. Speaking of freedom, opportunity, rugged
individualism, resourcefulness, and self-reliance, these visions
of a nation born of exiles who come of age taming wilderness
offer moving images of the hope that has inspired millions

> Well, I guess you can't break out of prison and into
> society in the same week.
> —RINGO KID

around the world to seek a new life in the New World. One of the great popularizers of this American mythology is the director of over thirty Westerns, John Ford, and this entry on the Vatican Film List presents a lively example of his work.

It opens with a stagecoach traveling across a sere landscape and then rolling into town, where it collects a ragtag band of passengers—society's "upstanding citizens" cramming in alongside folks scarcely holding onto the fringe. The finely dressed Mrs. Lucy Mallory, traveling to meet her cavalry officer husband, must endure the company of Dallas, a woman of ill repute, who is being frog-marched out of town by the local chapter of the Law and Order League. A diminutive whiskey salesman, Mr. Peacock, endeavors to protect his samples from the insolvent, perpetually inebriated medic, Dr. Josiah Boone, who is all too ready to relieve him of them. And the crooked banker, Mr. Gatewood, absconding with the payroll of the mining company, must squeeze in shoulder to shoulder with the "notorious gambler," Mr. Hatfield, who, after a lingering glance at Mrs. Mallory, chivalrously elects to ride along as protection for this "angel in a jungle."

Amounting to a cross-section of the nineteenth-century American border town, this assembly of complex individuals is also marked by broad ironies—for example, a gambler who displays more honor than a banker, and a "respectable" man who makes his living selling liquor to the "down and outs" who drink it. A contrast

> Ford once commented that the two most beautiful things the camera can record are a couple dancing and a horse running.

In preparation for making *Citizen Kane*, Orson Welles allegedly watched *Stagecoach* over forty times, and when asked which directors he most admired, replied, "John Ford, John Ford, and John Ford."

between these two classes of people runs throughout the film—the inhumane guardians of public decency set against the compassionate outcasts—and forms part of its overall subversive evaluation of polite society, which Doc Boone summarizes in a conciliatory remark to Dallas: "We're the victims of a foul disease called social prejudice, my child. . . . Come on. Be a proud, glorified dreg like me."

One more joins the retinue when, advised that there may be danger of outlaws and Apaches, the weapon-wielding sheriff, Curley, agrees to "ride shotgun" next to the garrulous driver Buck. Then, with the coach harnessed with fresh horses, the latter calls out, "All aboard for Dry Fork, Apache Wells, Lee's Ferry, and Lordsburg!" They set off across a majestic, wasted landscape punctuated by towering buttes and mesas, only to pull up short at the sound of rifle fire. The source turns out to be the Winchester-wielding, prison-breaking Ringo Kid—a thirty-two-year-old John Wayne who appears here in his first headlining role—whom Curley immediately places under arrest, insisting that this outlaw, too, climb into a stagecoach now crammed to capacity.

Tensions mount between the passengers at each stop as a promised escort of cavalry fails to materialize, and the respectables attempt to maintain their distance from the rest. Mrs. Mallory will not even eat next to Dallas, for instance, whereas the more egalitarian undesirables seize the journey west as a chance to start anew. Ringo *de facto* proposes to Dallas, inviting her to join him at "a nice place, a real nice place" he owns across the border, luxuriously equipped with

trees, grass, and a half-built cabin. She seems inclined to accept but hesitates, especially as he articulates the hope to shoot down a trio of thugs who murdered his brother, an encounter she fears he will not survive. "Well, there's some things a man just can't run away from," The Kid replies—an effective summary, on the one hand, of a classic Wild West readiness in the face of danger, and on the other, of the inescapable social prejudices the company will drag with them even to the outermost edge of the nation.

It turns out this sentiment is not *entirely* accurate, though: there are at least a few things a man can outrun, they find, when a band of Apaches descends upon the coach during the last stretch of the trip. In an action-packed chase, the stagecoach barrels at a full gallop, as Ringo, Curley, and Hatfield pick off dozens of attackers. Just when it looks like their rumbling microcosm of Euro-American society might fall to another of the film's symbols of savage incivility, a bugle call heralds deliverance by the long-expected cavalry.

They reach the ironically named end of the line, Lordsburg, which proves to be no paradisal city of God, but a shadowy city of men. Even here at the frontier, prejudice persists, vice reigns, and the only way for regular, well-meaning folks like Ringo and Dallas to start again is to press on even further "across the border." After each character meets his and her respective fate, Curley surprises everyone by setting free Ringo, who rides off in a one-horse wagon with Dallas at his side, under Doc Boone's backhanded benediction: "Well, they're saved from the blessings of civilization."

> We're the victims of a foul disease called social prejudice, my child. . . . Come on. Be a proud, glorified dreg like me.
> —DOC BOONE

It could be tempting to interpret this ending—the outcasts at the reins of a miniature stagecoach that is loaded, not coincidentally, with the minimum occupancy to establish a new society—as simple, syrupy wish-fulfillment. But the doctor's departing cynicism suggests something more equivocal. Will Ringo and Dallas really escape all that is unsavory about human civilization simply by slipping the border of the United States? Or is it more realistic to expect that, given time, wherever they settle down will end up exhibiting some version of what they would like to leave behind?

*Stagecoach* was released into theaters almost exactly six months before Germany invaded Poland, precipitating the Second World War, and for its original audience, there would have been little doubt that the utopian country it hints at had yet to materialize on the stage of world affairs. Indeed, there is little reason to expect that the United States was any less in the grip of dishonest bankers, unimaginative businessmen, and self-satisfied elites in the mid-twentieth century than it was in the mid-nineteenth, or for that matter, is in the twenty-first.

So, where does that leave the American dream and its promise of reinvention as communicated so imaginatively in *Stagecoach*? Is there any place like the one it hints at: a land of freedom and second chances, where the mistakes of the past

John Wayne's marginal yet lionized figure in the movie can be traced to "the Good-Bad Man," a staple character in many Westerns iconically played by silent-film star William S. Hart. "An outlaw who underwent moral reformation of a kind, yet stayed outside the law," write critics Richard Griffith and Arthur Mayer, the Good-Bad Man came to stand in for a way of life "secretly envied by all who were irked by civilized restraint."

> Well, there's some things a man just can't run away from.
> —RINGO KID

are wiped clean and ordinary folks get the chance to live a decent, honest life?

Considered in this way, the hope at the heart of a Western like this might be appreciated less as a terrestrial place we can travel to by bus, plane, or stagecoach, and more as an oblique insight into the eternal significance of forgiveness. The mythic promise of the New World might only be fully realized "in a place, a real nice place" over the border of history in the new creation. But this does not prevent our experiencing hints and glimpses of it now—in the Westerns of John Ford, perhaps, but much more certainly among that ragtag band of fellow travelers commonly called the Church, whose purpose is not to set individuals free from the constraints of society, but to introduce us all into a community of everlasting second chances.

*DPB*

## DISCUSSION QUESTIONS

- Travel by horse would have been a living memory amongst some in *Stagecoach*'s first audiences. Yet the film's original trailers strike a perhaps surprisingly nostalgic note for a simpler time before, for instance, "ultra-modern" travel by train, bus, and airplanes capable of circumnavigating the globe in a mere four days. Has more changed between our time and that of the first viewers of *Stagecoach* or between theirs and the days of the wagon-traveling folk it depicts?

- If a Western like *Stagecoach* shows something less like history and more like myth, what universal human desires and fears does it explore? Does any part of the Wild West suggest to you a (perhaps imperfect) picture of paradise?

- Across many of the films made by John Ford, who was a first-generation Irish American and (at least nominally) a Catholic, some viewers detect a consistently positive emphasis upon family and community life over individual interests. Do you find either of these qualities in *Stagecoach*? If so, how plausible is it to attribute these to the influence of Catholic Christianity?

# *The Wizard of Oz*

## 1939

*Kansas teenager Dorothy Gale is carried off in a tornado to an enchanted land, where she and her fantastical companions learn lessons in virtue and gratitude on their journey.*

*T*he *Wizard of Oz* epitomizes the Golden Age of Hollywood. Starring Judy Garland, Frank Morgan, Ray Bolger, Jack Haley, Bert Lahr, and a huge cast of other characters, *The Wizard of Oz*, adapted from the 1900 novel by L. Frank Baum, remains a beloved classic whose musical numbers have become deeply ingrained in modern Western culture. Even today, many of us are taken aback the moment Dorothy steps out of the black-and-white world of her destroyed midwestern farmhouse and into the astonishing technicolor of

> There's no place like home.
> —DOROTHY GALE

the fantastic landscape of Oz. *The Wizard of Oz* is cinematic escapism; but as Dorothy's famous closing line—"There's no place like home"—illustrates, the film ultimately serves to help the audience tighten its grip on reality.

*The Wizard of Oz* begins in rural Kansas, a place of no particular significance to outsiders. It is the Great Depression, and life is hard for its residents, signaled by the need for Henry and Emily Gale to raise their orphan niece, Dorothy, whom we meet just as she is being told, "Find yourself a place where you won't get into any trouble." Dorothy's response is the film's best-known song, the enduring ballad, "Over the Rainbow," which won the Academy Award for Best Original Song and became the most iconic moment in Judy Garland's cinematic career. Its colorful vision of a high-up place where "the dreams you dare to dream really do come true" evokes our own wishes for what the world cannot give.

For Dorothy to understand that she is in many ways already living her dream, she must face further adversity in the form of a devastating tornado that sends her house airborne. Dorothy does not die, but at least for a time she passes away from her old life on earth and enters an enchanted and dreamlike land. Dorothy's old life, including the people she knows, are transposed into fantastic creatures, including her familiar farmhands now in the guise of a talking scarecrow, a tin woodsman, and an anthropomorphic lion. Just moments earlier, Dorothy had wanted to be far away, but now she simply wants to go home, and her colorful companions help her find a new perspective on the world to which she eventually returns.

The cruel obstacle in the great adventure of Dorothy, the Scarecrow, the Tin Man, and the Cowardly Lion is the Wicked Witch of the West, whose desire to harm Dorothy is ostensibly motivated by the death of her sister, the Wicked Witch of the East, who was crushed by Dorothy's falling house. The Wicked Witch's outrage echoes that of Mrs. Gulch, who wanted to destroy Toto out of retribution for biting her. But the good witch Glinda remarks that "only bad witches are ugly," suggesting that inner malice manifests itself externally, and that both the Wicked Witch in Oz and Mrs. Gulch in Kansas are motivated by meanness, not justice. Here again, *The Wizard of Oz* shows us the fantastical in order to propose a deeper understanding of the way the ordinary world works.

In recent decades, we may have grown accustomed to thinking that if only we could understand an antagonist's motivations, we may not find such a person so villainous after all. Indeed, Gregory Maguire's 1995 novel *Wicked: The Life and Times of the Wicked Witch of the West* opened the door to a whole subgenre of sympathetic villain origin stories. Nonetheless, as the ongoing popularity of the *Wizard of Oz* suggests, there remains a timeless appeal to fairy tales, which are populated by heroes and villains. Margaret Hamilton's performance as both the Witch and Mrs. Gulch is still frightening to many viewers because, despite so many changes in society since this film premiered, we can still spot true evil when we see it, and there is nothing to do in the end but stand up to it and fight.

A loose musical adaptation of L. Frank Baum's novel for the stage opened on Broadway in 1903 and toured America for seven years, and it is widely regarded as one of the great triumphs of early American mass entertainment. Various attempts at silent film versions of *The Wizard of Oz* were unsuccessful.

The Wizard of Oz is also about self-discovery and the cultivation of basic virtues. "If I only had a brain," the unwittingly clever Scarecrow sings. "If I only had a heart," the selfless Tin Man declares. "If I only had the nerve," the assertive Cowardly Lion laments. Each of Dorothy's fellow travelers illustrates the concept of *anamnesis* as described in the Platonic dialogue *Meno*. Simply put, their desire for virtue is a sign that they already possess the seed of what they believe they require, but it must be drawn out of them to flourish fully. The Wizard cannot intervene supernaturally to provide what the Scarecrow, Tin Man, and Lion lack, but in the role of an educator (he was "Professor Marvel" back in Kansas), he manages to elicit the character traits already present within the creatures who come to him for help. Jesus, whom Christians believe *can* give us what we lack, nonetheless also draws out the virtue from us that he has already planted as a seed within us. Dorothy, on the other hand, requires magical intervention to get back to Kansas, and it comes neither from the Wizard, nor from Glinda, but rather from the alignment of her will with a mysterious power. Her ruby slippers may be enchanted, but they enable Dorothy to embrace reality, which Christians believe to be a heavenly kingdom that has come near to us on earth.

The Wizard of Oz opened in August 1939, just before the start of World War II. The film brought joy to millions in difficult times, and its cultural weight would only increase when, in 1956, it was shown for the first of countless times on American television as an annual event. When *Oz* aired

> You are under the unfortunate delusion that simply because you run away from danger, you have no courage. You're confusing courage with wisdom.
> —THE WIZARD OF OZ

> If I ever go looking for my heart's desire again, I won't look any further than my own back yard. Because if it isn't there, I never really lost it to begin with!
> —DOROTHY GALE

in 1959, it earned an audience share of 58%, and ever since it first became available on home video in 1980, it has been a staple in every family's movie library in every format. For many people, *The Wizard of Oz* is a touchstone for childhood memories, as well as the premier example of what movies used to be: larger-than-life yet intimately relatable to anyone who sits immersed in the colorful, musical story.

For some fans of *The Wizard of Oz*, the film also speaks to the profound spiritual need for safety and healing amid the trials of life. "There's no place like home" means more than just an appreciation of one's earthly stomping grounds, and anyone who has come into the Catholic Church, for example, has surely heard the familiar words from fellow Catholics: "Welcome home." The *Catechism of the Catholic Church* teaches, "We can view realities and events in terms of their eternal significance, leading us toward our true homeland: thus the Church on earth is a sign of the heavenly Jerusalem." Dorothy Gale does not stay in Oz, but her old drab life in Kansas takes on a new Oz-like joy. In light of the world beyond, Kansas is not a place to escape, but rather to embrace. Likewise, discovering the gift of Christian community and liturgy in the Church prepares our souls not for escape *from* the world but for flourishing *in* it—only

Well-known actor Buddy Ebsen was originally cast as the Scarecrow, then recast as the Tin Man. He fell victim to aluminum poisoning from his stage make-up and had to be replaced by Jack Haley.

Emilio Estevez's movie *The Way* (2010), about pilgrims walking "El Camino" to the shrine of St. James the Apostle in northern Spain, is a conscious reworking of *The Wizard of Oz*. Estevez remarked, "Martin Sheen's character is Dorothy, James Nesbitt's the scarecrow. . . . Instead of Oz, they're going to Santiago de Compostela."

now, to prepare for the life in the world to come.

*The Wizard of Oz* is a one-of-a-kind concoction of Munchkins, magic, and melody, but it is ultimately a conventional homecoming tale. Like most of the great stories in literature—from *The Odyssey* to *The Lord of the Rings*—the dazzling spectacle of *The Wizard of Oz* has the potential to hit us hard, because deep within the human soul most of us long for the place we know we belong. Moreover, even if we think we are lacking something on our journey—brains, heart, courage, you name it—everything will be made just right when we arrive. In this way, the enduring legacy of *The Wizard of Oz* is its exemplary use of images, music, dialogue, and all the spectacles of cinema to teach us the most important lessons about life.

*AP*

## DISCUSSION QUESTIONS

- Do the Scarecrow, the Tin Man, and the Cowardly Lion have all the brains, heart, and courage they need from the beginning, or does the journey to the Emerald City equip them with what they need before they reach their destination?

- What do you make of the mysterious character of the Wizard? Is his charlatanism and powerlessness meant to imply something about God, or might God even use such imposters to bless his people?

- What do you make of the unique look of the film? What is the effect on you when the film abruptly changes from the drab sepia tone of Kansas to the technicolor splendor of Oz?

# Notes

## INTRODUCTION

**"some important films"**: John Thavis, "'Some important films' applauded by Vatican," *The Catholic Northwest Progress*, November 16, 1995, https://washingtondigitalnewspapers. org/?a=d&d=CATHNWP19951116.2.17.1.

**"not all that deserve mention are included"**: Thavis.

**"the passion for the shows of the circus"**: Pius XI, *Divini Illius Magistri* 90, encyclical letter, December 31, 1929, vatican.va.

**"an ideal film"**: Pius XII, "To the Representatives of the Italian Cinematograph Industry," apostolic exhortation, June 21, 1955, vatican.va.

**"respite from the pressure of real existence"**: "To the Representatives of the Italian Cinematograph Industry."

**"lofty and positive mission"**: "To the Representatives of the Italian Cinematograph Industry."

**"Catholic Film critics can have much influence"**: Pius XII, *Miranda Prorsus*, encyclical letter, September 8, 1957, vatican.va.

**"consolidate, complete, and raise up the truth and the goodness":** *Catechism of the Catholic Church* 856.

**"a relationship offered in friendship, openness, and dialogue":** John Paul II, "Letter to Artists" 11, April 4, 1999, vatican.va.

**"go to the peripheries":** Francis, "Message of His Holiness Pope Francis—Signed by the Cardinal Secretary of State—To the Participants in the Meeting for Friendship Among Peoples," August 24–30, 2014, vatican.va.

**"subcreation":** J.R.R. Tolkien, "On Fairy-Stories," in *Tree and Leaf* (London: Allen & Unwin, 1964).

**"suspend disbelief":** Samuel Taylor Coleridge, *Biographia Literaria* (1817).

**"Even beyond its typically religious expressions . . .":** "Letter to Artists" 10.

**"to follow the path of the fruitful dialogue between the Church and artists":** "Letter to Artists" 1.

### ANDREI RUBLEV

**"noble peace, eternity, and harmony of the soul":** "The Three Andreis," directed by Dina Musatova, 1966, on *Andrei Rublev*, directed by Andrei Tarkovsky (1966; New York: Criterion, 2018), Blu-ray.

**a depiction of the Trinity modeled after the Old Testament story:** Andrei Rublev, *The Trinity*, c. 1425, depicted in *The Word* *on Fire Bible (Volume I): The Gospels* (Park Ridge, IL: Word on Fire, 2020), 118.

**"In the beginning, Rublev's belief was purely intellectual":** "The Three Andreis."

### BEN-HUR

**"He wanted to make a movie that a broad audience would like":** *Ben-Hur: The Making of an Epic*, directed by Scott Benson (Burbank, CA: Turner Home Entertainment, 1993).

### THE FLOWERS OF ST. FRANCIS

**"recreating an image for Italy":** "Isabella Rossellini on *The Flowers of St. Francis*," 2004, on The Criterion Channel, https://www.criterionchannel.com/videos/isabella-rossellini-on-the-flowers-of-st-francis.

**"Poor man, you don't know what you've done":** "Father Virgilio Fantuzzi on *The Flowers of St. Francis*," 2004, on The Criterion Channel, https://www.criterionchannel.com/videos/father-virgilio-fantuzzi-on-the-flowers-of-st-francis.

**"extends the frontiers of Christian love":** John XXIII, "Opening Address to the Council," in *The Word on Fire Vatican II Collection* (Park Ridge, IL: Word on Fire Institute, 2021), 9.

**"Praise be to you, my Lord, through our Sister, Mother Earth":** Francis of Assisi, Canticle of Creatures, quoted in Francis, *Laudato Si'* 1, encyclical letter, May 24, 2015, vatican.va.

### *THE GOSPEL ACCORDING TO ST. MATTHEW*

**"I may be an unbeliever . . .":** Pier Paolo Pasolini in a 1966 press conference, quoted in Gregory and Maria Pearse, "Pasolini: Quo Vadis? The Fate of Pier Paolo Pasolini," https://www.nga.gov/content/dam/ngaweb/calendar/film/pdfs/notes/heavenly-earth-notes.pdf.

**"true art has a close affinity with the world of faith":** John Paul II, "Letter to Artists" 10, April 4, 1999, vatican.va.

### *LA VIE ET PASSION DE NOTRE SEIGNEUR JÉSUS-CHRIST*

**"the common man and his family still used kerosene lamps . . .":** Richard Griffith and Arthur Mayer, *The Movies* (New York: Simon & Schuster, 1970), 17; quoting Benjamin B. Hampton, *A History of the Movies* (New York: Covici Friede, 1931), 13.

### *A MAN FOR ALL SEASONS*

**"The blood of the martyrs is the seed of the Church":** As with many famous statements that achieve currency in popular discourse, the original is slightly different. What Tertullian actually wrote, in his *Apologeticus pro Christianis*, was "plures efficimur, quotiens metimur a vobis; semen est sanguis christianorum": "we multiply whenever we are mown down by you; the blood of Christians is seed" (Tertullian, *Tertulliani's Apologeticus, the Text of Oehler*, trans. A. Souter [Cambridge: Cambridge University Press, 1917], 50).

### *NAZARÍN*

**"It's like someone falling asleep in bed"**: Luis Buñuel, in *A Mexican Buñuel*, produced by Emilio Maille, 1997, on The Criterion Channel, https://www.criterionchannel.com/videos/a-mexican-bunuel.

### *ORDET*

**"Every factor of division can be transcended"**: John Paul II, *Ut Unum Sint* 1, encyclical letter, May 25, 1995, vatican.va.

### *THE PASSION OF JOAN OF ARC*

**"Joan of Arc was not stuck at the cross-roads"**: G.K. Chesterton, *Orthodoxy* (Park Ridge, IL: Word on Fire Classics, 2017), 39.

### *THE SACRIFICE*

**"External chains of events . . ."**: "Directed by Andrei Tarkovsky," directed by Michal Leszczylowski, 1988, on *The Sacrifice: Special Edition*, directed by Andrei Tarkovsky (1986; New York: Kino Classics, 2018), Blu-ray.

### *THÉRÈSE*

**"To evangelize the evangelists"**: Thérèse of Lisieux, *Autobiography of a Saint: The Complete and Authorized Text of L'Histoire D'une Ame*, trans. Ronald Knox (London: Collins, 1963), 123.

**the greatest saint of modern times:** Pierre Descouvemont, *Therese and Lisieux*, trans. Salvatore Sciurba and Louise Pambrun (Toronto: Novalis, 1996), 4.

**"I felt charity enter into my soul":** Thérèse of Lisieux, *Story of a Soul: The Autobiography of Saint Thérèse of Lisieux*, trans. John Clarke (Park Ridge, IL: Word on Fire Classics, 2022), 101.

**"Often during my Communions . . .":** Thérèse of Lisieux, 82.

**"lit and led me through / More certain than the light of noonday clear":** John of the Cross, "Stanzas of the Soul," in *The Poems of St John of the Cross*, trans. Roy Campbell (New York: Pantheon Books, 1953), 11.

### *AU REVIOR LES ENFANTS*

**"In her rejection of every persecution against any man . . .":** Vatican Council II, *Nostra Aetate* 4, in *The Word on Fire Vatican II Collection: Declarations and Decrees* (Elk Grove Village, IL: Word on Fire Institute, 2023), 53.

### *BICYCLE THIEVES*

**"No doubt one's first and most superficial reaction . . .":** Cesare Zavattini, "Some Ideas on the Cinema," trans. Pier Luigi Lanza, in *Sight and Sound* 23, no. 2 (1953): 64–69.

**"reintroduce the dramatic into quotidian situations":** Vittorio De Sica, quoted in Godfrey Cheshire, "*Bicycle Thieves*: A Passionate Commitment to the Real," The Criterion Collection, February 12, 2007, https://www.criterion.com/current/posts/467-bicycle-thieves-a-passionate-commitment-to-the-real.

**"The thesis implied is wondrously, outrageously simple":** André Bazin, "Bicycle Thief," in *What is Cinema?: Volume II* (Berkeley: University of California Press, 2005), 51.

**"There wasn't even a trace of an organized movie industry":** Vittorio De Sica, "My Secret," in *On* Bicycle Thieves*: The Criterion Collection DVD Booklet* (New York: Criterion Collection, 2013).

**"I am bored to death with heroes more or less imaginary":** Zavattini, "Some Ideas on the Cinema."

**"not through its exceptional but through its normal quality":** Zavattini.

**"The high quality of this motion picture . . .":** "The 20th Academy Awards Memorable Moments," Oscars website, https://www.oscars.org/oscars/ceremonies/1948/memorable-moments.

## THE BURMESE HARP

**"I just felt I had to make it into a film":** Interview with Kon Ichikawa on *The Burmese Harp*, directed by Kon Ichikawa (1956; New York: Criterion, 2007), Blu-ray.

**"I heard that San Giorgio was the name of an Italian man . . .":** Interview with Kon Ichikawa.

## DEKALOG

**"can't quite find their bearings":** Krzysztof Kieslowski, quoted in *Kieslowski on Kieslowski, ed.* Danusia Stok (London: Faber & Faber, 1995), 79.

**"Everyone has their reasons":** Krzysztof Kieslowski, quoted in Paul Coates, "'And So On': Kieślowski's *Dekalog* and the Metaphysics of the Everyday," The Criterion Collection, September 27, 2016, https://www.criterion.com/current/posts/4235-and-so-on-kieslowski-s-dekalog-and-the-metaphysics-of-the-everyday.

**"They do this with such dazzling skill":** Stanley Kubrick, Foreword to Krzysztof Kieślowski and Krzysztof Piesiewicz, *Decalogue: The Ten Commandments* (London: Faber & Faber, 1991), vii.

## GANDHI

**"When I saw you in that tunic, I knew I could die in peace":** An echo of the Canticle of Simeon (Luke 2:29–32), which in the Latin Vulgate reads, "*Nunc dimittis servum tuum, Domine*" ("Now thou dost dismiss thy servant, O Lord").

**"Those also can attain to salvation who through no fault of their own . . .":** Vatican Council II, *Lumen Gentium* 16, in *The Word on Fire Vatican II Collection* (Park Ridge, IL: Word on Fire Institute, 2021), 66.

## IT'S A WONDERFUL LIFE

**"articulated in terms of 'friendship' or 'social charity'":** *Catechism of the Catholic Church* 1939.

## THE SEVENTH SEAL

**"Nobody today knows the names of those who built Chartres Cathedral":** "Ingmar Bergman on Life and Work," directed by

Jörn Donner, 1998, on *Wild Strawberries*, directed by Ingmar Bergman (1957; New York: Criterion, 2013), Blu-ray.

**"For me those eight hours were no hours at all"**: "Ingmar Bergman on Life and Work."

### THE TREE OF WOODEN CLOGS

**"even slowly, step by step . . .":** Interview with Ermanno Olmi, on *The Tree of Wooden Clogs*, directed by Ermanno Olmi (1978; New York: Criterion, 2017), Blu-ray.

**"made a treasure chest of all those emotions":** Interview with Ermanno Olmi.

**"As soon as the word got around . . .":** Interview with Ermanno Olmi.

### WILD STRAWBERRIES

**"a figure who on the outside looked like my father":** Ingmar Bergman, *Images: My Life in Film*, trans. Marianne Ruuth (New York: Arcade, 1994), 20.

**a celebrated Swedish hymn:** Johan Olof Wallin, "Vär är den vän som överallt jag söker?" English translation from http://musingsandasearchfortruth.blogspot.com/2011/01/ordet-vs-through-glass-darkly.html.

### 8 ½

**"director's block":** Federico Fellini, *Fellini on Fellini*, trans. Isabel Quigley (New York: Delacorte, 1976), 148.

**"Sex, circus, cinema, and spaghetti":** Fellini, 16.

**"After reading the script, I said no":** Fellini, 67.

### 2001: A SPACE ODYSSEY

**"God is dead":** Friedrich Nietzsche, *Thus Spoke Zarathustra: A Book for Everyone and No One*, trans. R.J. Hollingdale (London: Penguin, 1969), 41.

### CITIZEN KANE

**the spellbinding contrast:** Peter Bogdanovich, Commentary on *Citizen Kane*, directed by Orson Welles (1941; New York: Criterion, 2022), Blu-ray.

**_Citizen Kane_ did for the sound period what _Birth of a Nation_ did for the silent period:** Roger Ebert, Commentary on *Citizen Kane*.

### THE GRAND ILLUSION

**"Charity is the apostle's indispensable weapon":** Pius XI, *Mit Brennender Sorge* 35, encyclical letter, March 14, 1937, vatican.va.

### LA STRADA

**"When I was in the States with her . . .":** Federico Fellini, *Fellini on Fellini*, trans. Isabel Quigley (New York: Delacorte, 1976), 54.

**"I know little about Catholic dogma":** Fellini, 57.

**"the Franciscan element in neorealism"**: "Introduction to *La Strada*," Martin Scorsese, on *La Strada*, directed by Federico Fellini (1954; New York: Criterion, 2021), Blu-ray.

**"*La Strada* is about loneliness"**: Charlotte Chandler, *I, Fellini* (New York: Cooper Square, 2001), 103.

### THE LEOPARD

**"The Christian faithful are those . . ."**: *Catechism of the Catholic Church* 871.

### LITTLE WOMEN

**"a degenerate and misguided attempt"**: Paul Rotha, in *A Paul Rotha Reader*, ed. Robert Kruger and Duncan Petrie (Exeter: University of Exeter Press, 1999), 60.

### METROPOLIS

**"without God, before God, and not in accordance with God"**: *Catechism of the Catholic Church* 398.

### NAPOLÉON

**"lacked space in certain scenes"**: *The Charm of Dynamite*, directed by Kevin Brownlow, narrated by Lindsay Anderson (London: BBC, 1968).

**"amazed victims"**: Abel Gance, quoted in Paul Cuff, "Experiential Art: Musical Performance, Live Cinema, and Abel Gance's *Napoléon*," Alternate Takes, http://www.alternate-takes.co.uk/?2014,2,566.

**"Enthusiasm is essential in the cinema":** *The Charm of Dynamite.*

**"reality squared":** *Abel Gance's Napoleon - A Film from the Future*, YouTube video, August 18, 2019, https://www.youtube.com/watch?v=6dwRq-STdlE.

**"a moral religion":** Abel Gance, quoted in Paul Cuff, "Living History: Abel Gance's *Napoléon*," *Abel Gance's Revolutionary Silent Epic: Napoléon* (London: British Film Industry, 2016), 1.

**"the world's greatest director":** Gance, quoted in Cuff, 2.

### NOSFERATU

**"undiscovered country from whose bourn no traveler returns":** William Shakespeare, *Hamlet* 3.1.79–80.
**"I suspect that the whole obsession of our time with the monstrous in general . . .":** Frederick Buechner, *Telling the Truth: The Gospel as Tragedy, Comedy, and Fairy Tale* (New York: Harper & Row, 1977), 86.

### STAGECOACH

**"horses and men in all their brute strength":** Louis Delluc, quoted in Richard Griffith and Arthur Mayer, *The Movies* (New York: Simon & Schuster, 1970), 89.

**"An outlaw who underwent moral reformation of a kind":** Griffith and Mayer, 93.

## *THE WIZARD OF OZ*

"We can view realities and events in terms of their eternal significance": *Catechism of the Catholic Church* 117.

# Image Credits

### Andrei Rublev

*Portrait of Anatoliy Solonitsyn in Andrei Rublev (1966)* (p. 13): cineclassico / Alamy Stock Photo; *ANDREY RUBLYOV* (p.16): MOSFILM / Ronald Grant Archive / Alamy Stock Photo; *Andrei Rublev Andrei Rublyov Year: 1966 - Soviet Union Directed by Andrei Tarkovsky Anatoli Solonitsyn* (p. 16): Photo 12 / Alamy Stock Photo; *Holy Trinity (Troitsa)*, Andrei Rublev, 1427, Wikimedia Commons.

### Babette's Feast

*Mar 04, 1988; Copenhagen, DENMARK; Scene from the Gabriel Axel directed drama, "Babette's Feast."* (p. 22): Entertainment Pictures / Alamy Stock Photo; *Mar 04, 1988; Copenhagen, DENMARK; Scenes from the Gabriel Axel directed drama, "Babette's Feast."* (p. 26): Entertainment Pictures / Alamy Stock Photo.

### Ben-Hur

*Ben Hur* (p. 31): MARKA / Alamy Stock Photo; *Ben-Hur is a 1959 American epic historical drama film, directed by William Wyler, produced by Sam Zimbalist for Metro-Goldwyn-Mayer and starring Charlton Heston, Stephen Boyd, Jack Hawkins, Hugh Griffith and Haya Harareet.* (p. 34): Atlaspix / Alamy Stock Photo; *BEN-HUR 1959 MGM film with Claude Heater as Christ delivering the Sermon on the Mount* (p. 34): Pictorial Press Ltd / Alamy Stock Photo; *Ben-Hur* (p. 34): Photo 12 / Alamy Stock Photo; *Ben Hur* (p.34) MARKA / Alamy Stock Photo; *Charlton Heston & Jack Hawkins Film: Ben-Hur; Ben Hur (USA 1959) Characters: Judah Ben-Hur, Quintus Arrius Director: William Wyler 18 November 1959* (p. 34): ©MGM, Cinematic Collection / Alamy Stock Photo; *Original Film Title: BEN-HUR. English Title: BEN-HUR. Film Director: WILLIAM WYLER. Year: 1959. Credit: M.G.M. / Album* (p. 34): Album / Alamy Stock Photo.

### The Flowers of St. Francis

*Francesco, giullare di Dio* (p.40): Photo 12 / Alamy Stock Photo; *Les onze fioretti de Francois d Assise Francesco giullare di Dio 1950 Real Roberto Rossellini Aldo Fabrizi. Collection Christophel © Cineriz / Rizzoli Film* (p. 44): Collection Christophel / Alamy Stock Photo.

### Francesco

*Franziskus (Francesco) BRD/Italien 1989 Regie: Liliana Cavani Szene mit MICKEY ROURKE Regie: Liliana Cavani aka. Francesco* (p. 48) United Archives GmbH / Alamy Stock Photo; *Francesco 1989 Real Liliana Cavani Mickey Rourcke. Collection Christophel © Karol Film / Royal Film / Rai 1* (p. 52): Collection Christophel / Alamy Stock Photo.

### The Gospel According to St. Matthew

*Il Vangelo secondo Matteo Year: 1964 Director: Pier Paolo Pasolini Enrique Irazoqui* (p. 55) Photo 12 / Alamy Stock Photo; *Il Vangelo secondo Matteo Year: 1964 Director: Pier Paolo Pasolini Enrique Irazoqui* (p. 58): Photo 12 / Alamy Stock Photo.

### La Vie et Passion de Notre Seigneur Jésus-Christ

*La Vie du Christ aka La Vie et Passion de Notre Seigneur Jésus-Christ (1907) - French silent movie era* (p. 63): cineclassico / Alamy Stock Photo.

### A Man for All Seasons

*A MAN FOR ALL SEASONS 1966 Columbia film with Paul Scofield as Sir Thomas More at right and Robert Shaw as Henry VIII* (p. 70): Pictorial Press Ltd / Alamy Stock Photo; *WELLES, SCOFIELD, A MAN FOR ALL SEASONS, 1966* (p. 74): Allstar Picture Library Ltd / Alamy Stock Photo; *A MAN FOR ALL SEASONS* (p. 74): Ronald Grant Archive / Alamy Stock Photo.

### The Mission

*THE MISSION - 1986 Goldcrest film with Jeremy Irons* (p. 78): Pictorial Press Ltd / Alamy Stock Photo; *ROBERT DE NIRO, THE MISSION, 1986* (p. 82): Cinematic Collection / Alamy Stock Photo; *ROBERT DE NIRO, THE MISSION, 1986* (p. 82): Maximum Film / Alamy Stock Photo; *Mission The Mission 1986 Real Roland Joffe Jeremy Irons Robert De Niro. COLLECTION CHRISTOPHEL © Enigma Productions* (p. 82): Collection Christophel / Alamy Stock Photo.

### Monsieur Vincent

*Monsieur Vincent Year: 1947 France Director: Maurice Cloche Writing credits Jean Anouilh, Jean Bernard-Luc Jean Debucourt, Pierre Fresnay, Lise Delamare* (p. 86): Photo 12 / Alamy Stock Photo; *Pierre Fresnay & Francette Vernillat, on-set of the French Film, "Monsieur Vincent", 1947* (p. 90): Glasshouse Images / Alamy Stock Photo; *Monsieur Vincent Year: 1947 France Director: Maurice Cloche Writing credits Jean Anouilh, Jean Bernard-Luc Pierre Fresnay, Jean Carmet* (p. 90): Photo 12 / Alamy Stock Photo.

### Nazarín

*Nazarin, (NAZARIN) MEX 1958, Regie: Luis Bunuel, FRANCISCO RABAL, RITA MACEDO, MARGA LOPEZ* (p. 95): United Archives GmbH / Alamy Stock Photo; *NAZARIN 1958 de Luis Bunuel Francisco Rabal. d'apres le roman de Benito Perez Galdos based on the novel by Benito Perez Galdos Prod DB © Producciones* (p. 98): TCD/Prod. DB / Alamy Stock Photo; *Nazarin Nazarín Year: 1959 - mexico Director : Luis Buñuel* (p. 98): Photo 12 / Alamy Stock Photo.

### Ordet

*Prod DB Â© Palladium / DR ORDET (ORDET / LA PAROLE, titre français de sortie) de Carl Theodor Dreyer 1955 DAN avec Preben Lerdorff Rye bougies, chandelles, d'apres la piecede Kaj Munk* (p. 103): TCD/Prod.DB / Alamy Stock Photo; *Henrik Malberg, Publicity Portrait for the Danish Film, "Ordet", Kaj Munk & Carl Theodor Dreyer A/S, Kingsley-International Pictures, 1955* (p. 106): Glasshouse Images / Alamy Stock Photo.

### The Passion of Joan of Arc

*LA PASSION DE JEANNE D'ARC (1928) THE PASSION OF JOAN OF ARC (ALT) MARIA FALCONETTI CARL THEODOR DREYER (DIR)* (p. 111): Moviestore Collection Ltd / Alamy Stock Photo; *La Passion de Jeanne d Arc The Passion of Joan of Arc Year : 1928 France Director : Carl Theodor Dreyer Maurice Schutz, Eugene Silvain, Maria Falconetti* (p. 114): Photo 12 / Alamy Stock Photo.

### The Sacrifice

*Opfer Offret vlnr: Allan Edwall, Filippa Franzen, Susan Fleetwood *** Local Caption *** 1986* (p. 118): United Archives GmbH / Alamy Stock Photo; *Andrei Tarkovsky* (p. 122): Photo 12 / Alamy Stock Photo.

### Thérèse

*CATHERINE MOUCHET, THERESE, 1986* (p. 126): Cinematic Collection / Alamy Stock Photo; *THERESE* (p. 130): AFC / FILMS A2 / CNC / Ronald Grant Archive / Alamy Stock Photo; *The banner of St. Therese is carried into St. Peter's Basilica in Rome at her canonization ceremony, May 17, 1925,* artist unknown (p. 130): © Archives du Carmel de Lisieux. Used by permission.

### Au Revoir les Enfants

*Auf Wiedersehen, Kinder, (AU REVOIR LES ENFANTS) F 1987, Regie: Louis Malle, GASPARD MANESSE, RAPHAEL FETJÖ, Stichwort: Baskenmütze, Schüler, Frieren* (p. 137): United Archives GmbH / Alamy Stock Photo; *AU REVOIR LES ENFANTS RAPHAEL FEJTO, left, PHILIPPE MORIER-GENOUD, right Date: 1987* (p. 140): RGR Collection / Alamy Stock Photo; *AU REVOIR LES ENFANTS 1987 Real Louis Malle Gaspard Manesse. COLLECTION CHRISTOPHEL © Nouvelles Éditions de Films (NEF)* (p.140): Collection Christophel / Alamy Stock Photo.

### Bicycle Thieves

*MAGGIORANI,STAIOLA, BICYCLE THIEVES, 1948* (p. 145): Allstar Picture Library Ltd / Alamy Stock Photo; *Ladri di biciclette 28film29* (p. 148): Historic Images / Alamy Stock Photo; *Ladri di biciclette Bicycle Thieves Year : 1948 Italy Director : Vittorio De Sica Lamberto Maggiorani* (p. 148): Photo 12 / Alamy Stock Photo.

### The Burmese Harp

*Prod DB © Nikkatsu / DR LA HARPE DE BIRMANIE (BIRUMA NO TATEGOTO) de Kon Ichikawa 1956 JAP. avec Rentaro Mikuni WW2, guerre du pacifique, armée japonaise, camp de prisonniers, chorale, chanter autres titres: Harp of Burma, The Burmese Harp (USA)* (p. 153): TCD/Prod.DB / Alamy Stock Photo; *THE BURMESE*

*HARP* (p. 156): Ronald Grant Archive / Alamy Stock Photo; *Prod DB Â©Â Nikkatsu / DR LA HARPE DE BIRMANIE (BIRUMA NO TATEGOTO) de Kon Ichikawa 1956 JAP. avec Shoji Yasui WW2, guerre du pacifique, saluer, moine autres titres: Harp of Burma, The Burmese Harp (USA)* (p. 153): TCD/Prod.DB / Alamy Stock Photo.

### Chariots of Fire

*CROSS,CHARLESON, CHARIOTS OF FIRE, 1981* (p. 161): Allstar Picture Library Limited / Alamy Stock Photo; *CROSS,HAVERS, CHARIOTS OF FIRE, 1981* (p. 164): Allstar Picture Library Limited / Alamy Stock Photo; *DIE STUNDE DES SIEGERS Chariots of Fire UK 1981 Hugh Hudson Eric Liddell (IAN CHARLESON) and Harold Abrahams (BEN CROSS) Regie: Hugh Hudson aka. Chariots of Fire* (p. 164): United Archives GmbH / Alamy Stock Photo; *CHARIOTS OF FIRE* (p. 164): GOLDCREST / Ronald Grant Archive / Alamy Stock Photo; *ATHLETES ON THE BEACH, CHARIOTS OF FIRE, 1981* (p.164): Maximum Film / Alamy Stock Photo.

### Dekalog

*Krótki film o milosci Dekalog 6 Year: 1988 - Poland Director: Krzysztof Kieslowski Grazyna Szapolowska* (p. 169, 174): Photo 12 / Alamy Stock Photo; *DEKALOG 2 KRYSTYNA JANDA, ALEKSANDER BARDINI THOU SHALT NOT TAKE THE NAME OF THE LORD THY GOD IN VAIN \*\*\* Local Caption \*\*\* Date: 1988* (p. 174): RGR Collection / Alamy Stock Photo.

### Dersu Uzala

Dersu Uzala Year: 1975 - Soviet Union / Japan Yuriy Solomin, Maksim Munzuk Director: Akira Kurosawa (p. 179): Photo 12 / Alamy Stock Photo; *Dersou Ouzala Dersu Uzala 1975 Real Akira Kurosawa Maksim Munzuk Yuri Solomin Svetlana Danilchenko Dmitri Korshikov Collection Christophel © Atelier 41 / Daiei Studios / Mosfilm* (p. 182): Collection Christophel / Alamy Stock Photo; *DERSU UZALA* (p. 182): ATELEIER 41 / DAIEI STUDIOS / MOSFILM / Ronald Grant Archive / Alamy Stock Photo.

### Gandhi

*Gandhi, (GANDHI) GB-IND 1982, Regie: Richard Attenborough, BEN KINGSLEY, Stichwort: Brille* (p. 186): United Archives GmbH / Alamy Stock Photo; *GANDHI 1982 Columbia/Goldcrest film with Ben Kingsley as Gandhi* (p. 190): Pictorial Press Ltd / Alamy Stock Photo; *SETH,KINGSLEY,PADAMSEE, GANDHI, 1982* (p. 190): Maximum Film / Alamy Stock Photo.

### Intolerance

*Prod DB © Triangle Film Corporation / DR INTOLERANCE (INTOLERANCE) de D.W. Griffith 1916 USA autre titre: the mother and the law classique, histoire du cinema* (p. 194): TCD/Prod.DB / Alamy Stock Photo; *INTOLERANCE 1916 silent film by D.W.Griffith. Scene from the Babylon sequence showing the fall of the Empire to the Persians* (p. 198): Pictorial Press Ltd / Alamy Stock Photo.

### It's a Wonderful Life

*LIONEL BARRYMORE as Mr.Potter and JAMES STEWART as George Bailey in IT'S A WONDERFUL LIFE 1946 director FRANK CAPRA Liberty Films / RKO Radio Pictures* (p. 201): Masheter Movie Archive / Alamy Stock Photo; *Henry Travers & James Stewart Film: It's A Wonderful Life (USA 1946) Characters: Clarence, George Bailey Director: Frank Capra 20 December 1946* (p. 204): Cinematic Collection / Alamy Stock Photo; *IT'S A WONDERFUL LIFE 1946 RKO Radio Pictures film with Donna Reed and James Stewart* (p. 204): Pictorial Press Ltd / Alamy Stock Photo

### On the Waterfront

*ON THE WATERFRONT 1954 Columbia Pictures film with Marlon Brando* (p. 209): Pictorial Press Ltd / Alamy Stock Photo; On The Waterfront Year 1954 Director Elia Kazan Marlon Brando Karl Malden (p. 212): Photo 12 / Alamy Stock Photo; *1954 , USA : The celebrated movie actor MARLON BRANDO ( 1924 - 2004 ) and ROD STEIGER ( 1925 - 2002 ) in a pubblicity still for the movie ON THE WATERFRONT ( Fronte del porto ) by ELIA KAZAN , from a story by Budd Schulberg and Malcolm Johnson* (p. 212): ARCHIVIO GBB / Alamy Stock Photo.

### Rome, Open City

ANNA MAGNANI ROME OPEN CITY (1945) (p. 216): Allstar Picture Library Ltd / Alamy Stock Photo; Rome, ville ouverte Rome, open city Year : 1945 Italy Director : Roberto Rossellini Harry Feist, Aldo Fabrizi (p. 220): Photo 12 / Alamy Stock Photo.

### Schindler's List

*NEESON,KINGSLEY, SCHINDLER'S LIST, 1993* (p. 224): AJ Pics / Alamy Stock Photo; *Schindler's List* (p. 228): FlixPix / Alamy Stock Photo; *Film Still from "Schindler's List" Ralph Fiennes, Liam Neeson © 1993 Universal Photo Credit: David James* (p. 228): PictureLux / The Hollywood Archive / Alamy Stock Photo.

### The Seventh Seal

*THE SEVENTH SEAL 1957 Svensk Filmindustri production with Bengt Ekerot as Death and Max von Sydow as the Knight* (p. 232): Pictorial Press Ltd / Alamy Stock Photo; *THE SEVENTH SEAL (1957) MAX VON SYDOW INGMAR BERGMAN (DIR) 009 MOVIESTORE COLLECTION LTD* (p. 236): Moviestore Collection Ltd / Alamy Stock Photo.

### The Tree of Wooden Clogs

*L'Albero degli zoccoli The Tree of Wooden Clogs Year : 1978 Italy Director: Ermanno Olmi Palme d'or of the Cannes Film Festival of 1978* (p. 240, 244): Photo 12 / Alamy Stock Photo.

### Wild Strawberries

*1957, Film Title: WILD STRAWBERRIES, Director: INGMAR BERGMAN* (p. 248): Entertainment Pictures / Alamy Stock Photo; *Original Film Title: SMULTRONSTALLET. English Title: WILD STRAWBERRIES. Film Director: INGMAR BERGMAN. Year: 1957. Stars: BIBI ANDERSSON. Credit: SVENSK FILMINDUSTRI*

/ *Album* (p. 252): Album / Alamy Stock Photo; *Wild Strawberries 1957* (p. 252): PictureLux / The Hollywood Archive / Alamy Stock Photo.

## 8 1/2

*8 1/2 A 1963 Columbia/Embassy film with Marcello Mastroianni* (p. 259): Pictorial Press Ltd / Alamy Stock Photo; *8 1/2 (1963) MARCELLO MASTROIANNI, FREDERICO FELLINI (DIR) 005 MOVIESTORE COLLECTION LTD* (p. 262): Moviestore Collection Ltd / Alamy Stock Photo; *Huit et demi 8 1/2 / otto e mezzo Year: 1963 - italy Marcello Mastroianni Director: Federico Fellin* (p.262): Photo 12 / Alamy Stock Photo.

## 2001: A Space Odyssey

*2001 - Odyssee im Weltraum, (2001 - A SPACE ODYSSEY) GB 1968, Regie: Stanley Kubrick, GARY LOCKWOOD, KEIR DULLEA, Key: Raumschiff, Astronaut, Astronauten* (p. 267): United Archives GmbH / Alamy Stock Photo; *2001, L'ODYSSEE DE L'ESPACE 2001, A SPACE ODYSSEY 1968 de Stanley Kubrick scenario de Arthur C. Clarke screenplay by Arthur C. Clarke Prod DB © Metro* (p. 270): TCD/ Prod.DB / Alamy Stock Photo; *2001 l'odyssee de l'espace 2001: A Space Odyssey 1968 Stanley Kubrick COLLECTION CHRISTOPHEL* (p.270): Collection Christophel / Alamy Stock Photo; *2001: A Space Odyssey 1968. HAL* (p. 270): FlixPix / Alamy Stock Photo.

## Citizen Kane

*Citizen Kane 1941 réal : Orson Welles Orson Welles Collection Christophel* (p. 275): Collection Christophel / Alamy Stock Photo; *CITIZEN KANE 1941 RKO Radio Pictures with Orson Welles* (p. 278): Pictorial Press Ltd / Alamy Stock Photo; *CITIZEN KANE RKO Radio Pictures, Inc., 1941. Directed by Orson Welles. With Orson Welles* (p. 278): cineclassico / Alamy Stock Photo.

## Fantasia

*MICKEY MOUSE, FANTASIA, 1940* (p. 283): Allstar Picture Library Ltd / Alamy Stock Photo; *FANTASIA 1940 de James Algar, Samuel Armstrong, Ford Beebe, Norman Ferguson, Jim Handley, T. Hee, Wilfred Jackson, Hamilton Luke, Bill Roberts, Paul S* (p. 286): TCD/Prod.DB / Alamy Stock Photo; *FANTASIA (ANI - 1940) ANIMATED CREDIT DISNEY FNT 007FOH* (p. 286): Moviestore Collection Ltd / Alamy Stock Photo.

## The Grand Illusion

*Original Film Title: LA GRANDE ILLUSION. English Title: GRAND ILLUSION, THE. Film Director: JEAN RENOIR. Year: 1937. Stars: GASTON MODOT; JEAN GABIN. Credit: REALISATIONS D'ART CINEMATOGRAPHIQUE / Album* (p. 291, 294): Album / Alamy Stock Photo.

## La Strada

*Prod DB Â© Ponti-De Laurentiis / DR LA STRADA (LA STRADA) de Federico Fellini 1954 ITA avec Giulietta Masina et Anthony Quinn maquillage, clown, cirque, homme fort* (p. 299): TCD/Prod.DB / Alamy Stock Photo; *Giulietta Masina "La Strada" 1954 Ponti-De*

*Laurentiis Cinematografica File Reference # 33595 147THA* (p. 302): PictureLux / The Hollywood Archive / Alamy Stock Photo; *Prod DB Â© Ponti-De Laurentiis / DR LA STRADA (LA STRADA) de Federico Fellini 1954 ITA avec Giulietta Masina et Anthony Quinn* (p. 302): TCD/Prod.DB / Alamy Stock Photo.

### The Lavender Hill Mob

*ALEC GUINNESS and STANLEY HOLLOWAY in THE LAVENDER HILL MOB 1951 director CHARLES CRICHTON original screenplay T.E.B. CLARKE producer MICHAEL BALCON Ealing Studios / General Film Distributors (GFD)* (p. 307): Masheter Movie Archive / Alamy Stock Photo; *Prod DB © Rank Organisation / DR DE L'OR EN BARRES THE LAVENDER HILL MOB de Charles Crichton 1951 GB Stanley Holloway Alec Guinness Alfie Bass Sid Jam* (p. 310): TCD/Prod.DB / Alamy Stock Photo; *The Lavender Hill Mob (1951) , Alec Guinness* (p. 310): Mary Evans / STUDIOCANAL FILMS LTD / Alamy Stock Photo.

### The Leopard

*THE LEOPARD 1963 Titanus film with Burt Lancaster and Claudia Cardinale* (p. 315): Pictorial Press Ltd / Alamy Stock Photo; *THE LEOPARD 1963 TCF/Titanus film with Burt Lancaster and Claudia Cardinale* (p. 318): Pictorial Press Ltd / Alamy Stock Photo.

### Little Women

*Original Film Title: LITTLE WOMEN. English Title: LITTLE WOMEN. Film Director: GEORGE CUKOR. Year: 1933. Stars: KATHARINE HEPBURN; JEAN PARKER; JOAN BENNETT; FRANCES DEE. Credit: RKO / Album* (p. 323): Album / Alamy Stock Photo; *MONTGOMERY,HEPBURN, LITTLE WOMEN, 1933* (p. 326): Allstar Picture Library Ltd / Alamy Stock Photo; *LITTLE WOMEN 1933 RKO Radio Pictures film with Katherine Hepburn at top. From left: Frances Dee, Joan Bennett, Jean Parker* (p. 326): Pictorial Press Ltd / Alamy Stock Photo; *Original Film Title: LITTLE WOMEN. English Title: LITTLE WOMEN. Film Director: GEORGE CUKOR. Year: 1933. Stars: PAUL LUKAS; KATHARINE HEPBURN. Credit: RKO / Album* (p. 326): Album / Alamy Stock Photo; *Little Women Les quatre filles du Docteur March 1933 directed by George Cukor Katharine Hepburn Frances Dee Joan Bennett Jean Parker. COLLECTION CHRISTOPHEL / RnB © RKO Radio Pictures* (p. 326): Collection Christophel / Alamy Stock Photo.

### Metropolis

*METROPOLIS -1927* (p. 331): Moviestore Collection Ltd / Alamy Stock Photo; *Original Film Title: METROPOLIS. English Title: METROPOLIS. Film Director: FRITZ LANG. Year: 1927. Credit: U.F.A / Album* (p. 334): Album / Alamy Stock Photo; *Portrait of Brigitte Helm in Metropolis (1927) 001 - German weimar era cinema (1918 - 1935)* (p. 334): cineclassico / Alamy Stock Photo.

### Modern Times

*Original film title: MODERN TIMES. English title: MODERN TIMES. Year: 1936. Director: CHARLIE CHAPLIN. Stars: CHARLIE CHAPLIN. Credit: CHAPLIN/ UNITED ARTISTS / Album* (p. 338): Album / Alamy Stock Photo; *Movie poster:*

*Modern Times – a 1936 American silent comedy film written and directed by Charlie Chaplin.* (p. 342): JJs / Alamy Stock Photo; *CHARLIE CHAPLIN, MODERN TIMES, 1936* (p. 342): Allstar Picture Library Ltd / Alamy Stock Photo; *MODERN TIMES 1936 United Artists film with Charlie Chaplin and Paulette Goddard walking off into the dawn in the final scene. They were married the same year.* (p. 342): Pictorial Press Ltd / Alamy Stock Photo.

### Napoléon

*ALBERT DIEUDONNE NAPOLEON (1927)* (p. 345): Allstar Picture Library Ltd / Alamy Stock Photo; *ANTONIN ARTAUD as Marat ALEXANDRE KOUBITZKY as Danton EDMOND VAN DAELE as Robespierre and ALBERT DIEUDONNE as Napoleon Bonaparte in NAPOLEON Vu Par ABEL GANCE 1927 director ABEL GANCE Cine France / Films Abel Gance / Isepa - Wengeroff Film GmbH / Pathe Consortium Cinema / Societe Westi / Societe generale des films* (p. 348): Masheter Movie Archive / Alamy Stock Photo; *Napoleon vu par Abel Gance Year: 1927 France Director: Abel Gance Albert Dieudonne* (p. 348): Photo 12 / Alamy Stock Photo; *Josephine and Globe Triptych* (p. 348): Photoplay Productions. Used with permission.

### Nosferatu

*NOSFERATU, EINE SYMPHONIE DES GRAUENS Date: 1922* (p. 353): RGR Collection / Alamy Stock Photo; *Max Schreck "Nosferatu" 1922 File Reference # 31316 172THA* (p. 356): PictureLux / The Hollywood Archive / Alamy Stock Photo.

### Stagecoach

*DEVINE,CARRADINE,TREVOR,WAYNE, STAGECOACH, 1939* (p. 361): Allstar Picture Library Ltd / Alamy Stock Photo; *John Wayne, "Stagecoach", 1939 United Artists File Reference # 32603 190THA* (p. 364): PictureLux / The Hollywood Archive / Alamy Stock Photo.

### The Wizard of Oz

*THE YELLOW BRICK ROAD THE WIZARD OF OZ (1939)* (p. 369): Allstar Picture Library Ltd / Alamy Stock Photo; *RELEASED: Aug 12, 1939 - Original Film Title: The Wizard of Oz. PICTURED: MARGARET HAMILTON, JUDY GARLAND, BILLIE BURKE.* (p. 372): Entertainment Pictures / Alamy Stock Photo; *THE WIZARD OF OZ* (p. 372): Ronald Grant Archive / Alamy Stock Photo; *Judy Garland and the Cast, on-set of the Film, "The Wizard of Oz", 1939* (p. 372): Glasshouse Images / Alamy Stock Photo.

# Index